TOP ACCOUNTING ISSUES FOR 2013

CPE COURSE

CCH Editorial Staff Publication

CCH
a Wolters Kluwer business

Contributors

Contributing Editors... Steven C. Fustolo, CPA
Sharon R. Brooks, CPA
Julia K. Brazelton, PhD
Jan R. Williams, PhD, CPA
Joseph V. Carcello, PhD, CPA, CMA, CIA
Technical Review.................................Colleen Neuharth McClain, CPA
James F. Green, CPA
Production Coordinator..Sharon Sofinski
Production .... Lynn J. Brown
Layout & Design..Laila Gaidulis

ISBN: 978-0-8080-3082-9

4025 W. Peterson Ave.
Chicago, IL 60646-6085
800 344 3734
CCHGroup.com

Printed in the United States of America

FSC www.fsc.org
MIX
Paper from responsible sources
FSC® C101537

TOP ACCOUNTING ISSUES FOR 2013 CPE COURSE

Introduction

CCH's *Top Accounting Issues for 2013 CPE Course* helps CPAs stay abreast of the most significant new accounting standards and important projects. It does so by identifying the events of the past year that have developed into hot issues and reviewing the opportunities and pitfalls presented by these changes. The topics reviewed in this course were selected because of their impact on financial reporting and because of the role they play in understanding the accounting landscape in the year ahead.

Module 1 of this course reviews ongoing issues.

Chapter 1 focuses on the status of U.S. and worldwide adoption of International Financial Reporting Standards (IFRS) and examines the differences between IFRS and U.S. GAAP.

Chapter 2 discusses the pros and cons of fair value accounting and provides an overview of the FASB's fair value project.

In Chapter 3, the author summarizes the key advantages and disadvantages of using the last-in, first-out (LIFO) method for pricing inventory and explains how the 2013 U.S. budget proposal would affect inventory valuation methods.

Module 2 of this course reviews financial statement reporting.

Chapter 4 distills ASC Topic 220, *Comprehensive Income* (formerly FAS 130), which was issued to address the presentation of certain items (other comprehensive income items) that bypass the income statement and were recorded directly to equity.

Chapter 5 reviews the issues concerning revenue recognition and gives an overview of the FASB's revenue recognition project and other authoritative literature on the topic.

In Chapter 6, the author presents the results of several studies regarding restatements and discusses a few of the obvious financial reporting problems that have been announced by the SEC and the financial press.

Module 3 of this course reviews current developments.

Chapter 7 describes the accounting treatment of goodwill, including required disclosures, factors to consider when testing goodwill for impairment, and the purpose of ASU 2011-08.

In Chapter 8, the purpose and scope of ASU 2011-09 are examined, as well as the differences between multiemployer, single-employer, and multiple-employer plans.

Chapter 9 discusses generally accepted accounting principles (GAAP) affecting the presentation of a classified balance sheet and balance sheet offsetting—including new offsetting-related disclosures that many entities will have to start providing in the first quarter of 2013.

Finally, Chapter 10 examines selected accounting standards updates, including ASU 2010-09, ASU 2010-20, and ASU 2010-25.

Study Questions. Throughout the course you will find Study Questions to help you test your knowledge, and comments that are vital to understanding a particular strategy or idea. Answers to the Study Questions with feedback on both correct and incorrect responses are provided in a special section beginning on page 175.

Index. To assist you in your later reference and research, a detailed topical index has been included for this course beginning on page 191.

Quizzer. This course is divided into three Modules. Take your time and review all course Modules. When you feel confident that you thoroughly understand the material, turn to the CPE Quizzer. Complete one, or all, Module Quizzers for continuing professional education credit.

Go to **CCHGroup.com/PrintCPE** to complete your CPE Quizzers online for immediate results and no Express Grading Fee. Further information is provided in the CPE Quizzer Instructions on page 201.

September 2012

CCH'S PLEDGE TO QUALITY

Thank you for choosing this CCH Continuing Education product. We will continue to produce high-quality products that challenge your intellect and give you the best option for your Continuing Education requirements. Should you have a concern about this or any other CCH CPE product, please call our Customer Service Department at 1-800-248-3248.

COURSE OBJECTIVES

This course provides an overview of important accounting developments. At the completion of this course, the reader will be able to:

- Describe the phases involved in the IASB-FASB convergence project
- Cite differences between IFRS and U.S. GAAP
- Argue for and against fair value measurement
- Discuss the three-level hierarchy developed by ASC 820
- Describe the accounting treatment of certain items under ASC 320
- Summarize the key advantages and disadvantages of LIFO
- Describe what is included in other comprehensive income
- Explain the allowed presentation formats for other comprehensive income in the financial statements and notes
- Describe the revenue recognition issues that led to the revenue project
- List the disclosures that would be required under the revenue recognition proposal
- State the results of several studies regarding restatements
- Discuss reasons why Sarbanes-Oxley has been applied inconsistently by the SEC and the courts
- Describe the accounting treatment of goodwill
- Explain the purpose of and changes made by ASU 2011-08
- Discuss the differences between multiemployer, single-employer, and multiple-employer plans
- State the purpose and scope of ASU 2011-09
- Recall basic concepts related to presenting a classified balance sheet
- Apply criteria for offsetting assets and liabilities in a balance sheet
- Determine what is considered a subsequent event and when it must be evaluated
- Discuss the scope of ASU 2010-20

One **complimentary copy** of this course is provided with certain copies of CCH publications. Additional copies of this course may be downloaded from **CCHGroup.com/PrintCPE** or ordered by calling 1-800-248-3248 (ask for product 0-4285-500).

TOP ACCOUNTING ISSUES FOR 2013 CPE COURSE

Contents

MODULE 1: ONGOING ISSUES

MODULE 2: FINANCIAL STATEMENT REPORTING

MODULE 3: CURRENT DEVELOPMENTS

MODULE 1: ONGOING ISSUES — CHAPTER 1

International Accounting Standards Convergence

LEARNING OBJECTIVES

Upon completion of this chapter, the reader will be able to:

- State the number of companies that use IFRS worldwide
- Indicate what year it is likely that all countries will have adopted IFRS
- Describe the phases involved in the IASB-FASB convergence project
- Cite differences between IFRS and U.S. GAAP

INTERNATIONAL FINANCIAL REPORTING STANDARDS (IFRS)

During the past decade, a new set of International Financial Reporting Standards (IFRS) was adopted in Europe. The IFRS project is the first step at trying to internationalize global accounting standards to be used by all companies both inside and outside the United States.

Presently, United Kingdom companies are governed by IFRS issued by the International Accounting Standards Board (IASB). Effective in 2005, all companies listed on European stock exchanges (approximately 8,000) adopted IASB standards. As of 2010, approximately 120 countries required or allowed their companies to adopt the new international standards including the U.K., Australia, Japan, and New Zealand. Chile and South Korea adopted IFRS in 2009, Brazil in 2010, Canada and India in 2011, and Mexico adopted starting in 2012. Japan will decide in 2012 about an adoption in 2015 or 2016.

A total of more than 12,000 companies are now using IFRS worldwide.

The United States has not yet adopted IFRS, but is working with Europe's IASB at converging U.S. and International Standards over the next few years. Until then, with the new IFRS being issued, U.S. Securities and Exchange Commission (SEC) companies that also report in Europe will be required to report under two sets of standards: U.S. GAAP and IFRS.

By 2015, it is likely that all countries, including the United States, will adopt IFRS format in a move to globalize standards.

THE FIRST STEP: THE IASB-GAAP AGREEMENT TO CONVERGE STANDARDS

In 2002, both the IASB and FASB signed the *Norwalk Agreement* under which they agreed that convergence of both standards into one set of global standards is important. Both organizations included a convergence project in their agendas. The current move is for U.S. companies (including closely held entities), to adopt IFRS, rather than the other way around. Under the Norwalk Agreement, both sides agreed to move forward to:

- Remove differences between existing U.S. GAAP and IFRS in the short-term convergence project
- Converge future programs, either through joint or concurrent projects (long-term convergence project)

A key difference between U.S. GAAP and IFRS is that *IFRS are less rules-based and more principles-based.* The difference between the two concepts (rules versus principles) is pervasive and requires a dramatic change in the approach to accounting. According to the IASB, IFRS are principles-based standards that depend more on subjective determination and judgment of companies and their auditors in determining whether a transaction "faithfully represents" the economics of the transaction. In fact, the entire codification of IFRS fits into one volume as compared with the multiple volumes of information that encompasses U.S. GAAP. The result is that there is a great diversity in accounting and auditing under the IFRS system as compared with U.S GAAP (as noted in "Accounting's White Knight Sir David Tweedie wants to change the way the business world crunches its numbers" (*Fortune*, Sept. 30, 2002, **http://money.cnn.com/magazines/fortune/fortune_archive/2002/09/30/329306/index.htm**).

The IASB-FASB convergence project currently has two phases:

- **Phase one: Short-term convergence project.** Phase One is close to being complete and had as its objective the removal of a variety of small, individual differences between U.S. GAAP and the IFRS that are not within the scope of other major projects that are already in progress. The short-term convergence project is limited to those GAAP issues that both sides could resolve in the short-term. To date the FASB has issued three statements that are included within the short-term convergence project.
- **Phase two: Joint and concurrent (long-term) projects.** Phase Two is referred to as the long-term convergence project and consists of both organizations either working jointly or concurrently on larger more complex projects that include:
  - Revenue recognition
  - Consolidations and off-balance-sheet entities
  - Stock options
  - Leases
  - Financial performance reporting
  - Statement of comprehensive income
  - Reporting discontinued operations
  - Balance sheet offsetting

Both the FASB and IASB have as a larger goal the eliminating of significant differences between each side's GAAP, so that an ultimate convergence of standards would be seamless.

THE SHORT-TERM CONVERGENCE PROJECT

The FASB has taken a significant first step toward modifying U.S. GAAP to be consistent with IASB GAAP by issuing three standards to revise existing U.S. GAAP. Those three GAAP standards were issued as follows:

- *ASC 250, Accounting Changes and Error Corrections* (formerly FAS 154) eliminates the use of the cumulative effect of an accounting change for implementation of a voluntary accounting change, replacing it with a required restatement of financial statements, applied retroactively.
- *ASC 845, Nonmonetary Transactions* (formerly FAS 153) eliminates the use of a book-value approach to account for the exchange of similar productive assets (e.g., real estate exchanged for real estate) in situations in which the transaction does not have commercial substance.
- *ASC 330, Inventory (*formerly FAS 151) amends the language in ARB No. 43 (now codified as part of ASC Topic 505) to be consistent with IAS 2, with respect to inventory costs.

IASB CHANGES

On the other side, the IASB has issued a series of statements that cleaned up international standards to not only converge with the FASB, but also as part of the overall international standards convergence that took place. The chart on the following page presents the framework of the FASB-IASB short-term convergence project and long-term international standards project.

Why should small businesses care about the move toward international standards? Many accountants may look at the move toward international standards as an event that has no impact on domestic, non-public clients. But nothing could be further from the truth. The international standards will affect all companies, large and small, domestic and international, for two reasons:

1. Unless U.S. GAAP decides to create a separate GAAP for non-public companies, the change toward international standards will ultimately result in one set of standards to be used by all companies inside and outside of the United States, regardless of size and whether they are public or nonpublic.
2. The short-term convergence project has resulted in the FASB amending many commonly used FASB statements to bring U.S. GAAP in line with IFRS.

Move Toward International Standards

FASB-IASB's Norwalk Agreement

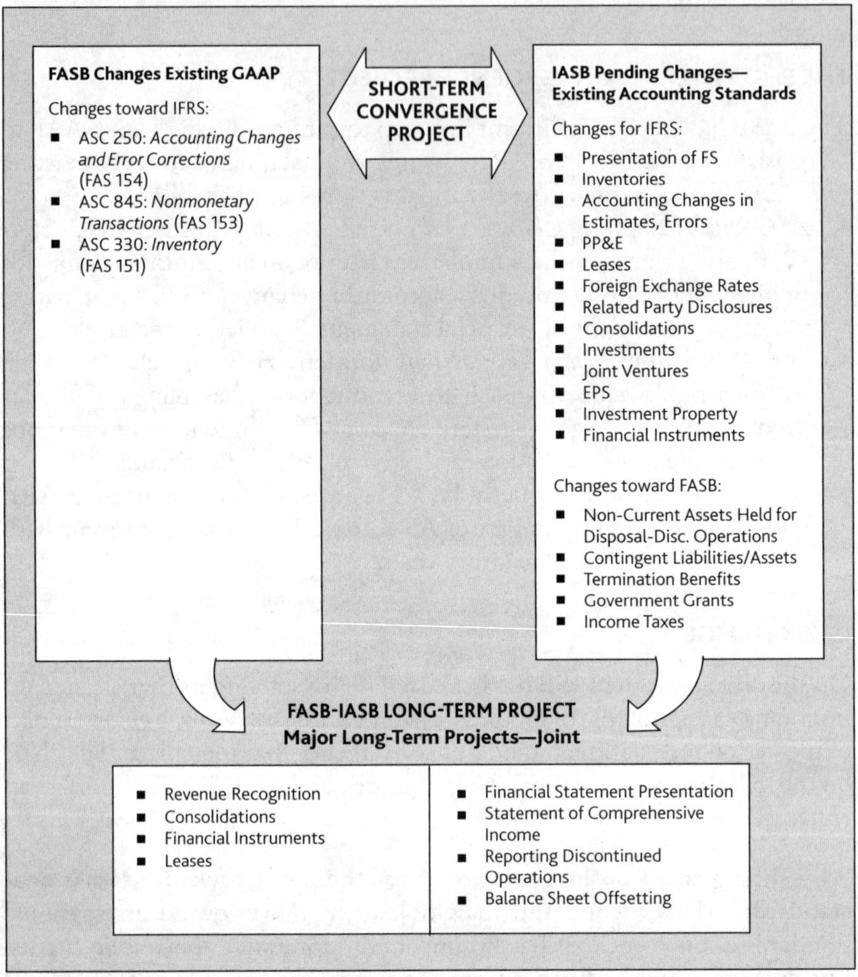

Is the convergence working? Apparently so. At its inception, critics stated that the project was doomed for failure for numerous reasons including the political and cultural difference between the FASB and IASB. Yet, it appears that both sides have succeeded at a pace not expected.

Consider the following:

- Since its inception, the IASB has been able to get 120 countries (at least 25 of them in the European Union (EU)) to adopt one set of international standards. The United States is not one of those 120 countries.
- In a relatively short period of time, both the FASB and IASB adopted new standards that reflect the other side's existing standards.

The FASB has issued three statements that amend U.S. GAAP under the short-term convergence project and has many standards about to be issued under its long-term convergence project. The following chart summarizes the status as of early 2012:

Status of FASB- IASB Convergence Project

Project	Influencing party	Status
Short-term project:		
Nonmonetary exchanges	IASB	Completed
Inventories	IASB	Completed
Voluntary accounting changes	IASB	Completed
Long-term project:		
Fair value measurement	FASB IASB	Completed
Statement of comprehensive income	FASB IASB	Completed
Balance sheet offsetting	FASB IASB	Completed
Accounting for financial instruments	FASB IASB	Pending high priority
Leases	FASB IASB	Pending high priority
Revenue recognition	FASB IASB	Pending high priority
Consolidation: Policy and Procedures	FASB IASB	Pending
Reporting discontinued operations	FASB IASB	Pending
Insurance Contracts	FASB IASB	Pending
Financial Statement Presentation	FASB IASB	Pending
Earnings per Share	FASB IASB	Not active
Income Taxes	FASB IASB	Not active
Postretirement Benefit Obligations including Pensions (Phase 2)	FASB IASB	Not active
Emissions Trading Schemes	FASB IASB	Not active
Financial Instruments with Characteristics of Equity	FASB IASB	Not active
Conceptual Framework Project	FASB IASB	Pending

Source: FASB

Both the FASB and IASB have announced that their goal is to prioritize the completion of three major projects: revenue recognition, leases, and financial instruments, and then focus on other areas that will facilitate the United States moving toward a full adoption of IFRS. The overall goal of the two organizations is for all major capital markets to be in position for the United States to adopt IFRS by 2015, subject to the SEC approving the convergence of U.S. standards.

THE SECOND PHASE: UNITED STATES MOVES TOWARD ADOPTING IFRS

Although the convergence project between the FASB and IASB is a first step toward trying to globalize standards, recent developments by the FASB, SEC, and Congress appear to be accelerating the United States' move toward adopting IFRS standards to replace U.S. GAAP.

This rapid action by the United States has many commentators shocked to think that U.S. GAAP, considered the gold standard, would be replaced by what some consider an inferior IFRS, for the sake of globalizing accounting standards.

Yet, in a recent survey of executives by the AICPA, 55 percent of those surveyed stated that they were preparing in some way for IFRS adoption (AICPA, International Financial Reporting Standards (IFRS): An AICPA Backgrounder).

Following is a quick analysis of what is going on at the IFRS front.

U.S. AND INTERNATIONAL SUPPORT TO MOVE TOWARD GLOBAL ACCEPTANCE OF IFRS

The years 2008 and 2009 created the impetus for IFRS to replace U.S. GAAP, while 2010 through early 2012 was a period during which the IFRS effort stalled.

In 2008, leaders from the G20 countries (An informal group of 19 countries and the EU, with representatives of the International Monetary Fund and the World Bank) stated that there was universal support for a single set of high-quality global accounting standards. The G20 reaffirmed their previous conclusions by agreeing for:

> international accounting bodies to redouble their efforts to achieve a single set of high quality, global accounting standards within the content of their independent standard setting process. (Leaders' Statement, The Pittsburgh Summit, September 24-25, 2009 (G20))

With continued support from Congress and the FASB, the SEC went public with its support as well.

In 2008, the SEC issued two proposals related to IFRS:

- A proposal to stop requiring certain foreign companies to reconcile their financial statements prepared under IFRS with GAAP
- A proposal to give U.S. companies the choice between using U.S. GAAP or IFRS to prepare financial statements

In November 2008, the SEC issued a document entitled *Roadmap for the Potential Use of Financial Statements Prepared in Accordance with International Financial Reporting Standards by U.S. Issuers* (the "Roadmap").

The Roadmap represented the first time that the SEC had embraced the possibility that U.S. issuers (SEC companies) ultimately would be required to adopt IFRS.

Specifically, the Roadmap outlined seven milestones that had to be met for the United States to move toward acceptance of IFRS. The seven milestones require:

1. Improvements in accounting standards
2. The accountability and funding of the IASC Foundation
3. The improvement in the ability to use interactive data for IFRS reporting
4. Education and training relating to IFRS
5. Limited early use of IFRS where this would enhance comparability for U.S. investors
6. The anticipated timing of future rulemaking by the SEC
7. The implementation of a mandatory use of IFRS by U.S. issuers

The SEC noted in its Roadmap that beginning with filings in 2010, the SEC would permit early use of IFRS by a limited number of U.S. issuers if companies used IFRS as the basis of financial reporting more than any other set of standards.

In its Roadmap, the SEC stated that by June 2011, it would assess whether the seven milestones had been achieved. If so, the SEC would decide whether to proceed with rulemaking that would require U.S. issuers to use IFRS beginning in 2014. In February 2010, the SEC moved the 2014 date to 2015.

In 2009, through a series of speeches, the SEC reaffirmed its commitment to assess IFRS by 2011 (e.g., October 2009 speech by James Kroeker, SEC Chief Accountant). Yet, in 2010, it appeared as if the SEC was wavering on its June 2011 decision date as well as the ultimate 2015 implementation date. In particular, in a 2010 speech, SEC Chairman Mary Schapiro stated that it would take a minimum of four years to adjust to IFRS if the SEC decided to require use of IFRS. Moreover, the Chairman noted that the SEC was not committed to a decision date of June 2011 (Speech by SEC Chairman Mary Schapiro, AICPA National Conference on Current SEC and PCAOB Developments, Washington D.C., December 2010).

In late 2011, the SEC announced that it needed additional time to issue a final report on the SEC's position as to the adoption of international standards.

Whether the SEC ultimately votes for adoption of IFRS and whether the 2015 implementation date holds, are unknown.

STUDY QUESTION

1. The FASB issued three statements to revise existing U.S. GAAP to be consistent with IASB GAAP. One modification:
   a. Amends the language in ARB No. 43 to be consistent with IAS 2, with respect to inventory costs
   b. Makes several changes to the computation of earnings per share (EPS)
   c. Requires the use of a book-value approach to account for the exchange of similar productive assets
   d. Requires the use of the cumulative effect of an accounting change for implementation of a voluntary accounting change

What would be the impact of U.S. companies being required to adopt IFRS? On more than one occasion, the SEC has stated that it is critical that FASB and IFRS standards reconcile many of their significant differences before any adoption of IFRS would be possible.

Currently, without reconciling many key differences, the impact of U.S. companies adopting IFRS would be significant because U.S. GAAP and IFRS are quite different. Consequently, as a prerequisite to U.S. companies adopting IFRS, the FASB and IASB are working on their convergence project to reduce, but not eliminate, the major differences between GAAP and IFRS.

Nevertheless, consider some of the more significant elements that would be impacted by the IFRS conversion:

- U.S. companies would be required to adopt new IFRS accounting standards.
- Accounting systems would have to be changed to capture revised IFRS data in order to be ready for 2015, or later, if the SEC extends the date.
- U.S. accountants, auditors, actuaries, and other parties would be required to receive extensive education and training in IFRS versus U.S. GAAP.

OBSERVATION

IFRS is now tested as part of the Uniform CPA examination in the United States.

- Costs to implement IFRS would likely be significant.

What would be the key differences between U.S. GAAP and IFRS? Although the list may change by 2015, based on current U.S. GAAP, the major differences between the two sets of standards are identified in the following chart:

Key Differences—U.S. GAAP and IFRS

Element	Treatment under IFRS	Treatment under U.S. GAAP
LIFO inventory	Does not permit use of LIFO inventory	Permits use of LIFO
Impairment of long-lived assets	Uses a one-step approach Permits companies to reverse impairment losses back to the amount of the basis when the reason for the impairment no longer exists	Uses a two-step approach Does not permit a reversal of impairment losses
Property, plant and equipment	Permits a company to evaluate its property, plant and equipment as long as the entire class is revalued Requires use of component depreciation in certain cases where the individual components can be separated and there are significant differences in the useful lives of the components	Does not permit such a revaluation Permits, but does not require, use of component depreciation
Uncertain tax positions	Not specifically addressed by IFRS	The tax benefit of a tax position recognized only if it is more likely than not that the position will be sustained upon examination
Revenue recognition	Limited IFRS guidance on revenue recognition	Has significant guidance on revenue recognition albeit scattered throughout GAAP
Research and Development (R&D)	Permits development costs to be capitalized if certain criteria are met, while research costs must be expensed	Requires R&D costs to be expensed in most cases
Disclosures	More extensive disclosures due to principles-based standards	Less extensive disclosures exist due to rules-based standards

Because IFRS is a principles-based system, the amount of authoritative literature for IFRS is small relative to the volumes of GAAP. Additionally, IFRS has minimal industry-specific guidance while GAAP has an abundance of industry-specific guidance.

Will IFRS directly impact non-public entities? The proposed changes to convert to IFRS are directed at public companies so, in theory, non-public entities would not be directly impacted by a convergence. However, the reality of the situation is that, under the current FASB structure, any convergence project will inevitably impact non-public entities. The FASB's "one-size, fits all" approach to accounting standards leaves no alternative for non-public entities. Consequently, if the FASB adopts international standards, non-public entities will be forced into using those new principles indirectly, solely because there will be no alternative.

The only savior for non-public entities is if a "little GAAP" alternative is adopted either within or outside the FASB.

The Blue Ribbon Panel's move toward a separate set of accounting standards for non-public companies means that accounting standards for non-public companies and those of public companies may move in different directions. If so, public companies' GAAP may become more complex with the adoption of IFRS, while non-public company standards may be streamlined under a GAAP alternative.

STUDY QUESTIONS

2. Which of the following is one of the milestones that had to be met for the United States to move toward acceptance of IFRS?

- **a.** The popularity of IFRS among U.S. investors
- **b.** Education and training relating to IFRS
- **c.** The implementation of an optional use of IFRS by U.S. issuers

3. The proposed changes to convert to IFRS would ___________.

- **a.** Directly affect both public and non-public companies
- **b.** Directly affect public companies but not directly affect non-public companies
- **c.** Not directly affect any companies

MODULE 1: ONGOING ISSUES — CHAPTER 2

The Move to Fair Value Accounting and the Mark-to-Market Controversy

LEARNING OBJECTIVES

Upon completion of this chapter, the reader will be able to:

- Argue for and against fair value measurement
- Discuss the three-level hierarchy developed by ASC 820
- Describe the accounting treatment of certain items under ASC 320
- Explain what is meant by an "orderly transaction"
- Discuss the criteria that should be used in determining the classification and measurement of financial assets

For the past decade, the historical cost model that has been the basis of GAAP accounting has slowly deteriorated, being gradually replaced by fair value accounting, but perhaps not fast enough for the investment community.

In a survey by the CFA Institute, *A Comprehensive Business Reporting Model*, investors noted 12 proposed changes to the business reporting model. Among them was the need for full fair value financial statements.

Given the fact that the source of the survey is the end user of many financial statements (i.e., the investor), its results should be looked at seriously.

As stated in the survey:

- "Fair value information is the only information relevant to financial decision making ... Decisions about whether to purchase, sell or hold investments are based upon the fair values. Financial statements based on outdated historical costs are less useful for making such assessments."
- Because current financial statements include a mixture of historical cost and fair value, investors who rely on fair values for decision making must expend considerable effort to restate cost to fair value.
- Historical cost itself is in reality historic market value—the amount of a past transaction—and is never comparable on a firm-to-firm basis because the costs were incurred at different dates by different firms.
- Investor conversion of historical cost components to fair value would be eliminated if GAAP recorded assets and liabilities at fair value at inception with a periodic revaluation to fair value.
- FASB should make a move to fair value accounting a priority.

The fact is that the historical cost model is inconsistent with the way in which investors and other third parties measure an entity—by the change in entity value. Presently, GAAP uses a fair value model to record the initial measurement of assets and liabilities. Thereafter, many assets are recorded at historical cost, such as fixed assets, while others are recorded at fair value or a hybrid of cost and fair value.

The following table illustrates the blend of historical cost, fair value, and other measurements presently used in GAAP.

Financial Measurements Under Existing GAAP

Item and Standard	Accounting Treatment
Cash	Carrying amount
Trade receivables	Net realizable value
Inventories—ASC 330	Lower of cost or market value
Securities including mortgage-backed securities—ASC 320	Measured at fair value or cost depending on category
Non-security investments—ASC 340	Historical cost, unless permanent writedown to market value
Loans receivable, including bank loans that are not securities—ASC 815	Carrying amount. Written down to fair value if the loan is impaired.
Fixed assets	Historical cost, depreciated or amortized
Goodwill—ASC 350	Initially recorded at historical cost (purchase price) and written down if there is an impairment in value
Intangibles other than goodwill with finite lives—ASC 350	Initially recorded at historical cost (purchase price) and amortized over the estimated useful lives
Intangibles other than goodwill with indefinite lives—ASC 350	Historical cost and written down if there is an impairment in value
Hedging derivatives—ASC 815	Fair value
Accounts payable and accrued expenses	Recorded at estimated amount at which obligation will be settled
Notes payable	Settlement amount
Asset retirement obligations—ASC 410	Recorded at fair value
Guarantee liabilities—ASC 460	Recorded at the fair value of the guarantee obligation at its inception
Stock options—ASC 718	External fair value model
Business combinations—ASC 805	Identified assets acquired, liabilities assumed, and noncontrolling interests in the acquiree are recorded at fair value at acquisition date
Disclosures	SEC companies are required to disclose the fair value of financial instruments.

The historical cost model has worked in terms of providing a format by which accountants can apply systematic and rational allocations of cost (such as in the case of depreciation and amortization) without the ambiguity of determining fair value. That is, the existing historical cost GAAP model has allowed accountants to follow a set of standard rules in preparing financial statements. But are historical cost financial statements meaningful to third parties?

The FASB is suggesting that the historical cost model no longer works and needs to be replaced or repaired with a fair value model whenever assets and liabilities can be reliably measured at fair value.

But simply measuring the change in entity wealth from period to period has its critics who note the following challenges to a fair value model:

- Fair value accounting is merely an appraisal of an entity's net assets from period to period. As a result, it may disguise the true performance of the entity as appreciation in certain assets may reward management for value enhancement for which they should take no credit.
- Fair value accounting introduces a degree of volatility to the accounting model as sharp increases and decreases in values may distort comparisons from period to period.
- Fair value accounting is too subjective as many assets and liabilities cannot be easily measured without making valuation assumptions. Such assumptions can vary and result in entities not being comparable.
- Although fair value accounting may be more relevant, the historical cost model is more reliable.
- The costs of moving to fair value accounting may exceed the benefit as companies would be required to perform asset valuations on a period-to-period basis.

How would a fair value model be implemented on a period-to-period basis? There are certainly challenges in applying a full fair value model to financial statements. For assets and liabilities with observable values (such as securities and other investments) fair value accounting is relatively easy to apply. However, for those assets that do not have such observable values, such as fixed assets and intangibles, measuring fair value from period to period is difficult and costly.

EXAMPLE

A company with property and equipment would be required to revalue such assets from year to year and may require outside services from an appraiser. Such a valuation would not only be costly but could delay the timely issuance of financial statements. Moreover, for many smaller companies, such cost of application may exceed the benefit derived from fair value information.

Is fair value a better system? There are arguments for and against a fair value system. However, the historical cost model does not purport to display the way third parties think in evaluating their investment. Unrealized gains and losses on assets should be an important element of total earnings for a period. More particularly, a company's performance for a period of time should be measured by the change in the fair value of its net assets from period to period as demonstrated below:

Fair Value of Net Assets

End of year	XX
Beginning of year	XX
Change = earnings for the period	XX

A common criticism of fair value accounting is that such a measurement may lack reliability and accuracy based on the fact that there is a range of fair value for each asset or liability. Yet, the counter-argument is that the worst fair value is far better than the best historical cost.

Another criticism is that use of fair value would introduce a high degree of volatility to financial statements from unrealized gains and losses on assets being recorded from year to year. However, volatility is an element of risk that an investor or third party should factor into its assessment of a company's value.

STATUS OF THE FASB'S FAIR VALUE PROJECT

Although the FASB's move toward fair value was slow at its inception, the pace has picked up in the past five years in part due to the Wall Street and banking troubles and the challenges in valuing the billions of dollars of non-performing bank loans and mortgage backed securities.

The fair value process actually began in September 2006, when the FASB issued ASC 820, *Fair Value Measurements* (formerly FAS 157).

ASC 820 defines fair value, establishes a framework for measuring fair value under GAAP, and enhances disclosures about fair value measurements. More specifically, ASC 820 does the following:

1. Defines fair value as the exit price which is:

   the price that would be received to sell an asset or paid to transfer a liability in an orderly transaction between market participants at the measurement date.

   a. The exit price (fair value) is market based, determined from the perspective of a market participant (the seller) that holds the asset or liability. An internally generated fair value is not relevant.

2. Develops a three-level hierarchy for valuation:

   Level 1: Observable market inputs that reflect quoted prices for identical assets or liabilities in *active markets* that the reporting entity has the ability to access at the measurement date

   Level 2: Observable market inputs other than quoted prices for identical assets or liabilities such as:
   – Quoted prices for similar assets and liabilities in active markets

   - Quoted prices for identical or similar assets and liabilities in markets that are not active
   - Market inputs other than quoted prices that are directly observable for the asset or liability, such as interest rates, yield curves, volatilities, and default rates

   Level 3: Unobservable market inputs, such as those derived through extrapolation or interpolation, which are not able to be corroborated by observable market data

3. Requires that in the absence of quoted prices for identical or similar assets or liabilities, fair value should be estimated using multiple valuation techniques consistent with the market approach, income approach, and cost approach whenever the information necessary to apply those techniques is available, without undue cost and effort. In all cases, the valuation techniques used for those estimates would emphasize relevant market inputs, including those derived from active markets.

4. Requires expanded disclosures about the use of fair value to remeasure assets and liabilities recognized in the statement of financial position, including information about the fair value amounts, how those fair value amounts were determined, and the effect of the remeasurements on earnings.

NEXT STEP: ASC 825 (FORMERLY FASB NO. 159) AND THE FAIR VALUE OPTION

After issuing ASC 820, the FASB introduced a project in ASC 825—the fair value option (FVO)—to consider whether to permit (but not require) entities a one-time election to report certain financial instruments (and certain non-financial assets) at fair value with the changes in fair value included in earnings.

The FVO project consists of two phases:

- Phase 1 addresses creating an FVO for financial assets and financial liabilities (issued as FAS 159, which is now part of ASC 825).
- Phase 2 addresses creating an FVO for selected nonfinancial assets.

In February 2007, the FASB commenced action on Phase 1 of the FVO project by issuing ASC 825, *Fair Value Instruments*.

ASC 825 provides the option of recording certain financial assets and liabilities at fair value for initial and subsequent measurement.

It applies to financial asset and liabilities that, in general, are not otherwise subject to fair value accounting. Further, *ASC 825 is optional*; that is, an entity may choose (but is not required) to record certain financial assets and liabilities at fair value, contrary to the way they are recorded and measured under other GAAP.

ASC 825 applies to financial asset and liabilities defined as follows:

> A *financial asset* is cash, evidence of an ownership interest in an entity, or a contract.
>
> A *financial liability* is a contract that imposes on one entity a contractual obligation to deliver cash or another financial instrument to a second entity or to exchange other financial instruments on potentially unfavorable terms with the second entity.

Examples of financial assets and liabilities to which the fair value option (FVO) applies and for which an entity has the option to use fair value accounting, include the following:

- Cash
- Investments
- Derivatives
- Receivables
- Trade payables
- Loans receivable and payable

ASC 825 applies to all financial assets and liabilities, *except*:

- Investments that would otherwise be consolidated
- Assets and liabilities covered under retirement and benefit plans
- Financial liabilities recognized under lease contracts under ASC 840 (formerly FAS 13)
- Written loan commitments not accounted for as derivatives
- Financial liabilities for demand deposit accounts

If an entity chooses to record a financial asset or liability at fair value under ASC 825, the change in the fair value is recognized in earnings as the changes occur.

STUDY QUESTIONS

1. In *A Comprehensive Business Reporting Model*, investors stated which of the following?

a. FASB should not move toward a fair value model.

b. Fair value information is the only information relevant for financial decision making.

c. Historical costs are more useful for making decisions about whether to purchase, sell, or hold investments.

d. The fair value model is inconsistent with the way in which investors measure an entity.

2. What inputs are placed into Level 3 inputs in the fair-value hierarchy?
   a. Inputs that are derived principally from or corroborated by observable market data by correlation
   b. Observable inputs other than quoted prices included in Level 1 that are observable
   c. Observable, unadjusted, quoted market prices in active markets for identical assets or liabilities that are accessible
   d. Unobservable inputs that should be used when observable inputs are unavailable

3. Which of the following does ASC 820, *Fair Value Measurements* do?
   a. Clarifies that book value is the price that would be received for an asset
   b. Develops a five-level hierarchy for valuation
   c. Requires expanded disclosures about the use of fair value to remeasure assets and liabilities
   d. Requires that fair value should always be estimated, even when quoted prices are available

4. The FASB commenced action on Phase 1 of the FVO (fair value option) project by issuing *The Fair Value Option for Financial Asset and Financial Liabilities,* which:
   a. Creates the option of recording certain financial assets and liabilities at fair value for initial and subsequent measurement
   b. Defines the exchange price
   c. Requires a fair value election to be made on an annual basis
   d. Would apply to investments that would otherwise be consolidated

THE MARK-TO-MARKET DEBATE IN AN ILLIQUID MARKET

In late 2008 and early 2009, Congress and third parties challenged the use of fair value accounting. The generic term used by the public is "mark-to-market accounting" which is nothing more than fair value accounting.

In the strong financial cycles of the early 2000s, fair value accounting was not an issue as financial institutions had ample capital and were not impacted by writedowns of financial assets. After all, the fair value of financial assets was increasing, not decreasing.

In 2008 and into 2009 and 2010, the severe decline in the stock market put pressure on entities to record writedowns of their financial assets that were securities and derivatives under both ASC 320, *Investments-Debt and Equity Securities* (formerly FAS 115) and ASC 815, *Derivatives and Hedging.*

Following is a quick review of ASC 320 rules before we look at how they have impacted mortgage-backed securities held by banks.

ASC 320 applies to securities. Under ASC 320, at the time of purchase, a security is placed into one of three categories based on management's positive intent and ability. Once a security is placed in a particular category, it generally can be changed only where there are significant unforeseeable circumstances. If there is a decline in the fair value of individual investments below amortized cost that is *other-than-temporary*, the cost basis should be written down to fair value with the recording of a realized loss. The written-down cost basis becomes the new basis going forward and cannot be reversed if the fair value increases in future years.

The following table summarizes the accounting treatment for investments:

	Securities		
	Debt securities held to maturity	**Trading securities**	**Available for sale securities**
Type	Debt	Debt and equity	Debt and equity
Intent	Hold to maturity	Sell in the near term	Undecided
Record at	Cost	Fair value	Fair value
Unrealized gains or losses	Not applicable	Presented on income statement	Presented in stockholders' equity, net of tax
Balance sheet	Based on maturity date	Current even if sale is expected beyond one year	Based on management's intent at year end
Other-than-temporary losses	Investment written down and realized loss recorded on income statement		

If the fair value of a security is less than its carrying amount, the security is impaired. Once impaired, the impairment is categorized as being either *temporary* or *other than temporary*.

Once a security is impaired (fair value is less than carrying value), a company is required to test to determine whether the impairment is temporary or other-than-temporary. If other-than-temporary, the loss should be realized and recorded on the income statement.

Generally, most investment unrealized losses are temporary in that there is an expectation that the losses will reverse (recover) within a reasonable period of time. Other losses may be other-than temporary in that it becomes unlikely that the loss will reverse within the reasonable period of time, or at all. Losses that are considered not temporary are referred to as *other-than-temporary*.

The result of having an investment loss that is other-than-temporary versus temporary is significant. If a security encounters an other-than-temporary loss, the result is that a realized loss is recorded on the income statement regardless of whether the investment is a security or non-security. In comparison, a temporary loss involving a held-to-maturity or available-for-sale security would not result in a realized loss affecting the income statement. For a trading security, the result of having an other-than-temporary loss is not significant because unrealized losses are presented on the income statement anyway. Further, trading securities are expected to be sold in the near term resulting in a realized gain or loss being recognized on the income statement.

When is a debt security impairment other than temporary? As it relates to most securities under ASC 320, the determination of whether an impairment loss is other than temporary was found in FASB Staff Position (FSP) FAS 115-1, *The Meaning of Other-Than-Temporary Impairment and Its Application to Certain Investments*, which provides factors that should be considered in determining when an impairment is other than temporary:

- The financial condition and near-term prospects of the issuer, including any specific events which may influence the financial condition of the issuer
- Ability and intent to hold an investment for a period of time sufficient to allow for any anticipated recovery

SEVERITY AND DURATION OF THE IMPAIRMENT

In 2009, in response to the problems related to impairments of mortgage-backed securities (MBS), the FASB issued two new pronouncements that address how financial institutions should evaluate debt securities (such as MBS) for impairment.

- FSP EITF 99-20-1: *Amendments to the Impairment Guidance of EITF Issue No. 99-20* (now found in ASC 325), and
- FSP FAS 115-2 and FAS 124-2: *Recognition and Presentation of Other-Than-Temporary Impairments* (now found in ASC 320)

In particular, FSP FAS 115-2 was issued to address how to determine other-than-temporary impairment for debt securities classified as available-for-sale and held-to-maturity under ASC 320.

FSP FAS 115-2 made the following changes to FSP FAS 115-1 with respect to debt securities only:

- The ability and intent to hold an investment was not a factor in determining impairment of a debt security, although it still applies to equity securities.
- An other-than-temporary impairment of a debt security (such as an MBS) shall be considered to have occurred if either one of the following two conditions is met:
  - An entity intends to sell the debt security (i.e., it has decided to sell the security).
  - It is more likely than not (more than 50 percent probability) that the entity will be required to sell the security before recovery of its amortized cost basis.
- If the entity does not expect to recover the entire amortized cost basis of the security, an other-than-temporary impairment shall be considered to have occurred.

- If an entity does not intend to sell the debt security, and it is not more likely than not that the entity will be required to sell the security before recovery of its amortized cost basis, any impairment loss is split. The portion of the loss representing the credit loss is recognized in earnings while the remainder is recorded in other comprehensive income, net of applicable taxes.

Regardless of the type of security, the decision as to whether an investment loss is temporary or other than temporary is significant and subject to management manipulation.

EXAMPLE

Company X has securities that are categorized as available-for-sale. The portfolio has an unrealized loss that is presented in stockholders' equity, net of the tax effect. X is having a great year and wishes to manage its earnings by accelerating future losses to the current year. X could argue that its investment losses are other-than-temporary and that the investment should be written down with a realized loss recorded on the income statement.

THE BANKS AND MORTGAGE-BACKED SECURITIES

Mortgage-backed securities have been blamed for many of the problems banks have had in the 2008 to 2012 downturn. Wall Street bundled various mortgage loans into securities that were sold to investors in tranches. The result is that individual assets (home loans) that individually were not considered securities became part of a security once they were bundled together and sold as a security. Once a bank held a mortgage-backed security as an asset, it was subject to the rules under ASC 320, which requires fair value accounting for certain categories of securities (trading securities and available for sale securities), and cost basis for those securities to be held to maturity.

It is important what management's intent is in deciding how to account for an MBS. If the plan is for the bank to collect the cash flows over the term of the security, the asset is held at cost and is categorized as held to maturity. If the goal is to trade the MBS for gain or loss, the security is in the trading security category and is recorded at fair value with the gain or loss going on the income statement. On the other hand, if bank management has not committed to hold the MBS to maturity (held to maturity) and is not trading MBS (trading security category), the security is categorized as available for sale and recorded at fair value with the gain or loss going to other comprehensive income (net of tax) in stockholder's equity.

MBS Accounting Treatment
ASC 320

	Assumes impairment is temporary			Other than temporary impairment
MBS management's intent	**ASC 320 category**	**MBS recorded at**	**Gain or loss treatment**	
Collect mortgage payments until maturity	Held to maturity	Cost	No gain or loss	Write down to fair value and record a loss on income statement
Buy and sell on a regular basis	Trading securities	Fair value	Gain or loss on income statement	
Undecided—not held to maturity and not trading securities	Available for sale	Fair value	Gain or loss in other comprehensive income (net of tax) in stockholder's equity	

In categorizing an MBS as held to maturity, trading security, or available for sale category, it is presumed that any impairment from an unrealized loss is temporary.

The problem comes when the MBS, regardless of category, has an unrealized loss and it is other than temporary. That is, there is a real question as to whether the loss will rebound within a reasonable period of time, or at all. If an impairment from an unrealized loss is other than temporary, the security is written down to fair value and the loss is recorded on the income statement. Once written down, the loss cannot be recovered if the fair value rebounds.

Many banks categorized MBSs as held to maturity with the plan to collect the mortgage payments until maturity and not sell the security. Thus, those MBSs were recorded at cost so that any losses were ignored because it has been presumed that those losses were temporary. Recording an MBS at cost in the held-to maturity category works fine as long as the mortgage loans that make up the security are not impaired. If the impairment is other than temporary, the MBS is written down to fair value and a realized loss is recorded on the income statement. Reversing that loss is not an option in future years if the fair value recovers.

Some of the bank MBSs were categorized as trading securities or available for sale securities in which case they were already recorded at fair value. Trading security gains and losses were recorded in the income statement so that any other-than-temporary impairment loss would have a minimal effect. As for MBSs categorized as available for sale, although it is true that those securities were already recorded at fair value, the gain or loss was recorded in other comprehensive income in stockholder's equity. Therefore, if an MBS that was categorized as available for sale had an impairment loss that was other than temporary, the unrealized loss or gain that was sitting in stockholder's equity was transferred to the income statement.

OTHER THAN TEMPORARY WRITEDOWNS OF MBSs

During the recent down market, because of declines in real estate values, banks have had to write down their MBSs under ASC 320. The presumption has been that the unrealized losses in the securities were other than temporary thereby requiring the banks to write down the MBS and record the loss on the income statement.

By writing down to fair value those securities that had been classified as held to maturity and recorded at cost, regulatory capital was reduced. The lower regulatory capital resulted in a restriction on the bank's ability to make loans. Such writedowns were non-cash entries that in some instances devastated the balance sheets of some (but not all) otherwise healthy banks. In some other cases where banks used the MBSs as collateral, the writedowns triggered margin calls and forced the banks to sell the MBSs at fire-sale prices to pay off the margin calls.

Thus began the cycle: asset writedowns drove a reduction in capital which triggered an inability to make loans and margin calls, which in turn resulted in fire sales of the assets to pay off the margin calls.

The cycle that created the problem looked like this:

- Housing prices declined.
- MBSs secured by the mortgages on those houses were written down to fair value by the banks, as the impairment losses are considered other than temporary with the loss on the income statement.
- Once the MBSs were written down to fair value, they created a capital shortfall for the banks and in some cases created margin calls for the banks if they used the MBSs as collateral for other loans received.
- The banks sold the MBSs at distressed prices to raise capital or to pay off margin calls.
- The distressed sales of the MBSs drove down the fair values of other MBSs, requiring a further writedown of MBSs.
- As the fair value of the assets declined, the credit rating of the bank's bond liabilities and issued stock declined.
- Suddenly, the banks had insolvent balance sheets and no ability to make loans or raise capital.

ASC 820 provides the framework of how to determine and measure fair value and provides that the fair value of an asset is the price that would be received for an asset or paid to transfer a liability in a transaction between market participants at the measurement date.

ASC 820 provides a three-level system of determining fair value. Assets that fall within Level 1 and 2 of the hierarchy are found within active markets where observable market values exist such as quoted market prices for identical or similar assets. In healthy, active markets, determining fair value for a Level 1 or 2 asset is relatively easy.

When assets are held within markets that are not active, distressed or disorderly (Level 3), fair value is unobservable and fair value must be obtained using assumptions such as used in a discounted cash flow model. Clearly, fair values obtained for Level 3 assets are far more subjective and can result in a range of values depending on the assumptions that are used.

THE PROBLEM WITH THE BANKS

When banks started selling MBSs at distressed discounted prices, those prices became the market value that was to be used to measure fair value for other MBSs. Thus, banks started writing down their impaired MBSs using distressed, undervalued prices of other MBSs that had been sold in the market. In many cases these reduced prices were well below the intrinsic value of the MBSs based on a discounted cash flow valuation.

Interestingly, banks also had problems on the liability side of their balance sheet. As the value of the MBSs and other financial assets fell, the value of the bank's bonds that it had issued also declined because of the higher risk associated with the bank. Thus, the same banks had to write down their liabilities and recorded the writedown as income under ASC 825.

What you had was a disaster with banks having grossly understated financial assets adversely affecting their ability to lend and sinking their credit rating. In some instances, the reduced credit rating reduced the fair value of the issued bond liabilities resulting in recording phantom income under ASC 825. Yet, most of the adjustments had no impact on cash flow. One example of this distortion occurred when Lehman Brothers recorded a $2.4 billion in pre-tax income by adjusting its bonds down to fair value right before it collapsed.

STUDY QUESTIONS

5. How is an other-than-temporary loss on an investment reflected on the income statement?

- **a.** A realized loss is recorded on the income statement only if the investment is a security.
- **b.** A realized loss is recorded on the income statement only if the investment is a non-security.
- **c.** A realized loss is always recorded on the income statement.
- **d.** A realized loss is not recorded on the income statement.

6. Under ASC 320, at the time of purchase, a security is placed into one of three categories including all of the following except:

   a. Debt securities held to maturity
   b. Trading securities
   c. Available for sale securities
   d. Undecided

THE SEC'S MARK-TO-MARKET STUDY

In October 2008, *The Emergency Economic Stabilization Act of 2008* (the Act) was signed into law and gave authority to the SEC to suspend application of ASC 820. As part of the Act, the SEC was required to conduct a study of mark-to-market accounting to assess its effects on the quality of financial information.

In January 2009, the SEC issued its study on mark-to-market accounting entitled, Report and Recommendations Pursuant to Section 133 of the Emergency Economic Stabilization Act of 2008: Study on Mark-To-Market Accounting (the Report).

The Report concluded the following as to whether fair value accounting (mark-to-market accounting) impacted the financial crisis found in the banks:

1. Fair value accounting did not appear to play a meaningful role in bank failures:

   – Bank failures in the United States appeared to be the result of growing probable credit losses, concerns about asset quality and eroding lender and investor confidence.
   – For banks that did recognize sizable fair value losses, the reporting of the losses was not the reason for the bank failure.

2. The Report recommends the following:

   – ASC 820 and mark-to-market requirements should be improved but not suspended.
   – The abrupt elimination of fair value would erode investor confidence.
   – Additional guidance for determining fair value in illiquid or inactive markets is needed, along with additional disclosures.
   – The accounting for financial asset impairments should be readdressed.
   – The accounting for investments in financial assets should be simplified.

Another study reached a similar conclusion that fair value accounting did not contribute to the U.S. banks' problems in the financial crisis in a major way. Instead, other factors played a role such as increased banks' leverage. The study analyzed 31 banks that failed and were seized by U.S. bank regulators in 2007 through 2009. Approximately 75 percent of the failed bank assets were loans that were recorded at amortized cost (subject to the impairment rules) with trading securities (recorded at fair value) playing no role (*Did Fair-Value Accounting Contribute to the Financial Crisis*?, Christian Laux and Christian Leux, 2010).

OBSERVATION

Although the empirical evidence points to the fact that fair value (mark to market) accounting played no significant role in the financial crisis, there is concern that the fear of a potential writedown and impact on a lender's capital requirements may stifle a bank's willingness to lend.

FASB DEALS WITH MARKETS THAT ARE NOT ORDERLY AND ACTIVE

The originally issued fair value model found in ASC 820 assumed that fair value was obtained within a market that was both orderly and active. But during the 2008 financial crisis, MBSs were being traded within markets that were not necessarily active nor orderly. The fair value guidance found in ASC 820 did not clearly address situations in which the market was not orderly and active because the volume of activity had declined. In such cases, use of a quoted market price was not representative of fair value.

In 2008 and 2009, the FASB issued FASB Staff Position FSP FAS 157-3, *Determining the Fair Value of a Financial Asset When the Market for That Asset is Not Active*, which was superseded by the 2009 issuance of FSP FAS 157-4: *Determining Fair Value When the Volume and Level of Activity for the Asset or Liability Have Significantly Decreased and Identifying Transactions That Are Not Orderly.*

Since its issuance, FSP FAS 157-4 has been incorporated into ASU 2011-04, *Fair Value Measurement (Topic 820), Amendments to Achieve Common Fair Value Measurement and Disclosure Requirements in U.S. GAAP and IFRSs.*

The amendments found in FSP FAS 157-4, as incorporated in ASU 2011-04, clarify the application of fair value measurement when there is a market that is not orderly or not active, such as in the case of the MBS market.

In general, the FASB reached the following conclusions to address situations in which a market may not be orderly and/or active:

Volume or level of activity for an asset or liability has significantly decreased; the market may not be active. The fair value of an asset or a liability might be affected when there has been a *significant decrease* in the volume or level of activity for that asset or liability in relation to normal market activity for the asset or liability (or similar assets or liabilities).

To determine whether, on the basis of the evidence available, there has been a significant decrease in the volume or level of activity for the asset or liability, a reporting entity shall evaluate the significance and relevance of factors such as the following:

- There are few recent transactions.
- Price quotations are not developed using current information.
- Price quotations vary substantially either over time or among market makers (e.g., some brokered markets).
- Indices that previously were highly correlated with the fair values of the asset or liability are demonstrably uncorrelated with recent indications of fair value for that asset or liability.
- There is a significant increase in implied liquidity risk premiums, yields, or performance indicators (such as delinquency rates or loss severities) for observed transactions or quoted prices when compared with the reporting entity's estimate of expected cash flows, taking into account all available market data about credit and other nonperformance risk for the asset or liability.
- There is a wide bid-ask spread or significant increase in the bid-ask spread.
- There is a significant decline in the activity of, or there is an absence of, a market for new issues (that is, a primary market) for the asset or liability or similar assets or liabilities.
- Little information is publicly available (e.g., for transactions that take place in a principal-to-principal market).

If a reporting entity concludes that there has been a significant decrease in the volume or level of activity for the asset or liability in relation to normal market activity for the asset or liability (or similar assets or liabilities), *further analysis of the transactions or quoted prices is needed.*

If a reporting entity determines that a transaction or quoted price does not represent fair value (e.g., there may be transactions that are not orderly), *an adjustment to the transactions or quoted prices* will be necessary if the reporting entity uses those prices as a basis for measuring fair value and that adjustment may be significant to the fair value measurement in its entirety.

Regardless of the valuation technique used, a reporting entity shall include appropriate risk adjustments, including a *risk premium* reflecting the amount that market participants would demand as compensation for the uncertainty inherent in the cash flows of an asset or a liability.

If there has been a significant decrease in the volume or level of activity for the asset or liability, *a change in valuation technique or the use of multiple valuation techniques may be appropriate* (e.g., the use of a market approach and a present value technique).

Estimating the price at which market participants would be willing to enter into a transaction at the measurement date under current market conditions if there has been a significant decrease in the volume or level of activity for the asset or liability depends on the facts and circumstances at the measurement date and requires judgment. A reporting entity's intention to hold the asset or to settle or otherwise fulfill the liability is not relevant when measuring fair value because fair value is a market-based measurement, not an entity-specific measurement.

Transactions are not orderly. The determination of whether a transaction is orderly (or is not orderly) is more difficult if there has been a significant decrease in the volume or level of activity for the asset or liability in relation to normal market activity for the asset or liability (or similar assets or liabilities). In such circumstances, it is not appropriate to conclude that all transactions in that market are not orderly (i.e., forced liquidations or distress sales).

A reporting entity shall evaluate the circumstances to determine whether, on the weight of the evidence available, the transaction is orderly.

Circumstances that may indicate that a transaction is not orderly include the following:

- There was not adequate exposure to the market for a period before the measurement date to allow for marketing activities that are usual and customary for transactions involving such assets or liabilities under current market conditions.
- There was a usual and customary marketing period, but the seller marketed the asset or liability to a single market participant.
- The seller is in or near bankruptcy or receivership (i.e., the seller is distressed).
- The seller was required to sell to meet regulatory or legal requirements (i.e., the seller was forced).
- The transaction price is an outlier when compared with other recent transactions for the same or a similar asset or liability.

If the evidence indicates the transaction is *not* orderly, a reporting entity shall place little, if any, weight (compared with other indications of fair value) on that transaction price.

If the evidence indicates that a transaction *is* orderly, a reporting entity shall take into account that transaction price. The amount of weight placed on that transaction price when compared with other indications of fair value will depend on the facts and circumstances, such as the following:

- The volume of the transaction
- The comparability of the transaction to the asset or liability being measured
- The proximity of the transaction to the measurement date

If a reporting entity does not have sufficient information to conclude whether a transaction is orderly, it shall take into account the transaction price. However, that transaction price may not represent fair value (i.e., the transaction price is not necessarily the sole or primary basis for measuring fair value or estimating market risk premiums). When a reporting entity does not have sufficient information to conclude whether particular transactions are orderly, the reporting entity shall place less weight on those transactions when compared with other transactions that are known to be orderly.

OBSERVATION

In most situations in which the market is not orderly and/or not active, an entity will determine fair value using *expected discounted cash flows*, and not the distressed prices in the market. The expected cash flows must reflect default and liquidity risk adjustments that would be added by a willing buyer of the instrument.

OTHER CHANGES TO FAIR VALUE MEASUREMENT

Throughout 2009 and 2010, the FASB continued with its efforts to fine tune the application of fair value measurements.

In September 2009, the FASB issued Accounting Standards Update (ASU) 2009-12: *Fair Value Measurements and Disclosures (Topic 820) Investments in Certain Entities That Calculate Net Asset Value per Share (or Its Equivalent)* to address the fair value measurement of investments in certain entities that calculate net asset value per share (or its equivalent).

The ASU states that an entity is permitted to measure the fair value of an investment on the basis of the net asset value per share of the investment (or its equivalent) if the net asset value of the investment (or its equivalent) is calculated in a manner consistent with the measurement principles of ASC 946, *Financial Services—Investment Companies.*

In January 2010, the FASB issued another ASU related to fair value measurement and disclosure, entitled ASU 2010-06: *Fair Value Measurements and Disclosures (Topic 820) Improving Disclosures about Fair Value Measurements.* ASU 2010-06 amends the fair value rules found in ASU 820 to require new disclosures involving transfers in and out of Level 1 and 2 fair value measurements and certain other information involving Level 3 fair value measurements.

Finally, in 2011, the FASB issued ASU 2011-04—*Fair Value Measurement (Topic 820) Amendments to Achieve Common Fair Value Measurement and Disclosure Requirements in U.S. GAAP and IFRS.* The ASU makes certain amendments to fair value measurement and disclosures.

FASB BATTLES THE BANKS ON LOAN PORTFOLIOS

Because MBSs are securities, they are subject to the fair value rules under ASC 820, and the other-than-temporary impairment rules of ASC 320.

But banks and other Wall Street firms have had significant portfolios of loans receivable that do not meet the definition of a security. Therefore, ASC 320 does not apply to these loans and the rules of ASC 310, *Accounting by Creditors for Impairment of Loans* (formerly FAS 114) apply instead.

Specifically, with respect to loans receivable held by banks and other institutions, ASC 310 requires that the loans be recorded at carrying value, and not fair value. The only time fair value comes into play is if a loan is impaired, in which case the loan must be written down to fair value, measured at the present value of cash flows.

The result is that a performing loan in which a borrower is making mortgage payments is not written down even if the underlying collateral (real estate) has declined. As long as the loan is not impaired, the loan continues to be recorded at carrying value (generally the note face value) and fair value does not come into play.

What is a loan impairment and when does it occur? When it comes to an impairment of a loan which is not a security, the authority is found in ASC 310, which defines a loan impairment as a loan in which:

> based on current information and events, it is probable that a creditor will be unable to collect all amounts due according to the contractual terms of the loan agreement.

"All amounts due according to the contractual terms" means that both the contractual interest payments and the contractual principal payments of a loan will be collected as scheduled in the loan agreement.

In general, a loan in which a borrower is making principal and interest payments is considered a performing loan and is not impaired. Even an insignificant delay or insignificant shortfall in amount of payments does not result in the loan being impaired. Most important for a loan receivable that is not a security, the fair value of the underlying collateral (e.g., real estate) is not a factor, as long as the borrower is making timely payments under the loan agreement.

What this means is that there is a profound difference in the way loans receivable and some MBSs are handled by banks under GAAP. MBSs are securities and may be recorded at fair value if the MBS is categorized as a trading security or available-for-sale security under ASC 320. In such cases, the MBS is recorded at fair value which is the price that the seller (bank) would receive if the MBS were to be sold in an orderly transaction.

If the underlying collateral of an MBS has declined below the face value of the notes, clearly the exit price of the MBS declines and there is a writedown of the MBS on the bank's balance sheet even if the loans are performing otherwise (e.g., even if the borrower is making payments timely).

Conversely, if a loan is not part of an MBS (such as a single mortgage loan that a bank holds in house), it is not a security and thus not subject to the ASC 320 rules. Consequently, the loan is recorded at carrying value as long as it is not impaired (e.g., as long as the borrower is making timely payments of interest and principal and not otherwise in default). If the value of the underlying collateral declines, and the borrower continues to making timely payments under the loan, generally there is no impairment and no possible writedown.

What if there is a loan impairment? Let's assume that the borrower is not making timely loan payments in accordance with the loan agreement. If the delay or shortfall amount is significant, the loan is likely to be impaired because "*based on current information and events, it is probable that a creditor will be unable to collect all amounts due according to the contractual terms of the loan agreement.*"

If the loan is impaired, fair value now comes into play. ASC 310 states that if there is an impairment of a loan, a creditor shall measure impairment based on one of the following:

- Present value of expected future cash flows discounted at the loan's effective interest rate
- Loan's observable market price
- The fair value of the collateral if the loan is collateral dependent

EXAMPLE

In 2008, Bank X made a loan in the amount of $1 million secured by a first mortgage on the borrower's real estate. The loan requires monthly principal and interest payments in the amount of $5,000 per month.

Assume at December 31, 2011 the loan looks like this:

- The borrower continues to make timely monthly principal and interest payments and there are no other defaults related to the loan.
- The fair value of the secured real estate has declined to $600,000. Based on the fair value of the secured real estate (the loan is under water), X estimates the fair value of the loan if sold in an orderly market would be $600,000, which is the fair value of the collateral.
- The Bank's business strategy is to continue to collect monthly payments on the loan and not sell the loan.

Scenario 1: Recorded at Amortized Cost with the Recording of an Impairment, if Applicable (Current Practice) Under ASC 310

Bank X would continue to record the loan at its cost which is $1 million. The $1 million should be written down only if there is an impairment.

An impairment exists if "based on current information and events, it is probable that a creditor will be unable to collect all amounts due according to the contractual terms of the loan agreement."

In this example, the borrower continues to make timely principal and interest payments. Therefore, X can reach the conclusion that based on current information and events, it is probable that the borrower will continue to make timely payments and X will collect all amounts in accordance with the contractual terms of the loan agreement. Thus, there is no impairment and no entry required.

Scenario 2: Recorded at Fair Value

If, instead, the FASB required bank loans to be recorded at fair value, there would be a huge writedown. In this case, the loan would have to be recorded at fair value even though there is no impairment.

Loss on writedown to fair value	400,000	
Allowance for writedown		400,000

OBSERVATION

The above example illustrates the potential disaster that could occur if bank loans were to be recorded at fair value instead of the current practice of amortized cost with an impairment loss, if applicable.

If fair value were to be required, banks would have to write down fully performing loans solely because the fair value of the loans (assuming sold) has declined due to a decline in the underlying collateral. Instead, current GAAP states that as long as the loan is performing (e.g., the borrower is making timely payments and it is probable that the payments will continue to be made under the loan agreement), there is no impairment and fair value is not relevant.

Given the fact that the bank, in this case, plans to collect payments under the loan and not sell the loan, the bank's return will happen through collecting the cash flows and not by selling the loan. Consequently, a dip in the fair value of the loan should not be a factor as long as the loan is performing.

STUDY QUESTIONS

7. Under ASC 310, a loan is impaired if ________________.

   a. The fair value is less than the carrying amount of the loan.
   b. It is reasonably possible that the borrower will not be able to pay some of the loan on a timely basis.
   c. It is probable that a creditor will be unable to collect all amounts due.
   d. The interest rate of the loan is higher than market value.

8. Under ASC 310, if a loan is impaired, which of the following is *not* a way to measure the impairment?

   a. Present value
   b. Loan's market price
   c. Fair value of the collateral
   d. Carrying value

WHAT HAPPENED AT THE FASB THAT ALMOST CREATED A CATASTROPHE AMONG U.S. BANKERS

In May 2010, the FASB tried to expand the use of fair value measurement to numerous financial instruments that are presently subject to the historical cost model and not subject to the fair value model that many securities must apply.

In particular, in its exposure draft entitled, Accounting for Financial Instruments and Revisions of the Accounting for Derivative Instruments and Hedging Activities-Financial Instruments (Topic 825) and Derivatives and Hedging (Topic 815), the FASB floated the idea of applying fair value to most financial instruments as follows:

- For financial instruments other than debt instruments (e.g., loans), the instruments would have been recorded at fair value with the change in fair value recorded in net income.
- For most debt instruments (including loans), for which the business strategy is to hold them for collection or payments of contractual cash flows, the instruments would been presenting both fair value and amortized cost information on the balance sheet with the fair value adjustment recorded as part of other comprehensive income.

As written, fair value accounting would have been expanded to a list of financial instruments that would have included the following:

- Accounts receivable and payable
- Other receivables and payables
- Originated and purchased loans
- Investments in debt securities
- Investments in equity securities (except investments in equity securities that qualify for the use of the equity method)
- Core and noncore deposits
- Issued debt
- Hybrid financial instruments
- Financial derivative instruments
- Certain financial guarantees
- Loan commitments and standby letters of credit (except certain loan commitments).

For some financial instruments (such as trading securities, securities available for sale, and certain derivatives), the proposed fair value requirement would represent no change from current practice. However, for certain other financial instruments (such as loans receivable), the change would be huge in that those loans would have to be written down to fair value while under existing GAAP, they are not written down unless they are impaired (e.g., unless the borrower is not making timely principal and interest payments).

Bankers Pressure the FASB to Cave in

Once the exposure draft was issued and it proposed recording loans receivable at fair value, the political storm started from constituents who wanted to remove loans receivable from the scope of the proposed fair value accounting standard.

Bank lobbyists started an aggressive campaign in Congress to eliminate the FASB's fair value proposal that came from various sources that included the following:

- Both Paul Volcker (former Fed Chairman) and William Isaac (former FDIC Chairman) publicly opposed the FASB's fair value proposal for bank loans (Bloomberg).
- The American Bar Association wrote a letter to the FASB opposing fair-value accounting noting that it was unreliable for bank loan portfolios and would create sizeable losses for banks (ABA letter dated August 31, 2010)
- One analyst concluded that if the FASB fair value proposal were passed, the 26 largest U.S. banks could have a writedown of about $4 trillion of loans by $138 billion or about 3.5 percent (ABA letter dated August 31, 2010).
- One analyst suggested that if fair value accounting were to be applied to bank loan portfolios, the four largest American banks (JP Morgan Chase, Wells Fargo, Bank of America, and Citibank) would become insolvent due to the writedowns based on the following analysis:

Equity and allowance available to absorb writedowns:	
Combined tangible common equity	$408 billion
Allowance for loan losses	$129 billion
Total equity and allowance for losses	$537 billion
Total loan portfolio	$2,958 trillion
Percent	18%

Source: Mark-to-Market Would Make Banks Insolvent, marktomarketdebate.com, June 2010.

OBSERVATION

The previous chart illustrates that the top four U.S. banks have total tangible common equity and allowances for loan losses equal to 18 percent of their total loan portfolios. That means they have enough equity and allowances to absorb not more than 18 percent writedown in the loan portfolio to reflect a decline to fair value. Given the fact that a large portion of that loan portfolio is secured by real estate, it is highly likely that the writedown would exceed 18 percent making the banks effectively insolvent.

According to Federal Reserve Bank, the median loan loss reserve by size of bank was approximately 3.5 percent for all banks.

Clearly a change to fair value accounting would result in a sizeable writedown of the loan portfolios well in excess of the loan-loss allowance.

The Result

The political pressure on the FASB was too much for it to continue with its proposal for fair value accounting for bank loans. At its December 21, 2010 meeting, the FASB decided that both the characteristics of the financial asset and an entity's business strategy should be used as criteria in determining the classification and measurement of financial assets.

On October 20, 2011, the FASB issued a revised document entitled, *Accounting for Financial Instruments, Summary of Decisions Reached to Date During Redeliberations*, which summarizes the conclusions reached by the FASB with respect to fair value for financial instruments. The document is the basis for final documents to be issued in the near future.

CONCLUSIONS TENTATIVELY REACHED BY THE FASB

Financial instruments shall be segregated into three categories, each of which shall be accounted for differently in applying fair value or cost accounting:

- **Fair value with all changes in fair value recognized in net income (FV-NI):** Those financial instruments in this category would be initially recorded at fair value. Subsequently, the instruments would be recorded at fair value with the unrealized gain or loss in fair value recorded on the income statement.
- **Fair value with changes in fair value recognized in other comprehensive income in stockholders' equity (FV-OCI):** Those financial instruments in this category would be initially measured and recorded at transaction price. Subsequently, the instruments would be recorded at fair value with the unrealized gain or loss in fair value recorded as other comprehensive income in stockholders' equity, net of the tax effect.
- **Amortized cost:** This category would consist of certain financial instruments of entities that follow specialized industry guidance in ASC Topic 946 for investment companies. Such instruments would initially be measured and recorded at transaction price (cost).

The classification and measurement of financial instruments within the three categories would be based on both:

- The characteristics of the financial instrument
- The entity's business strategy for the instrument

A financial instrument that meets the following criteria would be categorized in the three categories based on the business strategy.

It is a *debt instrument* held or issued that has all of the following characteristics:

- It is not a financial derivative instrument subject to the guidance in Topic 815 on derivatives and hedging.
- An amount is transferred to the debtor (issuer) at inception that will be returned to the creditor (investor) at maturity or other settlement, which is the principal amount of the contract adjusted by any discount or premium at acquisition.
- The debt instrument cannot contractually be prepaid or otherwise settled in such a way that the investor would not recover substantially all of its initial investment, other than through its own choice.

NOTE

Trade receivables and payables, and notes receivable and payable generally would meet the criterion above and therefore would be measured at cost or FV-OCI depending on the business strategy.

A financial instrument that does *not* meet the above criteria would automatically be measured at FV-NI.

Financial Assets

An entity that meets the criterion for the characteristics of a financial asset would be characterized into the three categories based on the entity's business strategy for the financial instrument:

Amortized cost category. The business activity for these financial assets must meet *all* of the following conditions:

- Financial assets issued or acquired for which an entity's business strategy, at origination or acquisition of the instrument, is to manage the instrument through customer financing or lending activities. These activities primarily focus on the collection of substantially all of the contractual cash flows from the borrower.
- Financial assets for which the holder of the instrument has the ability to manage credit risk by negotiating any potential adjustment of contractual cash flows with the counterparty in the event of a potential credit loss. Sales or settlements would be limited to circumstances that would

minimize losses due to deteriorating credit, or to exit a particular market for risk management purposes.
- Financial assets that are not held for sale at acquisition

FV-OCI category. The business activity for these financial assets must meet *both* of the following conditions:
- Financial assets issued or acquired in a business activity for which an entity's business strategy is to invest the cash of the entity *either* to *a)* maximize total return by collecting contractual cash flows or selling the asset; *or* b) manage the interest rate or liquidity risk of the entity by either holding or selling the asset
- Financial assets that are not held for sale at acquisition or issuance

FV-NI Category. The business activity for these financial assets must meet *either* of the following conditions:
- Financial assets that are held for sale at acquisition
- Financial assets that are actively managed and monitored internally on a fair value basis

Financial Liabilities

Financial liabilities that meet *either* of the following two conditions would be classified as FV-NI:
- Financial liabilities for which an entity's business strategy at acquisition, issuance, or inception is to subsequently transact at fair value
- Financial liabilities that are short sales

All other financial liabilities that meet the characteristics of the instrument criterion would be measured at amortized cost.

The FASB has stated that the following assets would be categorized within the three categories as follows:

Financial Instrument	Proposed Category
Trade receivables and payables	Generally at cost
Loans and notes receivable	Generally at cost
Derivatives:	
Those derivatives designated as the hedging instrument in a cash flow hedge or a hedge of a net investment in a foreign operation	FV-OCI
All other derivatives	FV-NI
Debt securities	FV-OCI
Equity securities	FV-NI
Investments in non-marketable-equity securities	FV-NI Special rule for non-public entities: Cost less impairment loss plus upward adjustments in fair value when information about a change in price is observable
Long-term debt	Generally recorded at cost

An entity would be required to classify its financial instruments upon initial recognition and would not be permitted to subsequently change that decision.

Specific rules would be provided for measuring and recording impairment of financial instruments and for the recognition of interest income.

Financial statement presentation should be as follows:
Balance sheet presentation:

- An entity would be required to separately present financial assets and financial liabilities on the statement of financial position by classification and measurement category.
- For financial assets and liabilities measured at amortized cost, a public entity would be required to present the fair value parenthetically on the face of the balance sheet. (The parenthetical disclosure would not apply to non-public entities. Moreover, receivables and payables due in less than one year would not be subject to parenthetical disclosure of fair value.)
- All entities would be required to separately present cumulative credit losses on the face of the statement of financial position.
- All entities would be required to present parenthetically on the face of the statement of financial position the amortized cost of an entity's own debt that is measured at fair value.

Statement of comprehensive income:

- An entity would be required to present in net income an aggregate amount for realized and unrealized gains or losses for financial assets measured at fair value with all changes in fair value included in net income.
- An entity would be required to separately present the following items in net income for both financial assets measured at fair value with changes in value recognized in other comprehensive income and financial assets measured at amortized cost:
  - Current-period interest income
  - Current-period credit losses
  - Realized gains and losses
- An entity would be required to present in net income an aggregate amount for realized and unrealized gains or losses for financial liabilities measured at fair value with all changes in fair value recognized in net income.
- An entity would be required to separately present the following items in net income for financial liabilities measured at amortized cost:
  - Current-period interest expense
  - Realized gains and losses

There would be changes made to the fair value option found in ASC 825 that would permit use of the fair value option on a conditional basis only, and only for a group of financial assets or liabilities.

Disclosures of financial instruments would be expanded including information on liquidity risk with financial institutions disclosing information on interest rate risk.

As of early 2012, the FASB is continuing to redeliberate the issues in this fair value financial instrument project and once those redeliberations are completed, the FASB will decide whether to re-expose those decisions for public comment. Regardless of the approach the FASB takes, the proposed changes to fair value accounting for financial instruments are likely to pass.

OBSERVATION

The proposed changes to the accounting for financial instruments protects the loan portfolios held by U.S. banks by allowing such loans to continue to be carried at amortized cost. This cost approach is the correct one in light of the fact that fair value accounting should not be relevant to loans that continue to be performing at their contracted terms and conditions. Unlike securities and other investments which are traded for profits, most bank loan portfolios are held, and the return is generated through collecting the contracted cash flows over the life of the loans. Consequently, fair value (the exit price) is really not relevant unless the lender has as its goal the buying and selling of the loans.

STUDY QUESTION

9. The FASB has concluded that financial instruments are to be segregated into three categories, including all of the following *except:*

a. Amortized Fair Value
b. Amortized Cost
c. FV-OCI
d. FV-NI

MODULE 1: ONGOING ISSUES — CHAPTER 3

Proposed Repeal of LIFO

LEARNING OBJECTIVES

Upon completion of this chapter, the reader will be able to:

- Summarize the key advantages and disadvantages of LIFO
- Describe the IFRS rules regarding LIFO
- State the percentage of U.S. companies that use LIFO
- Cover some of the special situations, problems, and opportunities when using LIFO
- Explain the political leanings regarding the use of LIFO
- State how the 2013 U.S. budget proposal would affect inventory valuation methods

A business that produces or purchases goods for sale to its customers is required to consider the value of unsold goods when determining its income. Sales revenues are reduced by the cost of goods sold to ascertain gross income. Cost of goods sold consists of the beginning inventory value plus the cost of producing or purchasing additional goods, minus the value of the inventory of unsold goods at the close of the accounting period. The value of the closing inventory has a significant effect on the amount of earnings. The higher the inventory value, the higher the earnings.

Since the 1930s, last-in, first-out (LIFO) has been an acceptable method for pricing inventory. During periods of rapidly increasing costs, LIFO tends to minimize profits from the turnover of low cost inventories and thereby reduces income tax liabilities. In general, under LIFO it is assumed that the inventories sold are those that were most recently purchased. Consequently, LIFO usually reflects cost of goods sold in relatively current terms.

Prior to the inflationary period of the 1970's, most businesses determined the value of ending inventories using the first-in, first-out (FIFO) method. Under FIFO, the ending inventory is priced at its most recent costs. This frequently coincides with the actual physical handling of the goods. In times of stable prices, FIFO produces reasonable matching of current costs and revenues. However, in times of extreme and rapid inflation, using FIFO might overstate profits or understate losses from an economic viewpoint.

WHY USE LIFO?

Advantages. The most significant advantage of adopting LIFO is the cash flow generated through income tax savings. Every business manager must consider the economic benefit derived from reduced taxes. LIFO produces substantial tax savings when inflation increases the value of inventory by charging the latest costs to cost of sales.

Disadvantages. One of the major disadvantages of LIFO historically was the conformity requirement. Conformity required that LIFO be used to report primary financial earnings to shareholders, creditors, etc., when LIFO has been adopted for tax purposes.

In 1981 the Internal Revenue Service (IRS) issued revised tax regulations allowing taxpayers using LIFO to report supplemental information to shareholders and creditors disclosing the FIFO results. This form of reporting is permitted if the information is supplemental or explains the primary LIFO financial statements. With these additional disclosures, the conformity requirement was not as onerous to taxpayers.

Another disadvantage of LIFO is that it is a cost method with specific rules that must be used consistently when pricing increases and decreases in inventory levels. Therefore, if a business has widely fluctuating prices or volumes, earnings may fluctuate without truly reflecting operations. This could result in an attempt to manage inventories artificially to achieve desired results. In addition, write-downs permitted under the FIFO method must be restored to income before adopting LIFO. To the extent these write-downs are significant, the initial cash flow benefits of adopting LIFO could be lessened.

The adoption of LIFO usually results in inventory records being maintained on both a FIFO and LIFO basis. Therefore, a company is faced with the annual costs of computing inventory on both a FIFO and LIFO basis in addition to the costs incurred in making the initial conversion to LIFO. These additional clerical costs must be considered along with the expected savings when evaluating the expected benefits. A simplified LIFO calculation using general published indices was made available and helped reduce costs. In most industries, absent other considerations, the costs versus cash flow benefits are tilted substantially in favor of adopting LIFO.

LIFO is a cost method, and write-downs to reflect lower market prices or a decline in the utility value of inventory are not permitted under this method for tax purposes. If prices decline below those existing when LIFO is first adopted, its use would result in a tax cost rather than a tax savings.

LIFO typically results in a conservative balance sheet amount for inventories. This also means that shareholders' equity is more conservatively stated than if FIFO had been used. When a company has a relatively high level of borrowing, the debt to equity ratio can be adversely affected by adopting LIFO. This may violate debt agreement covenants.

STUDY QUESTION

1. Which of the following is an advantage of using LIFO?
   a. It requires conformity.
   b. It is a cost method with specific rules that must be used consistently.
   c. It increases cash flow when there is inflation.

THE IFRS EFFECT

One key change that would be made if U.S. companies convert to International Financial Reporting Standards (IFRS) would be the elimination of the LIFO inventory method. IFRS does not permit use of LIFO while U.S. GAAP does.

Although some companies argue that they use LIFO to better match revenues and expenses, the reality is that LIFO is used for U.S. GAAP because it saves taxes. In a perfect situation, companies would prefer to use LIFO for tax purposes and use FIFO or average cost for GAAP. In doing so, they could have the best of both situations: a lower taxable income and a higher GAAP income.

However, use of LIFO is one of the few examples of accounting methods where the Internal Revenue Code (Code) interferes with GAAP by way of Code Sec. 472's LIFO Conformity Requirement.

In general, the LIFO Conformity Requirement states that if an entity uses LIFO for income tax purposes, it must also use it for GAAP to clearly reflect its income. Over the years, the Sec. 472 regulations have watered down the LIFO Conformity Requirement to allow non-LIFO disclosures and supplementary information. However, the current regulations allow for the following for U.S. GAAP if LIFO is also used for tax purposes:

- The primary income statement must be presented on LIFO.
- The balance sheet may be presented on a non-LIFO (e.g., FIFO) basis.
- Supplementary information and footnotes can present non-LIFO information such as in the case of presenting an income statement on a FIFO basis as a supplementary schedule.
- Interim income statements may be presented on a non-LIFO basis as long as the total of the interim statements does not aggregate to one annual statement (e.g., three quarterly non-LIFO income statements may be presented, but not four quarterly statements).

So what happens when GAAP LIFO is replaced with IFRS FIFO or average cost? What happens to the Code Sec. 472 LIFO Conformity Requirement?

The issue is more political than technical. The technical answer is that assuming no action is taken to change Code Sec. 472, companies that adopt

IFRS and convert to a non-LIFO method for financial statement purposes also will be required to convert to a non-LIFO method (e.g., FIFO) for tax purposes and pay the tax on the LIFO reserve recapture.

One 2008 study suggested that 36 percent of U.S. companies use LIFO and that a conversion from LIFO for both IFRS and income tax purposes would have the following impact based on a sample of 30 U.S. firms reviewed:

Impact of Converting from LIFO to Non-LIFO: Sample 30 U.S. Companies

Change in	Average Change Increase / (Decrease)
Pre-tax income	11.9%
Net income	7.4%
Inventory—percent of total assets	46.0%
Stockholder's equity	34.2%
Current ratio	26.2%
Debt/equity ratio	(23.1)%

Source: The Potential Consequences of the Elimination of LIFO as a Part of IFRS Convergence (Georgia Tech College of Management).

In addition, there would be other impacts including the fact that financial covenants, compensation plans, and contracts driven by income would be impacted by a higher non-LIFO income. Some of the drawbacks of using LIFO such as the ability to manage earnings through liquidating LIFO layers would be eliminated through a conversion to a non-LIFO method.

STUDY QUESTION

2. Current regulations allow which of the following for U.S. GAAP if LIFO is also used for tax purposes?
   - **a.** The primary income statement must be presented on a basis other than LIFO.
   - **b.** Interim income statements may be presented on a non-LIFO basis.
   - **c.** The balance sheet must be presented on a LIFO basis.

WILL CONGRESS REPEAL OR SAVE LIFO?

Although a conversion from LIFO to a non-LIFO inventory method would clearly result in financial statement improvement as shown in the previous table, the tax effects would severely impact cash flow. In essence, companies would be required to pay federal and state income taxes on the entire LIFO reserve. In some industries, such as oil and gas, the tax effect would be in the billions. Consider three U.S. oil companies—Exxon-Mobil, Chevron, and Conoco-Phillip—inventories at December 31, 2010:

At December 31, 2010:	At FIFO	At LIFO	LIFO Reserve
Exxon-Mobil	$31.1	$9.8	$21.3
Chevron	10.6	3.6	7.0
Conoco-Phillips	10.6	4.9	5.7
Total	$52.3	$18.3	$34.0
% LIFO reserve to total LIFO inventory			186%

Source: Annual Reports

Using the example in the previous chart, assuming a 40 percent federal and state income tax rate, collectively Exxon, Chevron and Conoco would have a current federal and state tax bill of approximately $13.6 billion ($34 billion LIFO reserve at a 40 percent income tax rate) that negatively impacts each entity's cash flow. Of the $13.6 billion of additional taxes, approximately $10.8 billion would be payable to the federal government, while the remaining $2.8 billion would be paid for state and local income taxes (using 32 percent federal tax rate, net of the state tax benefit).

The overall tax revenue pickup from companies converting from LIFO to a non-LIFO basis would be sizeable and welcomed by Congress at a time when it desperately needs tax revenue. The author's estimation is that Congress expects the LIFO reserve recapture from repeal to be approximately $185 billion. (The 2011 Congressional Budget estimates that the tax revenue pickup from repeal to be $59 billion. Computation: $59 billion / 32% federal tax rate, net of state tax benefit = $185 billion estimated federal tax revenue pickup.)

In theory, Congress does not have to do anything to raise this tax revenue because the mere conversion to IFRS creates the tax revenue from the LIFO recapture. But waiting for the conversion to IFRS to eliminate LIFO would mean that Congress has to wait until 2014, 2015, or longer for IFRS to be adopted. Given the federal budget deficits and the push to lower corporate tax rates, it is unlikely that Congress will wait for the adoption of IFRS to eliminate LIFO.

Politically, it looks like the repeal of LIFO by Congress is gathering steam in both political parties. Although there are plenty of groups that will challenge the LIFO repeal, the political landscape points toward repeal of LIFO with an eight to 10-year phase-in of the LIFO recapture. After all, Congress can repeal LIFO and hide behind two reasons to support its decision:

- The international community does not allow the use of LIFO in IFRS to which U.S. companies are headed to adopt.
- A significant portion of the LIFO reserves are held by U.S. oil companies (Exxon, Chevron, and Conoco). Based on the analysis noted previously, Exxon, Chevron, and Conoco would pay approximately $10.8 billion of the $59 billion of additional federal taxes due to the LIFO repeal. In general, taxpayers are not sympathetic toward U.S. oil companies paying higher taxes.

In 2010, actions were taken by the White House and Congress that lead to the conclusion that Congress will repeal LIFO regardless of whether U.S. companies adopt IFRS.

In February 2010, as part of its proposed 2011 budget, the Obama Administration recommended that both LIFO and lower of cost or market value be repealed for inventories. The proposed changes were estimated to increase federal tax revenue by $59 billion for LIFO repeal and $7.5 billion for lower of cost of market repeal, over a 10-year period through 2020.

In August 2010, the Joint Committee on Taxation recommended repeal of LIFO using as one of its excuses the fact that the SEC has recommended adoption of international standards which would eliminate the use of LIFO anyway (Description of Revenue Provisions Contained in the President's Fiscal Year 2011 Budget Proposal, Joint Committee on Taxation, August 16, 2010).

Then, in December 2010, the National Commission of Fiscal Responsibility recommended that LIFO be "eliminated with appropriate transition" (The National Commission on Fiscal Responsibility and Reform, *The Moment of Truth,* December 2010, page 33). What was most significant about the National Commission recommendation is that the Commission is bi-partisan, suggesting that both parties in Congress support the repeal.

Similarly, the 2013 budget proposal repeals both LIFO inventories and lower of cost or market value, resulting in an increase in tax revenue of $74 billion for LIFO over 10 years, and $13 billion for lower of cost or market over four years.

The U.S. Department of Treasury explains the reasons for the proposed repeal:

Reasons for Change

The repeal of the LIFO method would eliminate a tax deferral opportunity available to taxpayers that hold inventories, the costs of which increase over time. In addition, LIFO repeal would simplify the Code by removing a complex and burdensome accounting method that has been the source of controversy between taxpayers and the Internal Revenue Service. International Financial Reporting Standards do not permit the use of the LIFO method, and their adoption by the Securities and Exchange Commission would cause violations of the current LIFO book/tax conformity requirement. Repealing LIFO would remove this possible impediment to the implementation of these standards in the United States.

Proposal

The proposal would repeal the use of the LIFO inventory accounting method for Federal income tax purposes. Taxpayers that currently use the LIFO method would be required to write up their beginning LIFO inventory to its FIFO value in the first taxable year beginning after December 31, 2013. However, this one-time increase in gross income would be taken into account ratably over ten years, beginning with the first taxable year beginning after December 31, 2013.

Source: General Explanations of the Administration's Fiscal Year 2013 Revenue Proposals, Department of the Treasury, February 2012

The bet is that Congress does not save LIFO and either repeals it directly or allows the conversion to IFRS to eliminate its use.

LAST-MINUTE ADOPTION OF LIFO BEFORE REPEAL

With the likely repeal of LIFO, taxpayers have an opportunity to adopt LIFO and lock in a LIFO reserve and not pay it back for 10 years.

With transportation prices increasing, 2012 and 2013 are likely to be years in which prices rise despite the otherwise soft economy.

Here is a quick approach to converting to LIFO in 2011 or 2012 using an external index (producer price index, Table 6 of the PPI).

Facts. Company X has the following information at FIFO:

Ending inventory FIFO, 12-31-10	$2,622,000
Ending inventory FIFO, 12-31-11	$2,947,000
Table 6, producer price index (PPI):	
Category: 0915, Converted Paper and Paperboard Products:	
Index: 12-10 (base year)	202.1
Index: 12-11	212.3
Increase	10.2
% increase (2010 to 2011)	5.05%
2011 index	**1.0505**
Ending inventory: 12-31-11 FIFO	$2,947,000
Divided by 2011 index	1.0505
Ending inventory, converted back to 2010 base year costs	$2,805,000
Base year 2010 inventory	2,622,000
2011 new layer	$183,000

Year	EI base year 2010 prices	Index	EI LIFO 12-31-11
2011	$ 183,000	1.0505	$ 192,000
2010 base year	2,622,000	1.0000	2,622,000
	$2,805,000		
EI- LIFO 12-31-11			$2,814,000
EI- FIFO 12-31-11			2,947,000
LIFO RESERVE			$ 133,000

Entry: 12-31-11		
CGS- LIFO Adjustment	133,000	
LIFO Reserve		133,000
Ending inventory: 12-31-11:		
FIFO	$2,947,000	
LIFO Reserve	(133,000)	
EI at LIFO	$2,814,000	

Conclusion. By using the external index, found in Table 6 of the PPI, the company converts to LIFO as of December 31, 2011 and creates a LIFO reserve of $133,000. With an easy LIFO conversion calculation, the company reduces both GAAP and taxable income by $133,000. Presumably, if inflation continues in 2012 and beyond, the company would continue to add to its LIFO reserve in year 2012. At that point, if and when LIFO is repealed, the company would have to convert back to FIFO. In the meantime, the company would save taxable income in years 2011 and 2012.

What if IFRS is passed and LIFO is not allowed for U.S. public companies? How does that affect the LIFO Conformity Requirement? There would be a violation of the LIFO Conformity Requirement and such companies would have to get off LIFO for tax purposes.

STUDY QUESTION

3. Under the proposed repeal, taxpayers that currently use the LIFO method would be required to write up their beginning LIFO inventory to its FIFO value:

a. In the first tax year beginning after December 31, 2012
b. In the first tax year beginning after December 31, 2013
c. In the first tax year beginning after December 31, 2014

CPE NOTE: When you have completed your study and review of chapters 1–3, which comprise Module 1, you may wish to take the Quizzer for this Module.

Go to **CCHGroup.com/PrintCPE** to take this Quizzer online.

MODULE 2: FINANCIAL STATEMENT REPORTING — CHAPTER 4

Comprehensive Income (ASC Topic 220)

LEARNING OBJECTIVES

Upon completion of this chapter, the reader will be able to:

- Describe what is included in other comprehensive income
- Define comprehensive income
- State the differences that exist currently between U.S. GAAP and IFRS in regard to how other comprehensive income is presented
- Explain which entities must comply with ASC 220 and which are exempt
- Explain the allowed presentation formats for other comprehensive income in the financial statements and notes
- State the ASU 2011-05 requirements regarding reclassification adjustments
- State the effective date of the ASU 2011-12 deferral for public and nonpublic companies
- Discuss how a non-controlling interest in another entity is presented in comprehensive income

BACKGROUND

ASC Topic 220, *Comprehensive Income* (formerly FAS 130), was issued to address the presentation of certain items (other comprehensive income items) that bypass the income statement and were recorded directly to equity.

Without a means to present these other comprehensive income items, financial statement users who focused on net income as the prime measurement of results of operations would not be taking into account these other comprehensive income items in measuring the entity's financial performance.

Examples of other comprehensive income items that under present accounting literature bypass the income statement and are recorded directly to stockholders' equity consist of:

1. Certain foreign exchange transactions under ASC 830, *Foreign Currency Matters*
2. Certain derivative transactions under ASC 815, *Derivatives and Hedging*
3. Certain transactions involving available-for-sale securities under ASC 320, *Investments—Debt and Equity Securities*
4. Certain pension transactions under ASC 715, *Compensation—Retirement Benefits*

Prior to the issuance of FAS 130 (now codified as ASC 220), an entity was required to present only the accumulated balances of the above list of other comprehensive income items in the statement of stockholders' equity. Yet, there were no standards on how to present these items. Moreover, an entity was not required to present one total for these items such as a caption "other comprehensive income." Ultimately, users pressured the FASB to implement standards to report comprehensive income, which is a broader concept of income. In June 1997, the FASB issued FAS 130, *Comprehensive Income.*

To date, ASC 220 (formerly FAS 130) has required that comprehensive income be presented in a financial statement format using one of three options:

1. Present a separate statement of comprehensive income.
2. Combine the statement of income and comprehensive income.
3. Present comprehensive income as a section within the statement of stockholders' equity.

The following are examples of the three options under existing ASC 220 rules prior to the changes made by Accounting Standards Update (ASU) 2011-05.

CURRENT RULES

Option 1: Separate Statement of Comprehensive Income

XYZ Corporation
Statement of Comprehensive Income
For The Year Ended December 31, 20X2

Net income	$120,000
Other comprehensive income:	
Unrealized gain on securities available for sale (net of tax of $20,000)	30,000
Foreign currency translation adjustments (net of tax of $16,000)	24,000
Total other comprehensive income	54,000
Comprehensive income	$174,000

CURRENT RULES

Option 2: Combined Statement of Income and Comprehensive Income

XYZ Corporation
Statement of Income and Comprehensive Income
For The Year Ended December 31, 20X2

Revenue	$1,000,000
Expenses	800,000
Income from operations	200,000
Income taxes	80,000
Net income	120,000
Other comprehensive income:	
Unrealized gain on securities available for sale (net of tax of $20,000)	30,000
Foreign currency translation adjustments (net of tax of $16,000)	24,000
Total other comprehensive income	54,000
Comprehensive income	$174,000

CURRENT RULES

Option 3: Present Comprehensive Income As Part of the Statement of Stockholders' Equity

XYZ Corporation
Statement of Stockholders' Equity
For The Year Ended December 31, 20X2

	Total	Retained Earnings	Accumulated Other Comprehensive Income: Unrealized gains on securities	Accumulated Other Comprehensive Income: Foreign currency adjustments	Common Stock
Beginning balance	$2,525,000	$2,000,000	$10,000	$15,000	$500,000
Comprehensive income					
Net income	120,000	120,000			
Other comprehensive income:					
Unrealized gains on securities available for sale (net of taxes of $20,000)	30,000		30,000		
Foreign currency translation adjustments (net of taxes of $16,000)	24,000	0	0	24,000	0
	54,000				
Total Comprehensive income	174,000				
Ending balance	$2,699,000	$2,120,000	$40,000	$39,000	$500,000

Although the three presentation options for comprehensive income all achieve the same result of disclosing other comprehensive income components and total comprehensive income, many financial statement users have complained that the third option of presenting comprehensive income within the statement of stockholders' equity results in comprehensive income being displayed less prominently than if the Option 1 or 2 were used. Moreover, although current U.S. GAAP permits use of the Option 3 (presentation within the statement of stockholders' equity), international accounting rules under the (International Financial Reporting Standards (IFRS) do not permit the Option 3 format.

The FASB has decided to amend ASC 220 to eliminate some of the key differences that exist between U.S. GAAP and international standards. ASU 2011-05 makes those changes.

ASU 2011-05

ASU 2011-05 was issued in June 2011. It amends ASC Topic 220, *Comprehensive Income* to improve the transparency and increase the prominence of items reported in other comprehensive income, and to facilitate convergence of U.S. GAAP and IFRS.

The amendments in this ASU should be applied retrospectively: For public entities, fiscal years, and interim periods within those years, *beginning after December 15, 2011*. For nonpublic entities, fiscal years *ending after December 15, 2012*, and interim and annual periods thereafter. Early adoption is permitted, because compliance with the amendments is already permitted. The amendments do not require any transition disclosures.

In December 2011, the FASB issued ASU 2011-12, which defers certain applications of ASU 2011-05 related to reclassification adjustments.

This ASU was issued as part of a joint project conducted by the FASB and the IASB to improve the presentation of comprehensive income in a manner that is as convergent as possible.

GAAP VS. IFRS

Currently, there are differences between how U.S. GAAP and IFRS present comprehensive income, as follows:

U.S. GAAP	IFRS
Permits *three alternatives* for presenting comprehensive income: ■ Separate statement ■ Combined statement with income statement ■ As part of the statement of changes in stockholders' equity	Permits only *two alternatives* for presenting comprehensive income: ■ Separate statement ■ Combined statement with income statement IFRS does not permit presenting comprehensive income as part of the statement of changes in stockholders' equity.
Does not require a consecutive presentation of the statement of income and comprehensive income	Requires consecutive presentation of the statement of income and comprehensive income
Reclassification adjustments from other comprehensive income to net income may be displayed *either* on the face of the financial statement in which comprehensive income is reported, or may be presented in the notes to financial statements.	Reclassification adjustments from other comprehensive income to net income *must* be presented on the face of the financial statements.

According to the FASB, removing certain presentation options will make it easier to compare statements of comprehensive income prepared using U.S. GAAP with those prepared using IFRS.

There are also U.S. GAAP-IFRS differences in the types of items reported in other comprehensive income that are not addressed by ASU 2011-05.

KEY CHANGES

Following are the key changes made to ASC Topic 220 by ASU 2011-05:

- Companies must present comprehensive income in a single statement or two separate, consecutive statements (statement of income and statement of comprehensive income). If the two-statement approach is selected, the two statements must be consecutive, presented one directly after the other.
  - The option to present comprehensive income in the statement of stockholders' equity (Option 3) is eliminated.
- Reclassification adjustments from other comprehensive income to net income must be presented on the face of the statement(s). The previous option to present the adjustments in the notes is eliminated.

Although ASU 2011-05 does eliminate some of the key differences in the presentation of comprehensive income between U. S. GAAP and IFRS, it does not deal with other differences that exist, including those related to components included within the definitions of other comprehensive income and comprehensive income.

DEFINITION OF COMPREHENSIVE INCOME

The definition of comprehensive income has been around for some time and is defined in ASC 220-10-20 as follows:

> ... the change in equity (net assets) of a business enterprise during a period from transactions and other events and circumstances from non-owner sources.

In other words, comprehensive income consists of the sum of those changes in equity, the source of which has *nothing to do with the owners (shareholders).*

Following is a formula that depicts the computation of comprehensive income:

Formula: Comprehensive Income (changes in equity that are from non-owner sources)

Net income and all of its components	
+ (–)	Other comprehensive income (items not presented on income statement)
=	Comprehensive income

Comprehensive income consists of changes in equity that are from non-owner sources.

One of the components of comprehensive income is net income, which is a change in equity from a non-owner source. There are also other changes in equity that are from non-owner sources, which are captured under the heading "*other comprehensive income.*" These other comprehensive income items bypass the income statement and are presented directly in equity.

There are essentially four categories of other comprehensive income items:

1. Certain foreign exchange transactions (ASC 830)
2. Certain derivative transactions (ASC 815)
3. Certain transactions involving available-for-sale securities (ASC 320)
4. Certain pension transactions (ASC 715)

The following chart summarizes comprehensive income, consisting of net income (loss) and other comprehensive income:

Comprehensive Income

1. **Net income (loss) + (–)**
2. **Other comprehensive income**
   (Items presented in equity and not on the income statement):

   a. **Certain foreign exchange transactions (ASC 830)**
      - Foreign exchange translation adjustments
      - Gains/losses on foreign currency transactions that are designated as economic hedges of a net investment in a foreign entity
      - Gains and losses on intra-entity foreign currency transactions that are of a long-term investment nature, when the entities to the transaction are consolidated, combined, or accounted for by the equity method

   b. **Certain derivative transactions (ASC 815)**
      - Gains or losses on derivative instruments that are designated as cash flow hedges

   c. **Certain transactions involving available-for-sale securities (ASC 320)**
      - Unrealized gains and losses on securities available for sale
      - Unrealized gains and losses from transfers of securities from the held-to-maturity category to available-for-sale category
      - Amounts recognized in other comprehensive income for debt securities classified as available-for-sale and held-to-maturity related to an other-than-temporary impairment recognized if a portion of the impairment was not recognized in earnings
      - Subsequent decreases (if not an other-than-temporary impairment) or increases in the fair value of available-for-sale securities previously written down as impaired

   d. **Certain pension transactions (ASC 715)**
      - Gains or losses associated with pension or other postretirement benefits that are not recognized immediately as a component of net periodic benefit cost
      - Prior service costs or credits associated with pension or other postretirement benefits
      - Transition assets or obligations associated with pension or other postretirement benefits that are not recognized immediately as a component of net periodic benefit cost

= **Comprehensive Income**

EXAMPLE

Facts. Company A has the following at year-end:

Net income	$1,000,000
Other comprehensive income (presented directly in equity)	
Foreign exchange transaction adjustments	100,000
Unrealized gain on available-for-sale securities	50,000

Conclusion. Comprehensive income is computed as follows:

Net income	$1,000,000
Other comprehensive income (presented directly in equity)	
Foreign exchange transaction adjustments	100,000
Unrealized gain on available-for-sale securities	50,000
Total comprehensive income	$1,150,000

Comprehensive income *excludes:*

1. Changes in equity from investments by owners or distributions to owners:
   a. Issuance of stock or equity interests
   b. Payment of dividends or owners' draws
2. Items reported as direct adjustments to paid-in capital, retained earnings, or other non-income related equity accounts such as:
   a. A reduction of equity related to employee stock ownership plans (ESOP)
   b. Taxes not payable in cash
   c. Net cash settlement resulting from a change in the value of a contract that gives an entity a choice of net cash settlement or settlement in its own shares
   d. Prior-period adjustments

OBSERVATION

Even though the previous list of items in (2)(a), (b) and (c) does consist of items that are recorded directly to equity, these items are specifically excluded from the definition of comprehensive income because the FASB chose to do so.

By way of example, the FASB concluded that a reduction in equity related to an ESOP is not part of comprehensive income because such a transaction involves the company's own stock, so such a transaction could be considered a transaction with the owners excluded from the definition of comprehensive income.

The FASB also excluded from the definition of comprehensive income taxes not paid in connection with an entity reorganization under ASC 852, *Reorganizations* (formerly SOP 90-7). These taxes not paid may result from a reorganized enterprise suffering net operating losses prior to reorganization that provide it with significant tax advantages going forward. ASC 852 requires that a reorganized enterprise record a "full tax rate" on its pretax income although its actual cash taxes paid are minimal because of those net operating loss carryforwards. Taxes not payable in cash are reported in the income statement as an expense with a corresponding increase to additional paid-in capital (APIC) in stockholders' equity. Although the credit to APIC resulting from taxes not payable in cash is not a transaction with an owner, it does not qualify as comprehensive income because the APIC credit stems from transactions and accounting that took place upon reorganization. In effect, the APIC credit adjusts transactions that were recorded in equity in an earlier period and does not result from the current period debit to income tax expense.

SCOPE OF THE STATEMENT

ASC 220, as amended by ASU 2011-05, *applies to* all entities that provide a *full set of financial statements* including a statement of financial position, results of operations and cash flows.

NOTE

Investment companies, defined benefit pension plans and other employee benefit plans that are exempt from providing a statement of cash flows are not exempt from the requirements of comprehensive income, even though there is not a full set of financial statements.

ASC 220 *does not* apply to:

- An entity that does not have any items of other comprehensive income items in any period presented.
- A not-for-profit organization that is required to follow the provisions of ASC Subtopic 958-205, *Not-for-Profit Entities, Presentation of Financial* Statements (formerly FSP FAS 117-1)

EXAMPLE

Company A is presenting comparative financial statements for 20X2 and 20X1. Its only change in stockholders' equity for 20X2 and 20X1 is net income. There are no other comprehensive income items (e.g., foreign exchange gains/losses, unrealized gains/losses on securities, etc.).

Conclusion: The Company is exempt from the requirements of ASC 220 because it does not have any items of other comprehensive income. Consequently, there is no requirement to present other comprehensive income or comprehensive income in a statement format.

Change the facts. Same facts as the example above, except Company A has an unrealized gain on available-for-sale securities in the amount of $100,000 in 20X2.

Conclusion. The Company *must comply* with the requirements of ASC 220 because it has an item of other comprehensive income (unrealized gain on available-for-sale securities). Therefore, the Company is required to present comprehensive income in a financial statement format.

What happens when there are compiled financial statements that omit a statement of cash flows? SSARS 19, *Compilation and Review Engagements*, provides that an entity may elect to omit a statement of cash flows (and also substantially all disclosures) required by GAAP. In such a situation, the entity is not presenting a full set of financial statements (e.g., the statement of cash flows is not included).

EXAMPLE

Company A has the following changes in stockholders' equity for 20X1:

Net income	$500,000
Other comprehensive income:	
Unrealized gains on securities available for sale	50,000
Foreign exchange translation adjustments	20,000

The company's financial statements are being compiled and management has elected to omit substantially all disclosures and the statement of cash flows.

Conclusion. The company is *exempt* from complying with ASC 220 because it is not presenting a full set of financial statements. Consequently, even though the company has two other comprehensive income items (unrealized gains and foreign exchange adjustments), it is not required to present comprehensive income in a financial statement.

Further, in accordance with Interpretation 10 of AR §80 (SSARS 19): *Omission of the Display of Comprehensive Income in Compiled Financial Statements,* the compilation report should be modified to reflect the fact that a statement of comprehensive income is not presented even though there are other comprehensive income items.

The Interpretation requires the compilation report to be modified to reflect the fact that a statement of comprehensive income is not displayed.

The following is suggested modified wording (shown in italic) to the paragraph in the compilation report:

> Management has elected to omit substantially all the disclosures, the statement of cash flows, *and the display of comprehensive income* required by accounting principles generally accepted in the United States of America. If the omitted disclosures, the statement of cash flows, *and the display of comprehensive income* were included in the financial statements, they might influence the user's conclusions about the company's financial position, results of operations, and cash flows. Accordingly, these financial statements are not designed for those who are not informed about such matters.

Change the facts. The company is issuing a full set of financial statements including a statement of cash flows.

Conclusion. Because the company has other comprehensive income items (unrealized gains and foreign exchange adjustments), the company must comply with the requirements of ASC 220. That means that comprehensive income must be presented in a financial statement format (one or two statements).

Do the requirements to display comprehensive income apply when OCBOA statements are presented? No. ASC 220 only applies if a full set of financial statements is presented, including a statement of cash flows. When Other Comprehensive Basis of Accounting (OCBOA) statements are presented (e.g., income tax basis), a statement of cash flows is *not required* in accordance with ASC 230, *Statement of Cash Flows* (formerly FAS 95). Therefore, OCBOA statements do not provide a full set of financial statements and are not subject to the comprehensive income requirements. Even if the entity elects to include a cash flow statement in a set of OCBOA financial statements, the statement would still not apply; that is, a statement of comprehensive income would not be required. This is because, in general, OCBOA statements do not have any other comprehensive income items.

EXAMPLE

OCBOA income tax basis financial statements would not have any of the other comprehensive income items (e.g., unrealized gains/losses on securities, foreign translation gains/losses) posted directly to equity.

STUDY QUESTIONS

1. Which of the following is an example of an other comprehensive income item?
   - **a.** Certain transactions involving trading securities
   - **b.** Certain transactions involving available-for-sale securities
   - **c.** Certain transactions involving debt securities held to maturity
   - **d.** Certain transactions involving non-security investments

2. The formula for comprehensive income is which of the following?

   a. Net income +- change in equity
   b. Net income +- other comprehensive income
   c. Net income +- non-cash transactions
   d. Net income +- change in working capital

3. Which of the following is an example of a transaction involving available-for-sale securities that would be part of other comprehensive income?

   a. Unrealized gains and losses from transfers of securities from the available-for-sale category to the held-to-maturity category
   b. Subsequent increase in the fair value of available-for sale securities previously written down as an other-than-temporary impairment
   c. Amounts recognized in other comprehensive income for debt securities classified as available-for-sale and held-to-maturity related to an other-than-temporary impairment recognized if a portion of the impairment was recognized in earnings
   d. Unrealized gains on securities available-for-sale

4. ASC 220, as amended by ASU 2011-05, requires that comprehensive income be presented in a format. Which of the following is one of the format options available?

   a. Disclose comprehensive income only
   b. Present a single continuous statement of income and comprehensive income
   c. Present comprehensive income as a section within the statement of stockholders' equity

REQUIREMENTS OF THE STATEMENT

The Statement requires the following:

Comprehensive income. All components of comprehensive income must be presented in the financial statements in the period in which they are recognized segregated as follows:

Net income	$XX
Other comprehensive income:	
Certain foreign exchange transactions	XX
Certain derivative transactions	XX
Certain transactions involving available-for-sale securities	XX
Total comprehensive income	$XX

Presentation. An entity with other comprehensive income items must report comprehensive income either in:

- A single continuous statement of income and comprehensive income
- Two separate but consecutive financial statements consisting of:
  - Statement of income, followed by a
  - Statement of comprehensive income

Regardless of whether a single or two financial statements approach is used, all items that meet the definition of comprehensive income shall be presented for the period in which those items are recognized. An entity reporting a *single continuous financial statement* (statement of income and comprehensive income) shall present the following components in two sections; net income and other comprehensive income:

- A total amount for net income together with the components that make up net income (e.g., revenue, expenses, etc.)
- A total amount for other comprehensive income together with the components that make up other comprehensive income
- Total comprehensive income

An entity reporting comprehensive income in *two separate but consecutive statements* shall present the following:

In the statement of income:
- Components of and the total for net income in the statement of net income

In the statement of comprehensive income:
- Components of and the total for other comprehensive income
- Total comprehensive income

NOTE

If two separate statements are presented, the statement of comprehensive income shall be presented immediately after the statement of income. Moreover, the statement of comprehensive income may (but is not required to) start with net income.

The terms "comprehensive income" or "other comprehensive income" do not have to be used in the financial statements even though they are used throughout ASC 220. If an entity has an outstanding noncontrolling interest, the following must be presented in the financial statements in which net income and comprehensive income are presented:

- Amounts for both net income and comprehensive income attributable to the parent

- Amounts for net income and comprehensive income attributable to the noncontrolling interest in a less-than-wholly owned subsidiary
- Consolidated net income and comprehensive income

Tax effect of other comprehensive income items. An entity shall present components of other comprehensive income in the statement in which other comprehensive income is reported either:

- Net of tax effects
- Before the tax effects with one amount shown for the total income tax expense allocated to total other comprehensive income

An entity shall present the amount of income tax expense (or benefit) allocated to each component of other comprehensive income, including reclassification adjustments, either in the statement in which those components are presented, or disclose it in the notes to financial statements.

NOTE

In lieu of disclosing in the notes the income tax expense allocated to each component of other comprehensive income, that information can be presented parenthetically for each component of other comprehensive income in the statement in which other comprehensive income is presented.

Balance sheet and statement of equity. The total of other comprehensive income must be presented as a separate component in the equity section of the balance sheet under a caption similar to *accumulated other comprehensive income.*

Accumulated other comprehensive income shall be presented separately from retained earnings and additional paid-in capital in the equity section of the balance sheet at the end of the accounting period. An entity shall present on the face of the financial statements or disclosure in the notes the changes in the accumulated *balance* for each component of *accumulated other comprehensive income.* The components must correspond to those used in the presentation of other comprehensive income.

The following example illustrates the options available for presenting comprehensive income under ASU 2011-05 of ASC 220:

EXAMPLE

Facts. The following financial data applies to XYZ Corporation for the year ended December 31, 20X1.

Revenue	$1,000,000
Expenses	800,000
Income from operations	200,000
Income taxes	80,000
Net income	120,000
Retained earnings:	
Beginning of year	2,000,000
End of year	$2,120,000

Other comprehensive income items:
(posted directly to stockholders' equity)

Unrealized gains on available-for-sale securities	$50,000
Income taxes allocated	(20,000)
Net gain	$30,000

Foreign currency translation adjustments	$40,000
Income taxes allocated	(16,000)
Net amount	$24,000

Format 1: Single Continuous Statement Approach (Combined Statement of Income and Comprehensive Income)

XYZ Corporation
Statement of Income and Comprehensive Income
For The Year Ended December 31, 20X1

Revenue	$1,000,000
Expenses	800,000
Income from operations	200,000
Income taxes	80,000
Net income	120,000
Other comprehensive income:*	
Unrealized gain on securities available for sale (net of tax of $20,000)	30,000
Foreign currency translation adjustments (net of tax of $16,000)	24,000
Total other comprehensive income	54,000
Comprehensive income	$174,000

* *Alternatively, the tax effect of other comprehensive income could be presented as follows:*

Unrealized gain	50,000
Foreign currency adjustments	40,000
Other comprehensive income, before taxes	90,000
Income tax expense allocated	(36,000)
Other comprehensive income	54,000

Format 2: Two-Statement Approach (Two separate but consecutive financial statements)

- Statement of income, followed by a
- Statement of Comprehensive Income

Separate Statement of Income

XYZ Corporation
Statement of Income
For The Year Ended December 31, 20X1

Revenue	$1,000,000
Expenses	800,000
Income from operations	200,000
Income taxes	80,000
Net income	120,000
Retained earnings:	
Beginning of year	2,000,000
End of year	$2,120,000

Separate Statement of Comprehensive Income

XYZ Corporation
Statement of Comprehensive Income
For The Year Ended December 31, 20X1

Net income	$120,000
Other comprehensive income:	
Unrealized gain on securities available for sale (net of tax of $20,000)	30,000
Foreign currency translation adjustments (net of tax of $16,000)	24,000
Total other comprehensive income	54,000
Comprehensive income	$174,000

PRESENTATION OF CHANGES IN COMPONENTS OF ACCUMULATED OTHER COMPREHENSIVE INCOME IN THE STATEMENT OF STOCKHOLDERS' EQUITY

Regardless of whether a single or two-statement format is used to present comprehensive income, ASC 220 requires an entity to present on the face of the financial statements or in the notes to financial statements, the changes in the accumulated *balance* for each component of *accumulated other comprehensive income.*

The changes may be shown either in the statement of stockholders' equity or in the notes to financial statements. Continuing with the previous example, the two presentation options are presented below:

Option 1: Present the changes in each component of accumulated other comprehensive income in the statement of stockholders' equity.

XYZ Corporation
Statement of Stockholders' Equity
For The Year Ended December 31, 20X2

			Accumulated Other Comprehensive Income		
	Total	Retained Earnings	Unrealized gains on securities	Foreign currency adjustments	Common Stock
Beginning balance	$2,525,000	$2,000,000	$10,000	$15,000	$500,000
Comprehensive income					
Net income	120,000	120,000			
Unrealized gains on securities available for sale	30,000		30,000		
Foreign currency translation adjustments	24,000	0	0	24,000	0
Ending balance	$2,699,000	$2,120,000	$40,000	$39,000	$500,000

NOTE

The requirement is to present the changes in each component of accumulated other comprehensive income. The two changes in accumulated other comprehensive income (unrealized gains and foreign currency adjustments) are shown net of tax. However, there is no requirement to disclose the tax effect of these changes when presenting the changes in accumulated other comprehensive income. Notice also that there is no labeling required such as "other comprehensive income" or "comprehensive income."

Option 2: Present the changes in each component of accumulated other comprehensive income in the notes to financial statements

XYZ Corporation
Statement of Stockholders' Equity
For The Year Ended December 31, 20X2

	Total	Retained Earnings	Accumulated Other Comprehensive Income	Common Stock
Beginning balance	$2,525,000	$2,000,000	$25,000	$500,000
Comprehensive income				
Net income	120,000	120,000		
Other comprehensive income – current year	54,000		54,000	
Ending balance	$2,699,000	$2,120,000	$79,000	$500,000

Note X: Changes in Accumulated Other Comprehensive Income

Changes in each component of accumulated other comprehensive income follow:

	Accumulated Other Comprehensive Income		
	Unrealized gains (losses) – available-for-sale securities	Foreign exchange translation adjustments	Total
Beginning balance	$10,000	$15,000	$25,000
Other comprehensive income – current year	30,000	24,000	54,000
End balance	$40,000	$39,000	$79,000

NOTE

An entity is required to present the changes in accumulated other comprehensive income either in a statement (statement of stockholders' equity) or in the notes to financial statements. The author believes that the best place to present this change is in the statement of stockholders' equity and not in the notes which is represented by Option 1 above. Option 2 provides for presentation in the notes to financial statements. Under Option 2, the total accumulated other comprehensive income is shown in one column in the statement of stockholders' equity because GAAP requires that all changes in equity be presented. Because the changes in the two components of accumulated other comprehensive income (unrealized gains and foreign currency adjustments) are disclosed in the notes (NOTE X), only the total change in accumulated other comprehensive income is presented in the statement of stockholders' equity.

PRESENTATION OF BALANCE SHEET—ALL FORMATS

Regardless of the format for presenting comprehensive income, ***accumulated other comprehensive income*** must be presented as a *separate component* on the balance sheet as follows:

XYZ Corporation
Balance Sheet
December 31, 20X1

Assets:	
Cash	$XX
Accounts receivable	XX
Securities, available-for sale	XX
Property and equipment, net	XX
Total assets	$XX
Liabilities:	
Accounts payable	$XX
Accrued expenses	XX
Deferred income taxes	XX
Total liabilities	XX
Stockholders' equity:	
Common stock	XX
Retained earnings	XX
Accumulated other comprehensive income	**79,000***
Total stockholders' equity	XX
Total liabilities and stockholders' equity	$XX

* *Unrealized gains on securities ($40,000) plus foreign exchange adjustments (39,000) (total $79,000).*

NOTE

The Statement requires that accumulated other comprehensive income be presented as a separate component in the equity section of the balance sheet. It does not require that the individual components be presented as long as they are presented elsewhere such as in the statement of stockholders' equity or in the notes to financial statements.

ALTERNATIVE PRESENTATION OF TAX EFFECT OF OTHER COMPREHENSIVE INCOME ITEMS

ASC 220 requires disclosure of the tax effect of each item of other comprehensive income. In each of the preceding three formats, this requirement has been achieved by presenting the tax effect parenthetically next to each item of other comprehensive income. Alternatively, this requirement can be satisfied by presenting the total tax expense as one line item assigned to other comprehensive income, with a separate note provided that discloses the breakout of income tax expense assigned to each other comprehensive income component.

Facts. Assume Format 1 (a single continuous statement) is selected to present comprehensive income, except that the tax effect of each item of other comprehensive income is not parenthetically presented, as follows:

XYZ Corporation
Statement of Income and Comprehensive Income
For The Year Ended December 31, 20X1

Revenue	$1,000,000
Expenses	800,000
Income from operations	200,000
Income taxes	80,000
Net income	120,000
Other comprehensive income ***(before taxes):***	
Unrealized gain on securities available for ***sale (no tax effect disclosed)***	50,000
Foreign currency translation adjustments ***sale (no tax effect disclosed)***	40,000
Other comprehensive income before taxes	90,000
Income tax expense related to items of other comprehensive income	**(36,000)**
Other comprehensive income, net of taxes	54,000
Comprehensive income	$174,000

Note X: Comprehensive Income

The following summarizes the tax effect, by component, of other comprehensive income:

	Unrealized gains – available-for-sale securities	Foreign exchange translation adjustments	Total other comprehensive income
Amount before tax effect	$50,000	$40,000	$90,000
Tax effect	(20,000)	(16,000)	(36,000)
Amount, net of tax effect	$30,000	$24,000	$54,000

STUDY QUESTIONS

5. Which of the following is an acceptable presentation of the tax effect related to components of other comprehensive income?
   - **a.** Present each component net of tax effects
   - **b.** Present total other comprehensive income with one total allocation of income taxes, and no allocation or disclosure as to the individual components
   - **c.** The tax effects are not required to be allocated to other comprehensive income
   - **d.** Present other comprehensive income in the financial statements without the tax effect and disclose the tax effect in the notes to financial statements

6. ASC 220 requires which of the following?
   - **a.** If a single format is used to present comprehensive income, an entity must present the changes in the accumulated balance for each component of accumulated other comprehensive income. This is not required for the two-statement format.
   - **b.** The changes in the accumulated balance for each component of accumulated other comprehensive income may be shown in the statement of stockholders' equity.
   - **c.** Individual components of accumulated other comprehensive income must be presented in the equity section of the balance sheet.

RECLASSIFICATION ADJUSTMENTS

If applicable, adjustments must be made to avoid double counting of comprehensive income items that are presented as part of net income in one period, and as part of other comprehensive income in that period or earlier periods. ASC 220 refers to such adjustments as reclassification *adjustments*.

EXAMPLE

In year 1, an entity records an unrealized gain on securities available for sale which is shown as part of stockholders' equity and other comprehensive income.

In year 2, the company sells the security which results in a realized gain on the income statement.

Conclusion. In year 2, the gain must be deducted from other comprehensive income to avoid including the gain in comprehensive income twice—once as a realized gain on the sale, and once as an unrealized holding gain.

RULES FOR RECLASSIFICATION ADJUSTMENTS

- An entity shall determine reclassification adjustments for each component of other comprehensive income. The reclassification adjustment for foreign currency translation adjustments is limited to translation gains and losses realized upon sale or upon complete or substantially complete liquidation of an investment in a foreign entity.
- An entity shall present reclassification adjustments and the effects of those adjustments on net income and other comprehensive income in the statement in which the components of net income and other comprehensive income are presented. The previous option of presenting reclassification adjustments in the notes to financial statements is eliminated by ASU 2011-05.

EXAMPLE

The following example extracted from ASC 220 illustrates the application of the reclassification adjustment.

Facts. On December 31, 20X1, Company X purchases 1,000 shares of equity securities at $10 per share (total purchase price is $10,000). The securities are classified as available for sale.

Fair value of these securities at December 31, 20X3 and 20X2 follows:

Year End	Fair value/ share	Total fair value	Total cost	Unrealized gain	30% tax effect	Unrealized net gain
12-31-X2	$12	$12,000	$10,000	$2,000	$(600)	$1,400
12-31-X3	15	15,000	10,000	5,000	(1,500)	3,500

Federal and state tax rate is 30 percent.

On December 31, 20X3, the securities were sold for $15,000.

Conclusion. Because the security is categorized as available for sale, it is recorded at fair value with any unrealized gain or loss recorded as a component of other comprehensive income, net of the tax effect.

Entries as follows:

December 31, 20X1:

	dr	cr
Investment in equity security	10,000	
Cash		10,000
To record purchase of 1,000 shares at $10 per share		

December 31, 20X2 and 20X3 entries:

	20X2 Entries		20X3 Entries	
	dr	cr	dr	cr
Allowance for unrealized gain	2,000		3,000	
Unrealized gain on securities (equity)		2,000		3,000
Unrealized gain on securities (30%) (equity)	600		900	
Deferred income tax liability		600		900
To record unrealized holding gains on securities available for sale, net of related tax effect				

	20X3 Entries	
	dr	cr
Cash	15,000	
Investment in equity security		10,000
Gain on sale of securities		5,000
To record sale of investment on 12-31-X3		
Unrealized gain on securities	3,500	
Allowance for unrealized gain		5,000
Deferred income tax liability	1,500	
To reverse the unrealized gain and related tax effect related to the sale of investments.		

Presentation on Financial Statements:

Company X
Statements of Income and Comprehensive Income
For The Years Ended December 31, 20X3 and 20X2

	20X3	20X2
Revenue	$XX	$XX
Expenses	XX	XX
Income from operations	XX	XX
Other income:		
Gain on sale of securities	**5,000**	0
Income taxes	XX	XX
Net income (given)	400,000	300,000
Other comprehensive income ***(before taxes):***		
Unrealized gain on securities available for ***sale*** (net of taxes $900 in 20X3 and $600 in 20X2)	2,100	1,400
Reclassification adjustment (net of tax effect of $1,500)	**(3,500)**	**0**
Other comprehensive income	(1,400)	1,400
Comprehensive income	$398,600	$301,400

NOTE

Prior to the issuance of ASU 2011-05, ASC 220 permitted the reclassification adjustment to be presented net on the statement with a corresponding gross presentation in the notes to financial statements. For example, a net presentation would net the $2,100 unrealized gain with the reclassification adjustment of $3,500, for a net amount of $1,400.

In ASU 2011-05, the ASU eliminated the option to present the reclassification adjustment in the notes to financial statements in lieu of presenting it on the face of the statement. Consequently, use of a net method is not possible because, with the removal of the note option, there is no way to inform the reader of the components that make up that net amount.

What happens to the reclassification adjustment if there are purchases and sales of securities within the same year?

EXAMPLE

Assume in 20X1, a security is purchased and sold as follows:

March 1, 20X1 purchased	$10,000
November 1, 20X1 sold	13,000
Gain	3,000
Tax effect 40%	(1,200)
Net gain	$1,800

Should an unrealized gain be shown up to the date of sale ($1,800) with a corresponding reversal as a reclassification adjustment of $(1,800)? Or should the entire unrealized gain up to the date of sale be excluded with only the $3,000 realized gain shown?

Response. For ASC 320, (formerly FAS 115) purposes, there would be no unrealized gain recorded because the calculation is done at the balance sheet date. At that date, there were no securities owned. However, for ASC 220 presentation purposes, the unrealized gain must be reflected up to the date of the sale as follows:

Company X
Statement of Income and Comprehensive Income
For The Year Ended December 31, 20X1

Revenue	$XX
Expenses	XX
Income from operations	XX
Other income:	
Gain on sale of securities	**3,000**
Income before income taxes	XX
Income taxes	XX
Net income	XX
Other comprehensive income	
Unrealized gain on securities available for sale (net of taxes $1,200)	1,800
Reclassification adjustment (net of tax effect of $1,200)	**(1,800)**
Other comprehensive income	(0)
Comprehensive income	$XX

DEFERRAL OF RECLASSIFICATION ADJUSTMENTS: ASU 2011-12

ASU 2011-05 made changes to the presentation of the reclassification adjustments.

Before the issuance of Update 2011-05, under U.S. GAAP, companies had the option to present reclassification adjustments out of accumulated other comprehensive income either on the face of the financial statement in which comprehensive income is reported or in the notes to the financial statements. Further, before the issuance of Update 2011-05, U.S. GAAP did not require that the effect of reclassification adjustments on the components of net income be presented in the financial statements.

ASU 2011-05 changed previous accounting for reclassification adjustments by requiring an entity to present the effect of reclassification adjustments on net income and other comprehensive income in the statement in which components of net income and the components of other comprehensive income are presented.

Subsequent to the issuance of ASU 2011-05, constituents questioned the FASB's approach to dealing with reclassification adjustments and asked the FASB to reconsider its approach.

In December 2011, the FASB issued ASU 2011-12, *Comprehensive Income (Topic 220) Deferral of the Effective Date for Amendments to the Presentation of Reclassifications of Items Out of Accumulated Other Comprehensive Income in Accounting Standards Update No. 2011-05*.

ASU 2011-12 defers the application of the reclassification adjustments found in ASU 2011-05 while the FASB has time to re-deliberate as to how to present reclassification adjustments. In essence, ASU 2011-12 requires companies to use the pre-ASU 2011-05 approach to deal with reclassification adjustments.

All other requirements in ASU 2011-05 are not affected by ASU 2011-12, including the requirement to report comprehensive income either in a single continuous financial statement or in two separate but consecutive financial statements. Public entities are required to apply the ASU 2011-12 deferral for fiscal years, and interim periods within those years, beginning after December 15, 2011. Nonpublic entities should begin applying these requirements for fiscal years ending after December 15, 2012, and interim and annual periods thereafter.

PRESENTATION OF NON-CONTROLLING INTERESTS

If a company has a non-controlling interest in another entity, comprehensive income must be presented before and after the non-controlling interest.

Following is an example of a two-statement approach for a company that has a non-controlling interest in another entity.

Format 2: Two-Statement Approach

Separate Statement of Income

XYZ Corporation
Consolidated Statement of Income
For The Year Ended December 31, 20X1

Revenue	$1,000,000
Expenses	800,000
Income from operations	200,000
Income taxes	80,000
Net income	120,000
Less: net income attributable to noncontrolling interest	**(25,000)**
Net income attributable to XYZ Corporation	95,000
Retained earnings:	
Beginning of year	2,000,000
End of year	$2,095,000

Separate Statement of Comprehensive Income

XYZ Corporation
Consolidated Statement of Comprehensive Income
For The Year Ended December 31, 20X1

Net income	$120,000
Other comprehensive income:	
Unrealized gain on securities available for sale (net of tax of $20,000)	30,000
Foreign currency translation adjustments (net of tax of $16,000)	24,000
Total other comprehensive income	54,000
Comprehensive income	174,000
Less: comprehensive income attributable to non-controlling interest	**(32,000)**
Comprehensive income attributable to XYZ Corporation	$142,000

XYZ Corporation
Consolidated Balance Sheet
December 31, 20X1

Assets:	
Cash	$XX
Accounts receivable	XX
Securities, available-for sale	XX
Property and equipment, net	XX
Total assets	$XX
Liabilities:	
Accounts payable	$XX
Accrued expenses	XX
Deferred income taxes	XX
Total liabilities	XX
Stockholders' equity:	
Common stock	500,000
Retained earnings	2,095,000
Accumulated other comprehensive income	62,000
Total stockholders' equity- XYZ Corporation	2,657,000
Noncontrolling interest	**42,000**
Total equity	2,699,000
Total liabilities and stockholders' equity	$XX

XYZ Corporation
Consolidated Statement of Stockholders' Equity
For The Year Ended December 31, 20X1

	Total	Retained Earnings	Accumulated Other Comprehensive Income	Common Stock	Non-controlling interest
Beginning balance (given)	$2,525,000	$2,000,000	$15,000	$500,000	$10,000
Comprehensive income					
Net income	120,000	95,000			(1) 25,000
Other comprehensive income – current year	54,000		47,000		(1) 7,000
Ending balance	$2,699,000	$2,095,000	$62,000	$500,000	$42,000

(1): $25,000 + $7,000 = $32,000 comprehensive income attributable to noncontrolling interest.

INTERIM-PERIOD REPORTING

An entity shall report the components of net income and other comprehensive income, and the total for comprehensive income, in condensed financial statements of interim periods issued to shareholders.

OPTIONAL DISCLOSURE

One item missing within ASC 220 is a disclosure of the description of comprehensive income. Although not specifically required, the author recommends that the following language be included in the summary of significant accounting policies, educating the reader as to what comprehensive income is:

> **Summary of Significant Accounting Policies**
>
> **Comprehensive Income**
>
> Comprehensive income consists of certain changes in stockholders' equity not related to transactions with stockholders. They include net income and certain other items that are not presented on the statement of income and, instead, are recorded directly in stockholders' equity, net of the related tax effect. These items include unrealized gains and losses on sales of certain securities, certain foreign exchange gains and losses, and specific pension transactions, among others.

REPORTING ISSUES: COMPREHENSIVE INCOME

If a separate statement of comprehensive income or a combined statement of income and comprehensive income is chosen to present comprehensive income, the report wording must be changed to reflect the new statement.

SSARS 19 states that if the statement of comprehensive income is presented, reference to the statement should be made in the appropriate paragraphs. Thus, if a statement of comprehensive income is required, the compilation, review, and audit reports should be modified to include reference to the statement.

Assume that a statement of income and comprehensive income is issued. Examples of a compilation, review, and audit report that include reference to the statement of income and comprehensive income follow:

Example of Change in Report Language: Comprehensive Income

> **Example: Compilation Report**
> **Statement of Income and Comprehensive Income Presented**
>
> **Accountant's Compilation Report**
>
> Board of Directors
> XYZ Corporation
>
> We have compiled the accompanying balance sheet of XYZ Corporation as of December 31, 20X2, and the related **statements of income and comprehensive income**, and cash flows for the year then ended. We have not audited or reviewed the accompanying financial statements and, accordingly, do not express an opinion or provide any assurance about whether the financial statements are in accordance with accounting principles generally accepted in the United States of America.

Management is responsible for the preparation and fair presentation of the financial statements in accordance with accounting principles generally accepted in the United States of America and for designing, implementing, and maintaining internal control relevant to the preparation and fair presentation of the financial statements.

Our responsibility is to conduct the compilation in accordance with Statements on Standards for Accounting and Review Services issued by the American Institute of Certified Public Accountants. The objective of a compilation is to assist management in presenting financial information in the form of financial statements without undertaking to obtain or provide any assurance that there are no material modifications that should be made to the financial statements.

James J. Fox & Company
March 31, 20X3

Example: Review Report—Statement of Income and Comprehensive Income Presented

Independent Accountant's Review Report

Board of Directors
XYZ Corporation

We have reviewed the accompanying balance sheet of XYZ Corporation as of December 31, 20X2, and the related **statements of income and comprehensive income**, and cash flows for the year then ended. A review includes primarily applying analytical procedures to management's financial data and making inquiries of company management (owners). A review is substantially less in scope than an audit, the objective of which is the expression of an opinion regarding the financial statements as a whole. Accordingly, we do not express such an opinion.

Management is responsible for the preparation and fair presentation of the financial statements in accordance with accounting principles generally accepted in the United States of America and for designing, implementing, and maintaining internal control relevant to the preparation and fair presentation of the financial statements.

Our responsibility is to conduct the review in accordance with Statements on Standards for Accounting and Review Services issued by the American Institute of Certified Public Accountants. Those standards require me (us) to perform procedures to obtain limited assurance that there are no material modifications that should be made to the financial statements. We believe that the results of our procedures provide a reasonable basis for our report.

Based on our review, we are not aware of any material modifications that should be made to the accompanying financial statements in order for them to be in conformity with accounting principles generally accepted in the United States of America.

James J. Fox & Company
March 31, 20X3

Example: Audit Report—Statement of Income and Comprehensive Income Presented

Independent Auditor's Report

Board of Directors
XYZ Corporation

We have audited the accompanying balance sheet of XYZ Corporation as of December 31, 20X2, and the related **statements of income and comprehensive income**, and cash flows for the year then ended. These financial statements are the responsibility of the Company's management. Our responsibility is to express an opinion on these statements based on our audit.

We conducted our audit in accordance with auditing standards generally accepted in the United Statements of America. Those standards require that we plan and perform the audit to obtain reasonable assurance about whether the financial statements are free from material misstatements. An audit includes examining, on a test basis, evidence supporting the amounts and disclosures in the financial statements. An audit also includes assessing the accounting principles used and significant estimates made by management, as well as evaluating the overall financial statement presentation. We believe our audit provides a reasonable basis for our opinion.

In our opinion, the financial statements referred to in the first paragraph present fairly, in all material respects, the financial position of XYX Corporation as of December 31, 20X2, and the results of its operations and its cash flows for the year then ended in conformity with accounting principles generally accepted in the United States of America.

James J. Fox & Company
March 31, 20X3

STUDY QUESTIONS

7. Reclassification adjustments are made to ____________.

a. Ensure that items are not classified in the wrong financial statement
b. Avoid double counting of comprehensive income items
c. Make sure disclosures thoroughly present information on comprehensive income
d. Permit a company to present comprehensive income on the correct line in the statement of comprehensive income

8. ASU 2011-12 does which of the following?

a. Defers the requirement under ASU 2011-05 to report comprehensive income either in a single continuous financial statement or in two separate but consecutive financial statements.

b. Defers the application of all ASU 2011-05 requirements until 2014

c. Defers the application of the reclassification adjustments found in ASU 2011-05

9. Which of the following statements is true?

a. If a separate statement of comprehensive income is chosen to present comprehensive income, the report wording is not affected.

b. If the statement of comprehensive income is presented, reference to the statement should be made in the appropriate paragraphs.

c. If a statement of comprehensive income is required, audit reports should be modified to include reference to the statement. However, compilation and review reports do not need to be modified.

MODULE 2: FINANCIAL STATEMENT REPORTING — CHAPTER 5

Revenue Recognition: Proposed Changes

LEARNING OBJECTIVES

Upon completion of this chapter, the reader will be able to:

- Describe the revenue recognition issues that led to the revenue project
- Explain how SAB 101 determines when revenue should be recognized
- Describe the steps involved in applying the proposed revenue standard
- State when an entity should combine two contracts
- Describe how the revenue recognition proposal differs from current GAAP
- Define an onerous performance obligation
- List the disclosures that would be required under the revenue recognition proposal
- Describe which contract costs should be capitalized and which should be expensed
- State the FASB's estimated effective date for the revenue recognition proposal

INTRODUCTION

Revenue recognition has been an important topic and a primary concern in recent cases of fraud and accounting violations noted by the Securities and Exchange Commission (SEC). Traditional accounting rules for recognizing revenue have become outdated as more complex revenue transactions have become the norm.

According to the AICPA, revenue recognition issues account for approximately *50 percent of all financial statement frauds.* Some of the more important revenue issues discussed by the AICPA and SEC follow:

- Recognition of revenue prematurely such as:
  - "Channel stuffing" (shipping inventory in excess of orders, or giving customers incentives to purchase more goods than they need in exchange for future discounts or other benefits)
  - Reporting revenue after goods are ordered but before they are shipped
  - Reporting revenue when significant services have not been performed
  - Improper use of the percentage-of-completion method
  - Improper year-end cutoff procedures
- Recognition of revenue that has not been earned including:
  - Recognizing revenue on bill and hold transactions, consignment sales, sales subject to contingencies, and those with the right to return goods, sales coupled with purchase discounts or credits, and other side agreements.

- Reporting sales to fictitious or nonexistent customers
- Sales to related parties in excess of market value
- Recognizing transactions at fair value that relate to exchanges of similar assets
- Reporting peripheral or incidental transactions, such as nonrecurring gains.[1]

In addition to traditional revenue manipulation strategies, there are numerous methods that a company can use to recognize revenue, subject to certain limitations, including:

- Traditional sales method
- Percentage-of-completion method
- Completed contract method
- Installment sales method

Thus, it is clear that there are simply too many variations in both methods and applications related to such a key financial statement item such as revenue.

BACKGROUND

Revenue recognition continues to be at the top of the list of the FASB's top issues based on the annual survey of the Financial Accounting Standards Advisory Council (FASAC).

Revenue is usually the largest single item in the financial statements. According to the FASB, studies confirm that revenue is the single largest category of financial statement restatements (FASB *Proposal for a New Agenda Project: Issues Related to The Recognition of Revenues and Liabilities*). As a result, issues related to revenue recognition are important to tackle.

There is no general standard for revenue recognition although there are more than 200 separate pieces of authoritative literature scattered throughout GAAP. The result is that there is a gap between broad conceptual guidance in the FASB concept statements, and the more detailed guidance. Most of the detailed authority offers industry-specific guidance rather than a broader-based guidance. Further, authority has been scattered among previously issued APB Opinions, FASB Statements, AICPA Auditing and Accounting Guides, AICPA Statements of Position (SOP), FASB Interpretations and Emerging Issues Task Force (EITF) Issues, SEC Staff Accounting Bulletins (SABs), and other pronouncements.

Previously, the SEC issued Staff Accounting Bulletin (SAB) No. 101, *Revenue Recognition in Financial Statements*. SAB No. 101 concluded that revenue should not be recognized until it is realized.

[1] *Financial Statement Fraud, Integrity of Financial Information Continue to Be Burner Issues (AICPA)*

Realization occurs when four criteria have been met:

1. Persuasive evidence of an arrangement exists.
2. Delivery has occurred.
3. The seller's price to the buyer is fixed and determinable.
4. Collectibility is reasonably assured.

The four criteria mirrored the criteria for revenue recognition of software revenue noted in ASC 985, *Software Revenue Recognition* (formerly SOP 97-2).

Subsequent to its issuance, SAB No. 101 was criticized for applying the standards for one particular industry (software) across the board to all industries. Further, because the SEC issued the SAB guidance, SAB No. 101 was not given the full due process that is provided by the FASB rule-making process.

The EITF has also issued guidance on revenue recognition, particularly guidance related to e-commerce and revenue arrangements with multiple deliverables. However, because there is no general standard for revenue recognition, the EITF has been in a position to interpret, rather than establish, GAAP for revenue.

THE REVENUE PROJECT

The FASB cites several reasons for the project, including:

- Much of the existing U.S. GAAP for revenue was developed before the Conceptual Framework.
- U.S. GAAP contains no comprehensive standard for revenue recognition that is generally applicable.
- U.S. GAAP for revenue recognition consists of more than 200 pronouncements by various standard-setting bodies that is hard to retrieve and sometimes inconsistent.
- Despite the large number of revenue recognition pronouncements, there is little guidance for service activities, which is the fastest growing part of the U.S. economy.
- Revenue recognition is a primary source of restatements due to applicable errors and fraud. Those restatements decrease investor confidence in financial reporting.
- Users face noncomparability among entities and industries, with little information to assist in identifying and adjusting for the differences.
- Accounting policy disclosures are too general to be informative.
- Revenue data are highly aggregated, and users say they would like more detail about specific revenue-generating activities.

STATUS OF PROJECT

The FASB has decided that the revenue recognition project should result in the issuance of statements that:

- Remove inconsistencies and weaknesses in existing revenue requirements
- Provide a more robust framework for addressing revenue issues
- Improve comparability of revenue recognition practices across entities, industries, jurisdictions, and capital markets
- Provide more useful information to users of financial statements through improved disclosure requirements
- Simplify the preparation of financial statements by reducing the number of requirements to which an entity must refer

In June 2010, the FASB and IASB issued an exposure draft entitled, *Revenue Recognition (Topic 605), Revenue from Contracts with Customers.* The two Boards received nearly 1,000 comment letters on the exposure draft leading the two Boards to decide to reissue the exposure draft to reflect public comments.

In January 2012, the FASB and IASB issued a new exposure draft entitled, *Revenue Recognition (Topic 605): Revenue from Contracts with Customers* (including proposed amendments to the *FASB Accounting Standards Codification®).*

The new exposure draft, if passed as a final document, would make the following changes to existing GAAP for revenue recognition:

- Remove inconsistencies in existing requirements
- Create a new criterion for revenue recognition which is based on a transfer of control

NOTE

The percentage-of-completion method would be eliminated.

- Require that contracts be identified and segmented into performance obligations
- Require a determination of transaction price, taking into account certain factors such as credit risk and time value, among other factors
- Make changes to how contract costs are accounted for including requiring certain contract costs to be capitalized as assets
- Provide a new presentation of revenue-related accounts in the statement of financial position
- Require expanded disclosures

STUDY QUESTION

1. What reason does the FASB cite as a need for the revenue project?
   - **a.** Accounting policy disclosures are too general to be informative.
   - **b.** There is too much guidance for service activities, making it confusing.
   - **c.** U.S. GAAP contains a comprehensive standard for revenue recognition that is generally applicable.
   - **d.** U.S. GAAP for revenue recognition consists of only 15 pronouncements by various standard-setting bodies.

DETAILS

The proposal would create a single, principles-based revenue recognition standard for International Financial Reporting Standards (IFRSs) and U.S. GAAP that would be applied across various industries and capital markets.

The proposed statement would replace IAS 18 *Revenue,* IAS 11, *Construction Contracts* and related interpretations. In U.S. GAAP, the proposed statement would supersede most of the guidance on revenue recognition in ASC 605 of the *FASB Accounting Standards Codification* related to revenue recognition.

The proposed guidance would also apply to all contracts with customers except:

- Lease contracts
- Insurance contracts
- Contractual rights or obligations within the scope of the following:
  - Receivables
  - Debt and equity securities
  - Extinguishments of liabilities
  - Debt
  - Derivatives and hedging
  - Financial instruments
  - Transfers and servicing
- Guarantees (other than product warranties)
- Certain nonmonetary exchanges between entities in the same line of business

NOTE

The accounting for revenue (and some costs) arising from contracts within the scope of the proposed guidance would be the same in both U.S. GAAP and IFRSs. However, differences might exist between U.S. GAAP and IFRSs in the profit margin reported in those contracts because of differences in other standards relating to accounting for the costs of fulfilling a contract.

The core principle of the draft standard is that:

> An entity shall recognize revenue when (or as) the entity satisfies a performance obligation by transferring a promised good or service (that is, an asset) to a customer. An asset is transferred when (or as) the customer obtains control of that asset.

To apply that principle, an entity would apply a five-step approach:

- **Step 1:** Identify the contract(s) with a customer.
- **Step 2:** Identify the separate performance obligations in the contract.
- **Step 3:** Determine the transaction price.
- **Step 4:** Allocate the transaction price to the separate performance obligations in the contract.
- **Step 5:** Recognize revenue when (or as) the entity satisfies each performance obligation.

Step 1: Identify the Contract(s) with a Customer

In most cases, an entity would apply the proposed guidance to a single contract. However, the proposal specifies when an entity would combine two or more contracts, and account for them as a single contract or segment a single contract and account for it as two or more contracts if goods or services are priced independently.

A contract would exist when an agreement (written, oral, or evidenced otherwise) between two or more parties creates enforceable obligations between those parties.

A contract would exist only if:

- The contract has commercial substance (that is, the risk, timing, or amount of the entity's future cash flows is expected to change as a result of the contract).
- The parties to the contract have approved the contract (in writing, orally, or in accordance with other customary business practices) and are committed to perform their respective obligations.
- The entity can identify each party's rights regarding the goods or services to be transferred.
- The entity can identify the payment terms for the goods or services to be transferred.

A contract would *not* exist for the purpose of applying the proposed guidance if either party can unilaterally enforce the right to terminate a wholly unperformed contract without compensating the other party. A *wholly unperformed contract* is a contract under which the entity has not transferred any goods or services and the customer has not paid any consideration.

A contract modification would be accounted for as a separate contract if the modification results in the addition to the contract of both of the following:

1. Promised goods or services that are distinct
2. An entity's right to receive an amount of consideration that reflects the entity's standalone selling price of the promised good(s) or service(s) and any appropriate adjustments to that price to reflect the circumstances of the particular contract.

EXAMPLE

An entity would adjust the standalone selling price for a discount that the customer receives because it is not necessary for the entity to incur the selling-related costs that it would incur when selling a similar good or service to a new customer.

An entity would combine two or more contracts entered into at or near the same time with the same customer (or related parties) and account for the contracts as a single contract if one or more of the following criteria is met:

- The contracts are negotiated as a package with a single commercial objective.
- The amount of consideration to be paid in one contract depends on the price or performance of the other contract.
- The goods or services promised in the contracts (or some goods or services promised in the contracts) are a single performance obligation.

Step 2: Identify the Separate Performance Obligations in the Contract

An entity is required to evaluate the terms of the contract and its customary business practice to identify all promised goods or services and determine whether to account for each promised good or service as a separate performance obligation.

A performance obligation is an enforceable promise in a contract with a customer to transfer a good or service to the customer.

Examples of promised goods or services may include, but are not limited to, the following:

- Goods produced by an entity for sale, such as inventory of a manufacturer
- Goods purchased by an entity for resale, such as merchandise of a retailer
- Providing a service of arranging for another party to transfer goods or services to the customer (e.g., acting as an agent of another party)
- Standing ready to provide goods or services (e.g., when-and-if-available software products)
- Constructing, manufacturing, or developing an asset on behalf of a customer
- Granting licenses or rights to use intangible assets

- Granting options to purchase additional goods or services (when those options provide the customer with a material right)
- Performing a contractually agreed-upon task (or tasks) for a customer

If an entity promises to transfer more than one good or service, it would account for each promised good or service as a separate performance obligation only if the good or service is *distinct*.

A good or service is *distinct* if either of the following is true:

- The entity regularly sells the good or service separately.
- The customer can benefit from the good or service either on its own or together with other resources that are readily available to the customer.

If a promised good or service is not distinct, an entity would combine that good or service with other promised goods or services until the entity identifies a bundle of goods or services that is distinct and treats the bundle as a single performance obligation.

A good or service in a bundle of promised goods or services is not distinct and, therefore, the entity would account for the bundle as a single performance obligation if both of the following criteria are met:

- The goods or services in the bundle are highly interrelated and transferring them to the customer requires that the entity also provide a significant service of integrating the goods or services into the combined item(s) for which the customer has contracted.
- The bundle of goods or services is significantly modified or customized to fulfill the contract.

An entity would be permitted to account for two or more distinct goods or services promised in a contract as a single performance obligation if those goods or services have the same pattern of transfer to the customer.

EXAMPLE

If an entity promises to transfer two or more distinct services to a customer over the same period of time, the entity could account for those promises as one performance obligation if applying one method of measuring progress would faithfully depict the pattern of transfer of those services to the customer.

STUDY QUESTIONS

2. The proposed revenue recognition standard has a core principle based on which one of the following triggering events occurring?

a. A contract must be signed.
b. There must be a completion of the critical stage.
c. There must be a transfer of promised goods or services.
d. There must be a certain percentage of transaction completed.

> **3.** Under the proposed revenue recognition standard, a contract exists only if the contract has certain attributes that include which of the following?
>
> **a.** The entity's future cash flows are not expected to change as a result of the contract.
> **b.** One of the parties to the contract has approved the contract in writing.
> **c.** Each party's rights regarding the goods or services to be transferred will be determined at a later date.
> **d.** The entity can identify the payment terms for those goods or services.

Step 3: Determine the Transaction Price

The transaction price is the amount of consideration to which an entity expects to be entitled in exchange for transferring promised goods or services to a customer, excluding amounts collected on behalf of third parties (e.g., sales taxes). When determining the transaction price, an entity would consider the effects of the following four elements:

1. Variable consideration
2. Time value of money
3. Noncash consideration
4. Consideration payable to the customer

Variable consideration. If the promised amount of consideration in a contract is variable, an entity would estimate the transaction price by using either the expected value (i.e., probability-weighted amount) or the most likely amount, depending on which method the entity expects to better predict the amount of consideration to which it will be entitled.

The time value of money. An entity would adjust the promised amount of consideration to reflect the time value of money if the contract has a financing component that is significant to the contract.

Noncash consideration. If a customer promises consideration in a form other than cash, an entity would measure the noncash consideration (or promise of noncash consideration) at fair value. If an entity cannot reasonably estimate the fair value of the noncash consideration, it would measure the consideration indirectly by reference to the standalone selling price of the goods or services promised to the customer in exchange for the consideration.

Consideration payable to the customer. If an entity pays, or expects to pay, consideration to a customer (or to other parties that purchase the entity's goods or services from the customer) in the form of cash, credit, or other items that the customer can apply against amounts owed to the entity, the entity would account for the consideration payable to the customer as a reduction of the transaction price unless the payment is in exchange for a distinct good or service.

An entity would not consider the effects of customer credit risk (i.e., collectibility) when determining the transaction price.

If the promised amount of consideration in a contract is *variable* (because of discounts, rebates, refunds, credits, incentives, performance bonuses, penalties, contingencies, price concessions, or other similar items), an entity would be required to estimate the total amount to which the entity will be entitled in exchange for transferring the promised goods or services to a customer.

The entity would update the estimated transaction price at each reporting date to represent faithfully the circumstances present at the reporting date and the changes in circumstances during the reporting period.

To estimate the transaction price, an entity would use either of the following two methods, depending on which method the entity expects to better predict the amount of consideration to which it will be entitled:

- **The expected value.** The expected value is the sum of probability-weighted amounts in a range of possible consideration amounts. An expected value may be an appropriate estimate of the transaction price if an entity has a large number of contracts with similar characteristics.
- **The most likely amount.** This amount is the single most likely amount in a range of possible consideration amounts (i.e., the single most likely outcome of the contract). The most likely amount may be an appropriate estimate of the transaction price if the contract has only two possible outcomes (e.g., an entity either achieves a performance bonus or does not).

NOTE

When estimating the transaction price, an entity would apply one method consistently throughout the contract.

OBSERVATION

One key change in the proposed standard versus existing GAAP involves how variable consideration is handled. Existing GAAP generally provides that an entity records revenue when the price is fixed and determinable. The proposal allows for revenue to be recognized when consideration is variable provided the price can be estimated. The result is that some companies may be recording revenue earlier in their sales cycle under the proposal as compared with current GAAP.

If an entity receives consideration from a customer and expects to refund some or all of that consideration to the customer, the entity would recognize as a refund liability the amount of consideration that the entity reasonably expects to refund to the customer. The refund liability (and corresponding change in the transaction price) would be updated at each reporting period for changes in circumstances.

STUDY QUESTION

4. Which of the following is *not* one of the four elements used to determine the transaction price in the revenue project?

a. Variable consideration
b. Time value of money
c. Product or service demand
d. Consideration payable to the customer

Step 4: Allocate the Transaction Price to the Separate Performance Obligations

An entity would allocate the transaction price to each separate performance obligation in the amount that depicts the amount of consideration to which the entity expects to be entitled in exchange for satisfying each separate performance obligation.

To allocate an appropriate amount of consideration to each separate performance obligation, an entity would determine the *standalone selling price* at contract inception of the good or service underlying each separate performance obligation and allocate the transaction price on a relative standalone selling price basis.

The best evidence of a standalone selling price is the observable price of a good or service when the entity sells that good or service separately in similar circumstances and to similar customers. A contractually stated price or a list price for a good or service may be (but shall not be presumed to be) the standalone selling price of that good or service. If a standalone selling price is not observable, an entity would estimate it.

If the sum of the standalone selling prices of the promised goods or services in the contract exceeds the transaction price (i.e., if a customer receives a discount for purchasing a bundle of goods or services), an entity would allocate that discount to all separate performance obligations on a relative standalone selling price basis, with certain exceptions.

An entity would allocate to the separate performance obligations in a contract any subsequent changes in the transaction price on the same basis as at contract inception. Amounts allocated to a satisfied performance obligation would be recognized as revenue, or as a reduction of revenue, in the period in which the transaction price changes.

Step 5: Recognize Revenue When a Performance Obligation Is Satisfied

An entity would recognize revenue when (or as) it satisfies a performance obligation by transferring a promised good or service to a customer. A good or service is transferred when the *customer obtains control* of that good or service.

Goods and services are assets, even if only momentarily, when they are received and used (as in the case of many services).

A customer would obtain control of an asset when it has the *ability to direct the use of and obtain substantially all of the remaining benefits from the asset*. Control includes the ability to prevent other entities from directing the use of, and obtaining the benefits from an asset through the potential cash flows that can be obtained directly or indirectly in many ways, such as by:

- Using the asset to produce goods or provide services (including public services)
- Using the asset to enhance the value of other assets
- Using the asset to settle liabilities or reduce expenses
- Selling or exchanging the asset
- Pledging the asset to secure a loan
- Holding the asset

PROPOSED RULES FOR RECOGNIZING REVENUE AT A POINT OF TIME OR OVER TIME

For each separate performance obligation, an entity would determine at contract inception whether the entity satisfies the performance obligation over time by transferring control of a promised good or service over time. If an entity does not satisfy a performance obligation over time, the performance obligation is satisfied *at a point in time*.

If an entity transfers control of a good or service over time, it recognizes revenue over time if at least one of the following two criteria is met:

1. The entity's performance creates or enhances an asset (e.g., work in process) that the customer controls as the asset is created or enhanced.
2. The entity's performance does not create an asset with an alternative use to the entity and at least one of the following criteria is met:
   a. The customer simultaneously receives and consumes the benefits of the entity's performance as the entity performs.
   b. Another entity would not need to substantially reperform the work the entity has completed to date if that other entity were to fulfill the remaining obligation to the customer.
   c. The entity has a right to payment for performance completed to date and it expects to fulfill the contract as promised.

For each separate performance obligation that an entity satisfies over time, the entity would recognize revenue over time by consistently applying a method of measuring the progress toward complete satisfaction of that performance obligation.

Appropriate methods of measuring progress include:

- **Input methods,** which recognize revenue on the basis of the entity's efforts or inputs to the satisfaction of a performance obligation (e.g., resources consumed, labor hours expended, costs incurred, time lapsed, or machine hours used) relative to the total expected inputs to the satisfaction of that performance obligation. If the entity's efforts or inputs are expended evenly throughout the performance period, it may be appropriate for an entity to recognize revenue on a straight-line basis.
- **Output methods,** which recognize revenue on the basis of direct measurements of the value to the customer of the goods or services transferred to date (e.g., surveys of performance completed to date, appraisals of results achieved, milestones reached, or units produced) and can be the most faithful depiction of the entity's performance.

NOTE

If an entity has a right to invoice a customer in an amount that corresponds directly with the value to the customer of the entity's performance completed to date (e.g., a services contract in which an entity bills a fixed amount for each hour of service provided), the entity shall recognize revenue in the amount to which the entity has a right to invoice.

As circumstances change over time, an entity would update its measure of progress to depict the entity's performance completed to date.

PROPOSED RULES FOR RECOGNIZING REVENUE AT A POINT OF TIME

If a performance obligation is not satisfied over time, an entity satisfies the performance obligation *at a point in time.* To determine the point in time when a customer obtains control of a promised asset and an entity satisfies a performance obligation, the entity would consider indicators of the transfer of control that include, but are not limited to, the following:

- The entity has a present right to payment for the asset.
- The customer has legal title to the asset.
- The entity has transferred physical possession of the asset.
- The customer has the significant risks and rewards of ownership of the asset.
- The customer has accepted the asset.

STUDY QUESTION

5. Which of the following is an indicator that a customer has obtained control of a good or service?
   a. The customer has a conditional obligation to pay with nothing other than the passage of time required before payment is due.
   b. The customer has an option to obtain legal title.
   c. The customer has the ability to direct the use of the asset.

ONEROUS PERFORMANCE OBLIGATIONS

For a performance obligation that an entity satisfies over time and that the entity expects at contract inception to satisfy over a period of time greater than one year, an entity shall recognize a liability and a corresponding expense if the performance obligation is onerous.

A performance obligation is onerous if *the lowest cost of settling the performance obligation exceeds the amount of the transaction price* allocated to that performance obligation. (e.g., there is an indicated loss with the performance obligation.)

The lowest cost of settling a performance obligation is the lower of the following amounts:

- The costs that relate directly to satisfying the performance obligation by transferring the promised goods or services
- The amount that the entity would pay to exit the performance obligation, if the entity is permitted to do so, other than by transferring the promised goods or services.

An entity initially shall measure the liability for an onerous performance obligation at the amount by which the lowest cost of settling the remaining performance obligation exceeds the amount of the transaction price allocated to that remaining performance obligation.

When an entity satisfies an onerous performance obligation, the entity would derecognize the related liability with the offsetting adjustment credited to expense.

Before an entity recognizes a liability for an onerous performance obligation, the entity would test for impairment an asset recognized from the costs incurred to obtain or fulfill a contract with a customer.

A not-for-profit entity would not recognize a liability for an onerous performance obligation if the purpose of the contract is to provide a social or charitable benefit.

At each reporting date, an entity would update the measurement of the liability for an onerous performance obligation for changes in circumstances and would recognize changes in the measurement of that liability as an expense or as a reduction of an expense.

CONTRACT COSTS

Contract costs recorded as an asset. If the costs incurred in fulfilling a contract with a customer are in the scope of other GAAP (such as inventory, property, plant, and equipment, or software), an entity shall account for those costs in accordance with that other GAAP.

If the costs incurred are not within the scope of other GAAP, an entity would recognize those costs to fulfill a contract as an asset only if those costs meet all of the following criteria:

- The costs relate directly to a contract (or a specific anticipated contract).
- The costs generate or enhance resources of the entity that will be used in satisfying performance obligations in the future.
- The costs are expected to be recovered.

Costs that relate directly to a contract (or a specific anticipated contract) include the following:

- Direct labor (e.g., salaries and wages of employees who provide services directly to the customer)
- Direct materials (e.g., supplies used in providing services to the customer)
- Allocations of costs that relate directly to the contract or to contract activities (e.g., costs of contract management and supervision, insurance, and depreciation of tools and equipment used in fulfilling the contract)
- Costs that are explicitly chargeable to the customer under the contract
- Other costs that are incurred only because the entity entered into the contract (e.g., payments to subcontractors).

Contract costs recorded as an expense. An entity would recognize the following costs as expenses when incurred:

- General and administrative costs (unless those costs are explicitly chargeable to the customer under the contract)
- Costs of wasted materials, labor, or other resources to fulfill the contract that were not reflected in the price of the contract
- Costs that relate to satisfied performance obligations (or partially satisfied performance obligations) in the contract (i.e., costs that relate to past performance)
- Costs that relate to remaining performance obligations but that the entity cannot distinguish from costs that relate to satisfied performance obligations

Incremental costs of obtaining a contract. An entity shall recognize as an asset the incremental costs of obtaining a contract with a customer if the entity expects to recover those costs, subject to certain limitations. The incremental costs of obtaining a contract are those costs that an entity incurs in its efforts to obtain a contract with a customer and that it would not have incurred if the contract had not been obtained (e.g., a sales commission).

As a practical expedient, an entity may recognize the incremental costs of obtaining a contract as an expense when incurred if the amortization period of the asset that the entity otherwise would have recognized is one year or less.

Costs to obtain a contract that would have been incurred, regardless of whether the contract was obtained, shall be recognized as an expense when incurred, unless those costs are explicitly chargeable to the customer regardless of whether the contract is obtained.

Special amortization and impairment rules for costs capitalized. An asset recognized for a contract cost would be amortized on a systematic basis consistent with the pattern of transfer of the goods or services to which the asset relates.

With respect to those contract costs capitalized, an entity would be required to recognize an impairment loss to profit or loss under certain rules.

Sale with a right of return. In some contracts, an entity transfers control of a product to a customer and also grants the customer the right to return the product for various reasons (such as dissatisfaction with the product) and receive any combination of the following:

- A full or partial refund of any consideration paid
- A credit that can be applied against amounts owed, or that will be owed, to the entity
- Another product in exchange

The exposure draft would provide the following rules to account for the right to return a product:

To account for the transfer of products with a right of return (and for some services that are provided subject to a refund), an entity would recognize all of the following:

1. Revenue for the transferred products in the amount of consideration to which the entity is *reasonably assured* to be entitled (considering the products expected to be returned)
2. A refund liability
3. An asset (and corresponding adjustment to cost of sales) for its right to recover products from customers on settling the refund liability

An entity's promise to stand ready to accept a returned product during the return period would not be accounted for as a separate performance obligation in addition to the obligation to provide a refund.

NOTE

The cumulative amount of revenue the entity recognizes to date shall not exceed the amount to which the entity is reasonably assured to be entitled.

For any amounts to which an entity is not reasonably assured to be entitled, the entity would not recognize revenue when it transfers products to customers but would recognize any consideration received as a refund liability. Subsequently, the entity would update its assessment of amounts to which the entity is reasonably assured to be entitled in exchange for the transferred products and should recognize corresponding adjustments to the amount of revenue recognized. An entity would update the measurement of the refund liability at the end of each reporting period for changes in expectations about the amount of refunds. An entity would recognize corresponding adjustments as revenue (or reductions of revenue).

An entity would recognize an asset (and corresponding adjustment to cost of sales) for its right to recover products from customers on settling the refund liability. The asset would initially be measured by reference to the former carrying amount of the inventory less any expected costs to recover those products. Subsequently, an entity would update the measurement of the asset to correspond with changes in the measurement of the refund liability.

EXAMPLE

Right of return (from the Exposure Draft)

Facts.

- An entity sells 100 products for $100 each.
- The cost of each product is $60.
- The entity's customary business practice is to allow a customer to return any unused product within 30 days and receive a full refund.
- The entity estimates that three products will be returned. The entity's experience is predictive of the amount of consideration to which the entity will be entitled.
- The entity estimates that the costs of recovering the products will be immaterial and expects that the returned products can be resold at a profit.

Conclusion. Upon transfer of control of the products, the entity would not recognize revenue for the three products that it expects to be returned. Consequently, the entity would recognize:

Total sales	100 units x $100	$10,000
Estimated returns	3 units x $100	(300)
Sales not expected to be returned	97 units x $100	$9,700
Entry at date of transfer of control:		
Accounts receivable	10,000	
Revenue		9,700
Refund liability		300
Cost of sales (97 x $60)	5,820	
Recovery asset (3 x $60)	180	
Inventory (100 x $60)		6,000

Presentation. When either party to a contract has performed, the entity would present the contract in the statement of financial position as either a contract asset or a contract liability, depending on the relationship between the entity's performance and the customer's performance.

If a customer pays consideration, or an amount of consideration is due before an entity performs by transferring a good or service, the entity would present the contract as a contract liability. A contract liability is an entity's obligation to transfer goods or services to a customer for which the entity has received consideration from the customer.

If an entity performs by transferring goods or services to a customer before the customer pays consideration, the entity would present the contract as either a contract asset or as a receivable depending on the nature of the entity's right to consideration for its performance.

- A contract asset is an entity's right to consideration in exchange for goods or services that the entity has transferred to a customer, when that right is conditioned on something other than the passage of time (e.g., the entity's future performance).
- A receivable is an entity's right to consideration that is unconditional. A right to consideration is unconditional if nothing other than the passage of time is required before payment of that consideration is due.

An entity would present a liability for onerous performance obligations separately from contract assets or contract liabilities.

Disclosures. An entity would disclose qualitative and quantitative information about:

- Its contracts with customers
- The significant judgments, and changes in judgments, made in applying the proposed guidance to those contracts

An entity would consider the level of detail necessary to satisfy the disclosure requirements and how much emphasis to place on each of the various requirements.

NOTE

An entity would aggregate or disaggregate disclosures so that useful information is not obscured by either the inclusion of a large amount of insignificant detail or the aggregation of items that have different characteristics.

Detailed disclosures that would be required include:

1. Information about its contracts with customers to help users understand the amount, timing, and uncertainty of revenue and cash flows from those contracts, including:

- A disaggregation of revenue for the periods
- A reconciliation from the opening to the closing aggregate balance of contract assets and contract liabilities, and
- Information about the entity's performance obligations including additional information about its onerous performance obligations.

NOTE

An entity would disaggregate revenue into the categories that best depict how the amount, timing, and uncertainty of revenue and cash flows are affected by economic factors.

2. A reconciliation from the opening to the closing aggregate balance of contract assets and contract liabilities presented in the statement of financial position
3. Information about its performance obligations in contracts with customers
4. For contracts with an original expected duration of more than one year, the amount of the transaction price allocated to the performance obligations remaining at the end of the reporting period that are expected to be satisfied in each of the following periods: (a) not later than one year; (b) later than one year but not later than two years; (c) later than two years but not later than three years; and (d) later than three years
5. The amount of any liability recognized for onerous performance obligations together with a discussion of: (a) the nature and amount of the performance obligations for which the liability has been recognized; (b) why those performance obligations have become onerous; and (c) when the entity expects to satisfy the liability
6. A reconciliation from the opening to the closing balance of the liability recognized for onerous performance obligations
7. The judgments, and changes in judgments, made in applying the proposed guidance that significantly affect the determination of the amount and timing of revenue from contracts with customers
8. For performance obligations satisfied continuously, (a) the methods (e.g., output methods, input methods, and methods based on the passage of time) used to recognize revenue; and (b) an explanation of why such methods are a faithful depiction of the transfer of goods or services
9. Information about the methods, inputs, and assumptions used: (a) to determine the transaction price; (b) to estimate standalone selling prices of promised goods or services; (c) to measure obligations for returns, refunds, and other similar obligations; (d) to measure the amount of any liability recognized for onerous performance obligations (including information about the discount rate)
10. A reconciliation of the opening and closing balances of assets recognized from the costs incurred to obtain or fulfill a contract with a customer by

main category of asset (e.g., costs to obtain contracts with customers, precontract costs, and setup costs). An entity would also be required to describe the method it uses to determine the amortization of the asset for each reporting period.

Nonpublic entity disclosures. A nonpublic entity would be permitted to elect not to provide any of the following disclosures:

- A reconciliation of contract balances
- The amount of the transaction price allocated to remaining performance obligations and an explanation of when the entity expects to recognize that amount as revenue
- A reconciliation of liability balances recognized from onerous performance obligations
- A reconciliation of asset balances recognized from the costs to obtain or fulfill a contract with a customer
- An explanation of the judgments, and changes in judgments, used in determining the timing of satisfaction of performance obligations, and in determining the transaction price and allocating it to performance obligations

STUDY QUESTION

6. Under the exposure draft, which of the following contract costs should be recorded as an asset?

   a. Costs that are incurred only because the entity entered into the contract
   b. Costs that relate to satisfied performance obligations in the contract
   c. Costs that relate to remaining performance obligations that the entity cannot distinguish from costs that relate to satisfied performance obligations
   d. Costs of wasted materials, labor, or other resources to fulfill the contract that were not reflected in the price of the contract

EFFECTIVE DATE AND TRANSITION

An entity would apply the proposed guidance for annual periods beginning on or after the effective date to be determined in the final statement.

NOTE

The FASB has decided that the standard would not be effective sooner than the annual reporting periods beginning on or after January 1, 2015, for public companies.

The effective date for nonpublic entities would be a minimum of one year after the effective date for public entities. Earlier application will not be permitted.

An entity would apply the proposed requirements retrospectively by applying the guidance on accounting changes and error corrections. In the period of adoption, an entity would provide the disclosures required.

What would be the impact of ultimately implementing the proposed revenue recognition model on present practice? The FASB suggests that for some contracts (e.g., many retail transactions), the proposed guidance would have little, if any, effect on current practice. However, the proposed guidance would differ from current practice in the following ways:

Recognition of revenue only from the transfer of goods or services. Contracts for the development of an asset (e.g., construction, manufacturing, and customized software) would result in continuous revenue recognition only if the customer controls the asset as it is developed.

Identification of separate performance obligations. An entity would be required to divide a contract into separate performance obligations for goods or services that are distinct. As a result of that requirement, an entity might separate a contract into units of accounting that differ from those identified in current practice.

Licensing and rights to use. An entity would be required to evaluate whether a license to use the entity's intellectual property (for less than the property's economic life) is granted on an exclusive or nonexclusive basis. If a license is granted on an exclusive basis, an entity would be required to recognize revenue over the term of the license. That pattern of revenue recognition might differ from current practice.

Effect of credit risk. In contrast to some existing standards and practices, the effect of a customer's credit risk (that is, collectibility) would affect *how much* revenue an entity recognizes rather than *whether* an entity recognizes revenue.

Use of estimates. In determining the transaction price (e.g., estimating variable consideration) and allocating the transaction price on the basis of standalone selling prices, an entity would be required to use estimates more extensively than in applying existing standards.

Accounting for costs. The proposed guidance specifies which contract costs an entity would recognize as expenses when incurred and which costs would be capitalized because they give rise to an asset. Applying that cost guidance might change how an entity would account for some costs, such as commissions.

Disclosure. The proposed guidance specifies disclosures to help users of financial statements understand the amount, timing, and uncertainty of revenue and cash flows arising from contracts with customers. An entity would be required to disclose more information about its contracts with customers than is currently required, including more disaggregated information about recognized revenue and more information about its performance obligations remaining at the end of the reporting period.

The FASB has announced that it plans to issue a final statement in 2012 or 2013.

CONCERN BY THE CONSTRUCTION INDUSTRY

One industry that is likely to be significantly impacted by proposed revenue changes is the construction industry.

Of particular concern is that the proposal eliminates the use of the percentage-of-completion method and replaces it with the possible use of a similar version depending on the terms and conditions of the underlying construction contract.

Consider the following details:

A company would recognize revenue either *at a point of time* or *over a period of time* depending on when and how.

In order to record revenue over time (similar to the percentage-of-completion method), a company must decide whether it satisfies the performance obligation (construction of the building) over time by transferring control of the promised good or service over time. If control is transferred over time, revenue is recognized over time, which is similar to the percentage-of-completion method.

In recognizing revenue over time, the proposal would allow a company to apply a method that measures progress toward complete satisfaction of the construction project, such as:

- **Using input methods,** which recognize revenue on the basis of the entity's efforts or inputs to the satisfaction of the construction project, such as labor hours expended, costs incurred, time lapsed, or machine hours used, relative to the total expected inputs to the satisfaction of that performance obligation
- **Using output methods,** which recognize revenue on the basis of direct measurements of the value to the customer of the goods or services transferred to date (e.g., surveys of performance completed to date, appraisals of results achieved, milestones reached, or units produced) and can be the most faithful depiction of the entity's performance.

Using input methods, such as percentage of costs incurred, would be similar to use of the percentage completion method under existing GAAP.

If the company cannot demonstrate that it transfers control over time, it defaults to recording revenue at a point of time, which is typically the end of the contract, similar to the completed contract method.

Many in the construction industry are concerned that the revenue proposal fails to give enough guidance as to how to determine whether control is transferred over time. Under the FASB's principles-based approach to revenue recognition, the FASB appears unwilling to expand the proposal to expand the guidance for the construction industry. Thus, if the proposal is issued as a final statement without further detail, there could be ambiguity as to whether a contractor recognizes revenue over time or at a point in time (the end of the contract).

MODULE 2: FINANCIAL STATEMENT REPORTING — CHAPTER 6

Restatements and Other Financial Reporting Abuses

LEARNING OBJECTIVES

Upon completion of this chapter, the reader will be able to:

- State the results of several studies regarding restatements
- Discuss reasons why Sarbanes-Oxley has been applied inconsistently by the SEC and the courts
- Describe differences between the clawback provisions of Section 304 of the Sarbanes-Oxley Act and Section 954 of the Dodd-Frank Act

The public is inundated with warnings from the financial press that focus on discovering the early warning signs of corporate reporting abuses. *The Wall Street Journal, Business Week, New York Times*, and other publications continue to deliver a weekly education to the unsophisticated investor. In this chapter, the author discusses a few of the obvious reporting problems that have been announced by the SEC and the financial press.

RESTATEMENTS

In 2011, Audit Analytics published a report (*Financial Restatements—A Nine-Year Comparison*) comparing the number of financial statement restatements in 2010 with those in previous years.

Details from the study suggest:

1. The number of restatements in 2010 (735) represented a slight increase from the 2009 level of 683. Overall, restatements declined considerably during the period 2006 to 2009:

Restatements by Year	
735	in 2010
683	in 2009
920	in 2008
1,215	in 2007
1,795	in 2006
1,550	in 2005
945	in 2004

2. In 2010, 699 companies filed 735 restatements.
3. The average restatement reduced earnings by an average of $5.9 million in 2010 as compared with $4.6 million in 2009, $7.2 million in 2008, and $23.5 million as far back as 2006.

4. The top 10 reasons for the 2010 restatements noted in the report follow:

	% Restatements
Debt and equity security issues	22%
Expense recording issues such as payroll and selling, general, and administrative expenses	14%
Statement of cash flow classification errors	9%
Deferred, stock-based, and executive compensation issues	11%
Acquisitions, mergers, divestitures, and reorganization issues	9%
Revenue recognition issues	10%
Income tax accounting issues	9%
Liabilities, payables, reserves, and accruals	12%
Accounts/loans receivable, investments, and cash issues	10%
Consolidation issues including variable-interest entities and off-balance sheet items	7%

Note: The sum of the percentages exceeds 100% because there were multiple issues related to individual restatements.

Another 2010 report issued by Glass Lewis indicated that restatements for companies audited by the Big Four were about half of those for companies audited by other auditors. Approximately 2.5 percent of Big Four clients issued restatements in 2010. Moreover, historically, smaller companies restate more often than larger companies do, and those companies in services and technology industries filed the most restatements.

What caused the decline in restatements from their peak in 2006? Restatements peaked in 2006, then gradually declined in 2007 and 2008 before leveling off in 2009. The slight uptick in restatements in 2010 versus 2009 was not significant and should not be construed as an upward trend.

Although there is no evidence to support a conclusion, a consistent hypothesis is that the decline in restatements from 2007 to 2009 was a by-product of improved internal control from companies implementing Section 404 of the Sarbanes-Oxley Act. For the past several years, most public companies have complied with Section 404 by rectifying their internal control differences and correcting errors that were found. Years 2007, 2008, and 2009 represented the first three-year trend in the past six years in which restatements declined, representing a culmination of the internal control vetting process. Although there was a slight uptick in restatements in 2010, for all practical purposes, 2009 and 2010 restatements were statistically at the same level suggesting that, at worst, restatements have leveled off.

Evidence of the impact of Section 404 compliance is identified by Glass Lewis in that the number of adverse opinions given by auditors has declined by 78 percent over the past five years under Sarbanes-Oxley. Moreover, the percentage of companies with ineffective internal controls dropped to two percent in 2010 from six percent in 2008.

In addition, there are factors that contribute to continued restatements:

- Auditors are being more demanding and assertive in requiring companies to make adjustments.
- Materiality thresholds are being reduced in fear of heightened scrutiny.

Another study suggested that the decline in restatements is directly linked to the rate of auditor turnover, which declined by 33 percent in 2010 as compared with 2008. It is commonly expected that auditor turnovers indicate that there was an auditor dispute that may have led to restatements and material weaknesses being uncovered in subsequent periods.

RESTATEMENT IMPACT OF ASC 250

In 2005, the FASB issued ASC 250, *Accounting Changes and Error Corrections* (formerly FAS 154), as part of the FASB-IASB short-term convergence project. Under ASC 250, voluntary changes in accounting principles require restatement of financial statements. Previously, under APB No. 20, *Accounting Changes,* with few exceptions, changes in or adoption of an accounting principle were treated with the "catch-up" change being presented as a cumulative effect of an accounting change on the income statement, net of the related tax effect. Therefore, prior to the adoption of ASC 250, companies had an incentive to voluntarily adopt a new accounting principle as a means to increase current year income.

In the post-ASC 250 years, with the cumulative effect, income-statement approach being replaced with a *required restatement of financial statements,* entities are required to restate their financial statements each time they either adopt a new GAAP standard or change an accounting principle. What is not clear is whether the changes under ASC 250 have removed the incentive for a company to voluntarily change accounting principles as a means to increase income.

Does the market still punish companies that have restatements? In the early 2000s, after Enron and other financial frauds, investors appeared less forgiving about earnings restatements. At that time, a restatement was considered a red flag for financial statement fraud, regardless of whether the restatement was a result of an intentional or an unintentional (voluntary) misstatement. There was evidence that suggested that the market had no tolerance for restatements and actually punished companies on both a short- and long-term basis, if they restated financial statements.

One study (*A Review of Earnings Restatements*), published by Min Wu of the New York University Stern School of Business, reached conclusions such as:

- A restatement is generally considered bad news by the market.
- The market reacts quite negatively to a restatement by penalizing the stock price for the *three-day period* after the restatement announcement.
- Restated companies lose credibility in the marketplace as investors rate their earnings as being a lower quality after the announcement is made.
- Stock declines due to a restatement vary up to 10 percent depending on the type of restatement.

Since the Min Wu Report was published, the market has become used to restatements with four years of significant restatements from 2003 through 2006, followed by a period of decline and leveling off of restatements during 2007 to 2010. The question is whether the market still punishes those companies that restate their financial statements or has become exposed to "restatement fatigue."

Another more recent study *(Restatements: Investor Response and Firm Reporting Choices*, Plumlee and Lonbardi Yohn) was published that suggests that the public has not changed its reaction to restatements as follows:

- The magnitude of the market reaction to restatement filings has not diminished with the increased frequency of restatements.
- How an entity discloses its restatement (with or without filing an 8K) suggests how the market will react to a restatement. A change in stock price and trading volume was significant if an entity filed an 8K versus if it did not.

Another study reached a conclusion that stock prices fell more sharply after a restatement when insiders of the company were on record for selling some of their stock during the restatement period (*Earnings Restatements Aren't Necessarily Stock-Price Poison*, Brad Badertscher, University of Notre Dame). The theory is that insiders were aware of some internal issues that motivated them to sell their stock prior to a significant decline in stock price. Conversely, the fact that insiders purchased shares of company stock during a restatement period had the effect of mitigating the negative impact of the stock price decline.

STUDY QUESTIONS

1. According to the Min Wu study, the market reacts to a restatement by:
   - **a.** Being indifferent with no change in stock price
   - **b.** Penalizing the stock price for a period after the announcement
   - **c.** Reacting as though the company has gone bankrupt

> **2.** Although restatements leveled off in 2010, what may have been a primary reason for the decline in restatements in 2008 and 2007?
>
> **a.** Implementation of international accounting standards
> **b.** Auditors were less assertive in requiring companies to make adjustments
> **c.** Materiality thresholds were increased in fear of heightened scrutiny
> **d.** Sarbanes-Oxley's Section 404

Give back those bonuses when there is a restatement. On July 21, 2010, President Obama signed the Dodd-Frank Wall Street Reform and Consumer Protection Act (the Act) into law. The Act includes expanded requirements that companies have a clawback policy so that executives are required to pay back incentive compensation if there is a restatement of a public company's financial statements. The clawback provision of Dodd-Frank is discussed later in this chapter.

Since 2002, Section 304 of the Sarbanes-Oxley Act has been the overall authority for companies to "claw back" executive compensation.

Section 304 states that certain officers of a public company must return their bonuses related to a year for which there is a restatement of the company's financial statements due to a material noncompliance issue as a result of a misconduct with any financial reporting requirement under the securities law.

More specifically, Section 304 of the Sarbanes-Oxley Act provides that if an issuer (public company) is required to prepare an accounting restatement due to the material noncompliance of the issuer, as a result of *misconduct,* with any financial reporting requirement under the securities laws, the chief executive officer and chief financial officer of the issuer must reimburse the issuer for:

- Any bonus or other incentive-based or equity-based compensation received by that person from the issuer *during the 12-month period* following the first public issuance or filing with the SEC (whichever first occurs) of the financial document embodying such financial reporting requirement
- Any profits realized from the sale of securities of the issuer during that 12-month period

As to the companies that have had clawback provisions in their executive employment contracts, when there have been restatements, many companies have been reluctant to go after their executives to return bonuses due to several reasons including:

- There is a high cost of litigation and bad publicity.
- The bad publicity may bring into question the terms and conditions of the employment contract.

Interestingly, the SEC did not prosecute a Section 304 case until 2007 even though Sarbanes-Oxley was effective in 2002. Since 2007, the SEC has ratcheted up its Section 304 cases. In recent years, the authority of Section 304 of Sarbanes-Oxley has continued to be tested in the courts in light of the high number of restatements.

Although the intent of Section 304 is clear, its application has led to situations in which challenges have continued to be made as to whether certain executives actually have to return their bonuses in the wake of their companies' restatements. In particular, executives have taken the position that their employment contracts that were consummated prior to the effective date of Section 304 should prevail and such contracts do not necessarily have a return of bonus requirement.

Also, both the courts and SEC have been inconsistent as to when Section 304 can be used for several reasons:

- There is a legal question as to whether the amount of compensation that must be returned is limited to the portion directly attributable to the misstated financial statements, and the definition of "misconduct."
- Although it is clear that the SEC can use Section 304 to recover bonuses, there is ambiguity surrounding whether third parties can sue under Section 304.
- The term "misconduct" is not defined in Sarbanes-Oxley or within other securities statutes.
- An unresolved issue is whether the misconduct of an employee can trigger Section 304 against the CEO or CFO, even if the CEO or CFO had no knowledge of that employee's misconduct.

There is a recent trend to place a string on bonuses so they can be pulled back in the event of restatements or other events. Regardless of the requirements of Section 304 of Sarbanes-Oxley or Section 954 of Dodd-Frank, companies are amending compensation policies to provide for the return of bonuses from both the executives and rank-and-file workers in the event of fraud, intentional misconduct, or material financial statement misstatements.

Consider the following statistics:

- Sixty-four percent of the Fortune 100 companies have a clawback policy aimed at fraud, as well as accounting restatements and other errors ("SEC Orders Ex-CEO to Return Pay," *Wall Street Journal,* July 23, 2009)
- Eighteen percent of those companies with a clawback policy applied their policy to all employees, executives and rank-and-file alike (Equilar, Inc., www.journalnow.com)

Is the SEC using Section 304 to retrieve bonuses? Through 2007, the SEC did not use Section 304 to recover bonuses. In fact, its first Section 304 case did not occur until 2007. Then, in 2008 through 2011, the SEC began prosecuting Section 304 cases with vigor. In particular, recent SEC actions under Section 304 have involved officers who were not individually charged with fraud or securities law violations.

One critical case occurred when the SEC took action against a former CEO of CSX Auto Corporation, to claw back more than $4 million of bonuses and stock profits allegedly earned while the company (but not the CEO) was committing accounting fraud. CSX had two financial statement restatements due to over-inflated revenue that were included in Form 10-K filings, both signed by the CEO. During the year following the filing of the 10-K forms, the CEO received bonuses and stock compensation. Subsequently, the SEC sought recovery of the CEO's $4 million of compensation and charged four former CSX executives with securities fraud, even though the CEO was not charged. What is most peculiar about the CSX case is that it represents the first case in which the SEC used the Section 304 clawback provision against an executive, even though individually he was not charged with fraud or other SEC violations.

OBSERVATION

Consistent with the broad philosophical direction of the Risk Assessment Standards, SAS 105 emphasizes the need to closely link the understanding of the entity, and the risk assessment, to the design of further audit procedures. Thus, whenever an auditor, as a result of obtaining an understanding of a client, assesses a significant risk of material misstatement, the audit procedures should respond to that risk. Conversely, in areas with low assessed risk, audit procedures would ordinarily be less intensive. This results in a more efficient allocation of audit resources, and a more effective audit. The practical result of this new emphasis will likely be a need to more closely tailor standardized audit programs to the unique risks of each individual engagement.

The CSX case is one example of several recent enforcement actions by the SEC that appear to be overly aggressive. Some commentators suggest that the SEC is merely applying a tone that is needed in a financial market the public believes is laced with fraud and corruption.

NEW CLAWBACK PROVISION UNDER DODD-FRANK

Arguably, the Dodd-Frank Act represents one of the most significant changes to corporate governance and financial regulation since the Great Depression.

The Act includes many executive compensation and corporate governance provisions.

One example is a requirement that at least once every three years, public companies allow their shareholders to make a nonbinding vote related to the compensation packages of its named executive officers including any agreements the company may have with those officers.

Another key change found in the Act is an executive compensation "clawback" provision.

Section 954 of the Act states:

> The rules of the Commission (SEC) ... shall require each issuer to develop and implement a policy providing—
>
> (1) for disclosure of the policy of the issuer on incentive based compensation that is based on financial information required to be reported under the securities laws; and
>
> (2) that, in the event that the issuer is required to prepare an accounting restatement due to the *material noncompliance of the issuer with any financial reporting requirement* under the securities laws, the issuer will recover from any current or former executive officer of the issuer who received incentive based compensation (including stock options awarded as compensation) during the 3-year period preceding the date on which the issuer is required to prepare an accounting restatement, based on the erroneous data, in excess of what would have been paid to the executive officer under the accounting restatement.

In essence, the Act requires the SEC to require all public companies to implement and disclose a clawback policy. Under this policy, if there is an accounting restatement due to a material noncompliance with financial reporting requirements, the company would have to recover any incentive-based compensation (e.g., bonuses, etc.) from any current or former executive officer for the three-year period prior to the restatement period.

Such recovery of incentive compensation would be required regardless of whether the executive officer was involved in the misconduct that led to the restatement.

Does the clawback provision found in Dodd-Frank's Section 954 overlap with the Section 304 clawback provision in Sarbanes-Oxley? There is a question as to whether the clawback provision found in Dodd-Frank is really necessary given the fact that Section 304 of Sarbanes-Oxley already has a clawback provision.

When one looks closely and compares the Section 954 Dodd-Frank clawback provision with the one found in Section 304 of Sarbanes-Oxley, it is clear that Dodd-Frank's version is far-reaching and much more expansive than Section 304 of Sarbanes-Oxley.

Although the SEC regulations for the Dodd-Frank clawback provision have not been issued, here are the obvious differences between the two clawback provisions:

- Section 304 of Sarbanes applies only to a CEO and CFO, while Section 954 of Dodd-Frank applies to "any current or former executive."
- Section 304 of Sarbanes requires that the misstatement be due to "misconduct" while Section 954 does not require that there be any misconduct.

NOTE

Section 954 applies when a company is "required to prepare an accounting restatement due to the *material noncompliance of the issuer with any financial reporting requirement.*" Arguably, all reported restatements meet the "material noncompliance" threshold because only material adjustments are required to be made by GAAP.

- Section 304 requires "any bonus or other incentive-based or equity-based compensation" be repaid as well as any profits realized from the sale of securities of the issuer. Section 954 only requires the repayment of the amount of incentive-based compensation (including stock options) that exceeds what would have been paid under the restatement.
- Section 304 applies to a 12-month period, while Dodd-Frank extends back three years from the year of restatement.

OBSERVATION

The Dodd-Frank clawback provision is far more mechanical than Section 304 of Sarbanes. Under Sarbanes, not only must there be a restatement, but there also must be misconduct associated with that misstatement. With Section 954 of Dodd-Frank, there is no "misconduct" threshold. Consequently, if a company restates its financial statements for any reason, it must recover any excess incentive-based compensation from its current and former executive officers. Although Dodd-Frank requires that the restatement represent "material noncompliance," an argument can be made that all required restatements represent "material noncompliance" with GAAP. Otherwise, such restatements would not be made due to immateriality.

As previously noted, 64 percent of Fortune 100 companies have clawback provisions in their executive compensation contracts. Most, if not all of them, have language that allows for a repayment of executive compensation when there is some sort of negligence or fraud on the part of the executive. The problem is that Dodd-Frank extends to situations in which an executive has done no wrong and for periods for which the executive may no longer be employed. The result is that an executive's clawback exposure under Dodd-Frank may certainly extend beyond the executive contract period.

STUDY QUESTION

3. Which of the following statements is true?
   a. The number of Section 304 cases prosecuted by the SEC has declined since Sarbanes-Oxley became effective in 2002.
   b. Eighteen percent of Fortune 100 companies have a clawback policy aimed at fraud, accounting restatements, and other errors.
   c. When there have been restatements, many companies that have had clawback provisions in their executive employment contracts have been reluctant to make their executives return bonuses.
   d. One requirement under Dodd-Frank is that at least once every five years, public companies allow their shareholders to make a nonbinding vote related to the compensation packages of its named executive officers including any agreements the company may has with those officers.

Should a company that records a restatement include the clawback recovery as part of the restatement entry? If a public company is required to restate its financial statements, a part of that entry should include a receivable due from the executives for recovery of compensation under Section 954 of Dodd-Frank.

EXAMPLE

In 2012, Company X discovers a material error related to years 2009, 2010, and 2011 due to an accrual that was not recorded for each of the three years.

X is going to make an entry in 2012 to record the accrual and restate the financial statements for 2009, 2010, and 2011. Income for each of the three years will decrease significantly.

X has an incentive compensation plan under which executives received sizeable bonuses for 2009–2011. Those bonuses were based on profitability.

Conclusion. Assuming the error is material, it would satisfy the material noncompliance threshold under Section 954 of Dodd-Frank. The result is that X must claw back the bonuses from its executives, including any executive that was employed during 2009–2011 that is no longer employed by the company in 2012.

Executive bonuses should be recomputed based on the restated income for 2009–2011 and the executives must repay the difference between the amount paid and the recomputed amount after the restatement.

The company makes the following entry in 2012, and restates the financial statements for 2009–2011:

Entry in 2012:

	dr	cr
Restatement adjustment 2009*	XX	
Restatement adjustment 2010*	XX	
Restatement adjustment 2011*	XX	
Accrual		XX
Executive clawback receivable**	XX	
Restatement adjustment 2009*		XX
Restatement adjustment 2010*		XX
Restatement adjustment 2011*		XX

*Retained earnings

**The amount of executive compensation that would have to be repaid under Dodd-Frank

The entry is made in 2012 with X restating each of the three years' financial statements to reflect the change. Tax effects are not considered in the above example, but obviously current and deferred tax entries would be required.

CPE NOTE: When you have completed your study and review of chapters 4–6, which comprise Module 2, you may wish to take the Quizzer for this Module.

Go to **CCHGroup.com/PrintCPE** to take this Quizzer online.

MODULE 3: CURRENT DEVELOPMENTS — CHAPTER 7

Accounting for Goodwill and Other Intangibles

LEARNING OBJECTIVES

Upon completion of this chapter, the reader will be able to:

- Describe the accounting treatment of goodwill when it is internally generated
- Describe the accounting treatment of goodwill when it is purchased in the acquisition of another company
- State the required disclosures relating to goodwill
- Discuss the factors considered when testing goodwill for impairment
- Explain the purpose of and changes made by ASU 2011-08

Goodwill is defined as "An asset representing the future economic benefits arising from other assets acquired in a business combination that are not individually identified and separately recognized" (Topic 805, Master Glossary).

FAS 142 (now codified as Topic 350) specifies the accounting and reporting requirements for goodwill and other intangible assets. Issued in June 2001, FAS 142 superseded APB Opinion No. 17, and AICPA Interpretations related to Opinion No. 17 and ARB No. 43, and amended several other accounting principles.

FAS 142 was amended by FAS 141(R) (Topic 805), effective for business combinations during periods beginning December 15, 2008.

A company records acquired intangible assets at fair market value (or relative fair value, if acquired in a lump-sum purchase), which is usually cost when the company purchases the intangible assets in an arm's-length purchase. The company amortizes the costs of these intangible assets over their useful lives if the assets are deemed to have a finite life.

A company determines the useful life of an intangible asset by using the time period that the company estimates the intangible asset will contribute directly or indirectly to future cash flows. A company does not amortize intangibles with indefinite lives but tests them for impairment.

A company does not amortize goodwill acquired in a business combination, but instead assigns the goodwill to reporting units and tests it for impairment. The costs related to internally generated intangibles (except goodwill and those costs determined to constitute research and development costs) are capitalized and amortized under certain conditions.

A company should aggregate intangible assets (except goodwill) and report them as a separate line item in the balance sheet. A company may elect to report individual intangibles separately or by class on the balance sheet. A company should report goodwill, however, as a separate line item on the balance sheet.

A company should report impairment losses and amortization expense related to intangibles on the income statement under income from continuing operations as a line item. If a goodwill impairment loss results from a discontinued operation, the company should report the impairment with discontinued operations.

ACQUISITION OF INTANGIBLES

A company should report an intangible asset acquired individually, such as the purchase of a patent, Internet domain name, or customer lists, as an asset at its fair market value, which is usually cost in an arm's-length purchase.

Generally, the amount of the cash exchanged is considered the fair value. If a company uses noncash assets, liabilities, or equity securities to acquire the intangible asset, the company should use the fair market value, which is the amount that would be received if the unit was sold at the measurement date in an orderly transaction between market participants.

When a company purchases an intangible in combination with other assets, the company allocates the acquisition price to the intangible based on its fair market value relative to the fair market values of all assets acquired.

A company should amortize an intangible asset with a finite life over its estimated useful life. However, a company should not amortize an intangible with an indefinite life, but the company should test it for impairment when appropriate.

A company determines the useful life of an asset by estimating the period of time that the asset contributes to future cash flows.

Factors to consider when determining useful life include asset use, useful life of related assets, legal limits, legal rights that extend useful life, the impact of obsolescence, and the relationship between maintenance costs and future cash flows.

After a company determines the useful life of an intangible asset, the company amortizes the intangible over that useful life using the amortization method that most accurately reflects the pattern of use.

A company should review the useful life each accounting period. A company should restate any changes attributable to an amended useful life prospectively and amortize the remaining book value over the revised useful life.

EXAMPLE

On January 1, Company Y acquired a patent at a cost of $100,000. The patent is estimated to have a useful life of 10 years.

Solution. The annual amortization expense for the patent amounts to $10,000. If the asset is used up faster in early years and less in later years, some form of accelerated amortization should be used. If the asset is used up equally each period, then straight-line amortization is appropriate.

EXAMPLE

A patent has a cost of $100,000, no residual value, and accumulated amortization amounting to $20,000. The estimated useful life was originally 10 years. The revised estimate indicates that only four years remain.

Solution. The new amortization expense amounts to $20,000 per year ($100,000 less $20,000/4 years). The residual value of an intangible asset is often zero.

In actuality, it is the asset's fair market value at the end of its useful life reduced by any expected disposition costs.

It is assumed to be zero unless it is expected to have a useful life to another enterprise later, or its future value is readily determinable from existing market transactions.

In addition, entities should test the intangible asset for impairment.

IMPAIRMENT

Impairment results when the company may not recover the carrying value of assets over future accounting periods. In the case of intangibles, this most often occurs when there is a major decline in the asset's fair value.

The following process is utilized to determine an impairment loss.

- After dividing the entity's assets into groups using the lowest level of assets that generate independent cash flows, the enterprise should estimate the net cash flows for each asset group.
- The company should compute the cash flows on a gross basis (not discounted to present value) and include any cash flows related to the use and disposition of the asset group.
- If the cash flow is less than the carrying value of the asset group, the company should test it for possible impairment. This requires a comparison of fair market values of the assets in the potentially impaired group.
- If fair value is less than the carrying amount of the asset group, the company reports an impairment loss equal to the difference between the carrying amount and the fair value.

- The asset is reduced by the loss, and the company amortizes the new basis over the remaining useful life.
- A subsequent recovery in the fair value of the intangible does not result in a reversal of the loss writedown.

EXAMPLE

Pattent Corporation is reviewing its intangibles using the provisions of Topic 360 because the company has a history of operating losses. The company has assets in other categories, but only its intangible asset generates cash flows in the category under consideration.

The carrying amount of the intangible asset is $10 million, with estimated net future cash flows of $8 million, and a fair market value of $7.5 million.

Solution. Because of the history of operating losses, Pattent Corporation must assess its intangible for impairment. Because the estimated future net cash flow of $8 million is less than the carrying amount of the asset ($10 million), the company must record an impairment loss.

The amount of the loss is $2.5 million, which is the difference between the carrying value ($10 million), and the fair value of the asset ($7.5 million). The following journal entry records the impairment of the intangible:

Estimated loss from impairment of intangible	$2,500,000	
Intangible		($2,500,000)

STUDY QUESTION

1. Goodwill acquired in a business acquisition must be:

   a. Expensed in the year acquired
   b. Capitalized and amortized over its useful life
   c. Capitalized and amortized over 40 years
   d. Capitalized and analyzed periodically for impairment

INTERNALLY GENERATED INTANGIBLES

A company capitalizes the costs related to internally generated intangibles when three conditions are satisfied:

- The costs must be related to an intangible asset that can be specifically identified, such as legal fees connected with obtaining a patent.
- The asset must have a determinable life.
- The intangible must not be inherent in a going concern and related to the enterprise as a whole.

For instance, consider the costs incurred to defend a patent held by the company.

The costs would be identifiable with the patent, have a determinable life, and not be related to the enterprise as a whole.

Goodwill

Goodwill exists when a purchasing company pays more for a business than the fair market value of the net assets if purchased separately.

EXAMPLE

If the value of a company's net assets is $1 million but the purchase price is $1.4 million, goodwill exists in the amount of $400,000. The company records the payment in excess of fair market value of the assets in the Goodwill account.

A company does not amortize goodwill resulting from a business combination.

Instead, the company tests it for impairment using the special impairment rules for goodwill contained in Topic 350. The test involves a two-step reporting level basis.

First, the company compares the carrying amount of the reporting unit to its fair market value, including goodwill. If the carrying value is less than its fair value, no impairment exists, and the second step is not required.

If the fair value is less than the carrying value, impairment is assumed. In this case, the company performs the second step to determine the amount of the impairment loss.

The fair value of the reporting unit is the amount that a willing buyer would pay the seller. Although a quoted market price is the best estimate of fair market value, the company may use other acceptable methods.

Three methods are possible:

- Prices paid for similar assets and liabilities.
- Present value of future cash flows.
- Valuation using multiples of earnings or revenue from other operations or activities of an entity, for which the multiples are known and are comparable in nature, scope, or size as the reporting unit for which fair value is being estimated.

In the second step, the company compares the carrying value of the goodwill to the implied fair value of the goodwill. This implied value is distinguished from the fair value because an estimate is used. One cannot directly determine the fair value of goodwill.

A company computes the implied fair value using the same procedures an entity would use when initially computing goodwill in a business combination.

The price paid for the unit (assumed to be fair market value) is allocated to all assets, including any intangibles. Any excess of price paid over the fair value allocated to the assets is the implied fair value of the goodwill.

So, if the implied fair value of the goodwill is less than the related carrying amount of the goodwill, an impairment loss equals the difference.

The loss is limited to the book value of the goodwill. A new basis for the goodwill is created. Reversal of prior impairment losses in subsequent periods is not permitted.

Testing for goodwill impairment under Topic 350 uses a process of assigning assets, liabilities, and goodwill to reporting units.

Assets and liabilities assigned may be part of a business combination, purchased separately, or as a part of a group purchase. They are typically assigned to the reporting unit on the date of acquisition.

A company should assign goodwill to reporting units that will benefit from it on the acquisition date, using a method that is reasonable, supportable, and applied on a consistent basis.

An entity should test for impairment of goodwill on at least an annual basis, and earlier if evidence suggests that testing is warranted.

The company must perform the testing at the same time each year, although each entity within a company may have different test dates during the year.

EXAMPLE

LeadJerr Company computed $1 million of goodwill in a business combination on January 1, 20X1. The goodwill was allocated to Reporting Units L and J. At the end of 20X3, the values for each reporting unit are:

Unit	Fair Value	Book Value	Book Value GW	Fair Value GW
L	$20,000,000	$16,000,000	$600,000	$700,000
J	$18,000,000	$19,500,000	$400,000	$375,000

Step 1. Compare the fair value of the reporting unit with its carrying value. For Unit L, the fair value of $20 million exceeds the $16 million book value; therefore, there is no goodwill impairment. For Unit J, the fair value of $18 million is less than the book value of $19.5 million; so, the company must test goodwill for impairment.

Step 2. Compare the fair value to the carrying value of the goodwill. This step is only relevant to Unit J. Unit J's goodwill has a book value of $400,000 and a fair value of $375,000. Since the fair value is less than the carrying value by $25,000, the company reports a goodwill impairment loss on the income statement in the amount of $25,000. The new goodwill carrying value amounts to $975,000 (600,000 + 375,000).

A company should not amortize goodwill computed using the equity method, but the company should test it for impairment under the provisions of ASC 350. A company should test goodwill from a business combination with a minority interest using the minority interest at the date of acquisition.

A company tests subsidiary goodwill for impairment at the subsidiary level, using its reporting units. Only if the goodwill is impaired at the consolidated level does the company report an impairment loss in the consolidated financial statements.

A company should consider goodwill when computing the gain or loss on the disposition of all or part of a reporting unit. If the transaction is a disposition of the entire unit, the company should include goodwill in the book value. On the other hand, if the disposal involved only part of the unit, the amount of goodwill included in the book value is based on its relative fair market value.

EXAMPLE

A company disposes of a part of its business. The fair value of the disposed portion of the business prior to disposition was $100,000.

The fair value of the remaining portion of the business after the disposition is $400,000. Goodwill is $1,000.

What is the amount of the goodwill allocated to the disposition?

Solution. The goodwill allocated to the disposition is $200, {$1,000 x [$100,000/($100,000 + $400,000)]}.

Goodwill Disclosures

For intangible assets not subject to amortization, the total carrying amount and the carrying amount for each major intangible asset class must be disclosed. In addition, the changes in the carrying amount of goodwill during the period must be disclosed showing the following separately (Topic 350-20-50, par. 1):

- The gross amount and accumulated impairment losses at the beginning of the period
- Additional goodwill recognized during the period, except goodwill included in a disposal group that, on acquisition, meets the criteria to be classified as held for sale in accordance with Topic 360-10-45, par.9
- Adjustments resulting from the subsequent recognition of deferred tax assets during the period
- Goodwill included in a disposal group classified as held for sale and goodwill derecognized during the period without having previously been reported in a disposal group classified as held for sale
- Impairment losses recognized during the period
- Net exchange differences arising during the period
- Any other changes in the carrying amount during the period
- The gross amount and accumulated impairment losses at the end of the period

STUDY QUESTION

2. An impairment loss for goodwill equals the excess of its:

a. Carrying value over its implied fair market value
b. Implied fair value over its carrying value
c. Net realizable value over its carrying value
d. Carrying value over its fair value

ASU 2011-08: TESTING GOODWILL FOR IMPAIRMENT

In September 2011, the FASB issued ASU 2011-08—Intangibles—Goodwill and Other (Topic 350) Testing Goodwill for Impairment The objective of this ASU is to introduce an optional qualitative assessment in testing goodwill for impairment.

Background

Prior to the issuance of ASU 2011-08, an entity with a material amount of goodwill has been required to test it annually. In doing so, the only method available has been to use the two-step formula found in ASC 350, which requires, at a minimum, that an entity perform the first step by comparing the fair value of the reporting unit (entity) to the carrying value of the reporting entity (entity). What this has meant is that in performing its annual test of goodwill, an entity has had to compute fair value, which can be tedious, costly, and time-consuming. Companies complained to the FASB that they needed a simpler method by which to screen a company to determine whether there was a potential impairment of goodwill.

In response to requests by companies to simplify the annual test for goodwill impairment, the FASB issued ASU 2011-08 to allow (but not require) use of a qualitative assessment to test impairment of goodwill. This optional qualitative assessment may be performed prior to performing the first step in the two-step approach and may alleviate an entity from having to perform either the first or second step.

Rules under ASU 2011-08

Under ASU 2011-08, an entity has the option to first make a qualitative assessment to determine whether it is necessary to perform the two-step goodwill impairment test.

If, based on the qualitative assessment, it is more likely than not (more than 50 percent probability) that the fair value of a reporting unit (entity) *is not* less than its carrying amount, the entity may bypass the two-step test for impairment as there is no impairment. If, based on the qualitative assessment, it is more likely than not that the fair value of an entity *is* less than its carrying amount, the entity must perform the first step of the two-step impairment test and then, if necessary, perform the second step.

NOTE

The qualitative assessment is optional so that an entity has an unconditional option not to perform the qualitative assessment and, instead, perform the two-step goodwill impairment test. An entity may resume performing the qualitative assessment in any subsequent period.

In making the qualitative assessment, an entity may assess qualitative factors to determine whether it is more likely than not (that is, a likelihood of more than 50 percent) that the fair value of a reporting unit is less than its carrying amount.

Examples of such qualitative factors (events and circumstances) include the following:

- Macroeconomic conditions such as:
  - a deterioration in general economic conditions
  - limitations on accessing capital
  - fluctuations in foreign exchange rates
  - other developments in equity and credit markets
- Industry and market considerations such as:
  - a deterioration in the environment in which an entity operates
  - an increased competitive environment
  - a decline in market-dependent multiples or metrics (consider in both absolute terms and relative to peers)
  - a change in the market for an entity's products or services, or a regulatory or political development
- Cost factors such as increases in raw materials, labor, or other costs that have a negative effect on earnings and cash flows
- Overall financial performance such as:
  - a negative or declining cash flows
  - a decline in actual or planned revenue or earnings compared with actual and projected results of relevant prior periods
- Other relevant entity-specific events such as changes in management, key personnel, strategy, or customers; contemplation of bankruptcy; or litigation
- Events affecting a reporting unit such as:
  - a change in the composition or carrying amount of its net assets
  - a more-likely-than-not expectation of selling or disposing all, or a portion, of a reporting unit

  - testing for recoverability of a significant asset group within a reporting unit
  - recognition of a goodwill impairment loss in the financial statements of a subsidiary that is a component of a reporting unit
- If applicable, a sustained decrease in share price (consider in both absolute terms and relative to peers)
- Other relevant events and circumstances that affect the fair value or carrying amount in determining whether to perform the first step of the goodwill impairment test

An entity shall consider the extent to which each of the qualitative factors (events and circumstances) could affect the comparison of an entity's fair value with its carrying amount considering the following guidelines:

- An entity should place more weight on the factors that most affect the entity's fair value or the carrying amount of its net assets.
- An entity should consider positive and mitigating factors that may affect its determination of whether it is more likely than not that the fair value of a reporting unit is less than its carrying amount.
- If an entity has a recent fair value calculation, it also should include as a factor in its consideration the difference between the fair value and the carrying amount in reaching its conclusion about whether to perform the first step of the goodwill impairment test.
- An entity shall evaluate, on the basis of the weight of evidence, the significance of all identified factors in the context of determining whether it is more likely than not that the fair value is less than its carrying amount.

NOTE

None of the individual examples of factors are intended to represent stand-alone events or circumstances that necessarily require an entity to perform the first step of the goodwill impairment test. The existence of positive and mitigating factors is not intended to represent a rebuttable presumption that an entity should not perform the first step of the goodwill impairment test.

ASU 2011-08 eliminates use of the special goodwill impairment test carry-forward rule that was included in the originally issued ASC 350.

Under that rule, ASC 350 offered a special relief provision under which, if certain criteria were met, an entity was able to test for impairment in the first year, and carry forward the test to each successive year, without updating it. ASU 2011-08 amends ASC 350 to officially remove the special carryforward rule.

ASU 2011-08 provides clarification with respect to disclosures involving the goodwill impairment by stating that the quantitative disclosures about significant unobservable inputs used in fair value measurements categorized within Level 3 of the fair value hierarchy are not required for fair value measurements related to the financial accounting and reporting for goodwill after its initial recognition in a business combination.

Effective Date and Transition

Use of the qualitative assessment found in ASU 2011-08 shall be applied prospectively for annual and interim goodwill impairment tests performed for fiscal years *beginning after December 15, 2011*. Earlier application is permitted.

Earlier application is also permitted for annual and interim goodwill impairment tests performed as of a date before September 15, 2011, if the entity's financial statements for the most recent annual or interim period have not yet been issued or, for nonpublic entities, have not yet been made available for issuance.

STUDY QUESTION

3. **Facts:** An entity is performing a qualitative assessment of impairment of its goodwill. The entity concludes that it is more likely than not that the fair value of the entity is not less than its carrying amount. Which of the following is correct?

   a. The entity must perform the first step of the two-step impairment test.
   b. The entity may bypass the first step and go directly to the second step.
   c. The entity may bypass the two-step test for impairment.
   d. The entity must perform both steps of the two-step impairment test.

MODULE 3: CURRENT DEVELOPMENTS — CHAPTER 8

ASU 2011-09: Multiemployer Plan Disclosures

LEARNING OBJECTIVES

Upon completion of this chapter, the reader will be able to:

- Discuss the differences between multiemployer, single-employer, and multiple-employer plans
- State the purpose and scope of ASU 2011-09
- Compare U.S. GAAP and IFRS in regard to the recognition, measurement, and disclosure requirements for multiemployer plans
- List the disclosure requirements of ASU 2011-09
- State the effective date of ASU 2011-09

INTRODUCTION

The objective of Accounting Standards Update (ASU) 2011-09, *Compensation—Retirement Benefits—Multiemployer Plans (Subtopic 715-80) Disclosures about an Employer's Participation in a Multiemployer Plan*, is to expand the required disclosures for employers that participate in multiemployer pension plans and multiemployer other postretirement benefit plans.

For employers that participate in multiemployer pension plans, the amendments in ASU 2011-09 require an employer to provide additional quantitative and qualitative disclosures to provide users with more detailed information about an employer's involvement in multiemployer plans.

BACKGROUND

It is common for employers of defined benefit pension plans and other postretirement benefit plans to provide benefits to their employees through multiemployer plans. In general, such plans allow individual employers to pool investment assets with other employers, and reduce administrative costs, particularly with respect to a group of individually smaller employers who seek the economies of scale that a larger multiemployer plan can afford them. Another group that uses multiemployer pension plans is companies with union contracts.

Contrary to multiemployer plans, single-employer plans may not have the benefits of pooling investment assets and driving down administrative costs, but they offer other benefits such as being able to maintain separate accounts for each employer so that each employer's contributions benefit only the employees of that contributing employer.

One particular difference between multiemployer and single-employer plans is that multiemployer plans may lack some of the transparency of single-employer plans for several reasons:

- Such plans may be part of collective-bargaining agreements.
- It may be difficult for individual employers and employees to obtain timely information about the multiemployer plan, particularly if such information is not published.
- The regulatory environment of such plans may vary across industries and restrict access to certain information about the plans.

U.S. GAAP for multiemployer pension plans is found in ASC Subtopic 715-80, *Multiemployer Plans*, which, prior to the application of ASU 2011-09, requires individual employers to make disclosures limited primarily to disclosing the historical contributions made to the plans.

Although a multiemployer pension plan is a defined benefit plan, on each employer's individual financial statements, U.S. GAAP treats the plan as if it were a defined contribution plan. In doing so, GAAP requires that an employer recognize its required contribution to the plan as pension or other postretirement benefit cost for the period and recognize a liability for any contributions due at the reporting date. The actuarial present value computations and extensive disclosures required of a typical single-employer defined benefit plan are not applicable when the plan is a multiemployer one.

There are also several unique characteristics of a multiemployer plan, some of which may expose one employer to the risks of other employers within the plan as follows:

- Assets contributed by one employer for its own employees may be used to provide benefits to employees of other participating employers as those assets are not specifically earmarked only for its employees.
- If a participating employer fails to make its required contributions, the unfunded obligations of the plan may be borne by the remaining participating employers.
- If an employer chooses to stop participating in a multiemployer plan, the withdrawing company may be required to pay to the plan a final payment (the withdrawal liability).

Financial statement users have continued to have concerns that U.S. GAAP has failed to provide sufficient transparency about a particular employer's participation in a multiemployer pension plan. Because the risk of exposure for any one particular employer within a multiemployer plan could expand beyond that employer's obligations to its employees, users of financial statements have requested that the FASB require additional disclosures to increase awareness of the commitments and risks involved with participating in multiemployer pension plans. In response, the FASB issued ASU 2011-09 in September 2011 to require additional disclosures about an employer's participation in multiemployer pension plans and other postretirement plans such as those that provide retirees with health and life insurance benefits.

According to the FASB, in developing the ASU, the FASB had several goals which were to help users:

- Assess the potential future cash flow implications relating to an employer's participation in multiemployer pension plans
- Assess the financial health of all of the significant multiemployer plans in which the employer participates
- Access additional information about the multiemployer plan that is available outside the financial statements

STUDY QUESTION

1. Which of the following is a unique characteristic of a multiemployer plan?
   - **a.** Assets contributed by one employer for its own employees may not be used to provide benefits to employees of other employer plans.
   - **b.** If a participating employer fails to make its required contributions, the unfunded obligations of the plan are not borne by the remaining employers.
   - **c.** A company that withdraws from a plan may be required to pay a withdrawal liability.
   - **d.** A multiemployer plan consists of one employer who administers several plans.

KEY CHANGES

Key changes made by ASU 2011-09 include the following:

- It applies to nongovernmental, multiemployer pension plans and other postretirement plans, but does not apply to single-employer plans.
- The amendments require additional separate disclosures for multiemployer pension plans and multiemployer other postretirement benefit plans.
- The ASU amendments require an employer to provide additional quantitative and qualitative disclosures, as well as more detailed information about an employer's involvement in multiemployer pension plans, including:
  - The significant multiemployer plans in which an employer participates, including the plan names and identifying number so that a user can obtain additional information about the multiemployer plan
  - The level of an employer's participation in the significant multiemployer plans
  - The financial health of the significant multiemployer plans
  - The nature of the employer commitments to the plans
  - Other information that includes a description of the extent to which the employer could be responsible for the obligations of the plan including benefits of employees of other employers
- In addition to disclosures of multiemployer pension plans, the ASU expands disclosures for multiemployer other postretirement benefit plans.

ASU 2011-09 does not change the recognition provisions of existing GAAP under which an employer recognizes its required contribution to the plan as pension or other postretirement benefit cost for the period and recognizes a liability for any contributions due at the reporting date. That guidance is unchanged by these ASU amendments.

COMPARISON OF U.S. GAAP WITH IFRS

U.S. GAAP differs from International Financial Reporting Standards (IFRS) in recognition and measurement of an employer's participation in multiemployer plans for both plans that provide pension benefits and those that provide other postretirement benefits. Under U.S. GAAP, the current recognition and measurement guidance for an employer's participation in a multiemployer plan requires that an employer treat the transaction as if it was a defined contribution plan by recognizing its required contribution to the plan as pension or other postretirement benefit cost for the period and recognizing a liability for any contributions due at the reporting date. Unlike a single-employer plan, an employer of a multiemployer plan does not record the actuarial benefit obligation.

International standards require that an employer account for a defined benefit multiemployer plan as a defined benefit plan, recognizing a defined benefit asset or liability, if sufficient information is available to do so. However, under IFRS, an employer may account for a defined benefit multiemployer plan as a defined contribution plan if there is insufficient information to apply defined benefit accounting, as is often the case.

On the disclosure side, ASU 2011-09 brings U.S. GAAP disclosures for employers of multiemployer plans closer in line with IFRS. In June 2011, the International Accounting Standards Board (IASB) issued amendments to international standards by issuing IAS 19, *Employee Benefits,* to enhance disclosures about an employer's participation in a multiemployer plan.

Even after the issuance of ASU 2011-09, U.S. GAAP disclosures are similar, but not identical, to the IFRS disclosures with the key remaining differences consisting of the use of information, terminology, and the greater level of specificity found in the FASB's disclosure requirements.

STUDY QUESTION

2. Which of the following is a key change made by ASU 2011-09?

a. The amendments require that the disclosures of multiemployer pension and other postretirement benefit plans be combined.
b. The disclosures apply to governmental and nongovernmental plans.
c. The changes apply to both single-employer and multiemployer plans.
d. The ASU affects disclosures for multiemployer other postretirement benefit plans.

REQUIREMENTS OF ASU 2011-09

Scope

The amendments in ASU 2011-09 apply to nongovernmental entities (public and nonpublic) that participate in:

- Multiemployer pension plans
- Multiemployer plans that provide postretirement benefits other than pensions

The ASU amendments *do not apply* to plans that are not multiemployer plans such as:

- Single-employer plans
- Multiple-employer plans
- Subsidiaries who participate in one, single parent plan

NOTE

ASU 2011-09 does provide a modified disclosure for certain subsidiaries and not-for-profit organizations, which is discussed later in this chapter.

NOTE

Multiple-employer plans are, in substance, aggregations of single-employer plans combined to allow participating employers to pool plan assets for investment purposes or to reduce the costs of plan administration. Contrary to multiemployer plans, multiple-employer plans ordinarily do not involve collective-bargaining agreements and generally maintain separate accounts for each employer so that contributions provide benefits only for employees of the contributing employer. In comparison, a multiemployer plan combines assets so that the assets of the plan are not maintained in separate accounts, by employer.

Definitions

The following ASC 715 definitions relate to ASU 2011-09:

Multiemployer plan. A pension or other postretirement benefit plan to which two or more unrelated employers contribute, usually pursuant to one or more collective-bargaining agreements. A characteristic of multiemployer plans is that assets contributed by one particular employer may be used to provide benefits to employees of other participating employers since assets contributed by an employer are not segregated in a separate account or restricted to provide benefits only to employees of that employer. A multiemployer plan is usually administered by a board of trustees composed of management and labor representatives and may also be referred to as a joint trust or union plan. Generally, many employers participate in a multiemployer plan, and an employer may participate in more than one plan. The employers participating in multiemployer plans usually have a common industry bond, but for some plans the employers are in different industries and the labor union may be their only common bond. Some multiemployer plans do not involve a union.

EXAMPLE

Local chapters of a not-for-profit entity (NFP) may participate in a plan established by the related national organization.

Single-employer plan. A pension plan that is maintained by one employer. The term also may be used to describe a plan that is maintained by related parties such as a parent and its subsidiaries.

Multiple-employer plan. In substance, an aggregation of single-employer plans, combined to allow participating employers to pool plan assets for investment purposes or to reduce the costs of plan administration. Such plans ordinarily do not involve collective-bargaining agreements. They may also have features that allow participating employers to have different benefit formulas, with the employer's contributions to the plan based on the benefit formula selected by the employer.

Nonpublic entity. An entity that does not meet any of the following criteria:

- Its debt or equity securities are traded in a public market, including those traded on a stock exchange or in the over-the-counter market (including securities quoted only locally or regionally).
- It is a conduit bond obligor for conduit debt securities that are traded in a public market (a domestic or foreign stock exchange or an over-the-counter market, including local or regional markets).
- Its financial statements are filed with a regulatory agency in preparation for the sale of any class of securities.

Pension benefits. Periodic (usually monthly) payments made pursuant to the terms of the pension plan to a person who has retired from employment or to that person's beneficiary.

Postretirement benefits other than pensions. All forms of benefits, other than retirement income, provided by an employer to retirees. Those benefits may be defined in terms of specified benefits, such as health care, tuition assistance, or legal services, that are provided to retirees as the need for those services arises, such as certain health care benefits, or they may be defined in terms of monetary amounts that become payable on the occurrence of a specified event, such as life insurance benefits.

STUDY QUESTION

3. Which of the following is correct with respect to multiemployer plans?
   a. Such a plan is usually administered by a board of trustees.
   b. All such plans involve a union.
   c. Such plans are from different industries.
   d. Assets contributed by an employer are segregated into a separate account.

Disclosures

Disclosures required by ASU 2011-09 include the following:

Disclosures for employers of multiemployer pension plans. Following are the new disclosures required by ASU 2011-09 for multiemployer pension plans, and they include all items recognized as net pension costs. The disclosures are based on *the most recently available* information through the date at which the employer has evaluated subsequent events.

An employer that participates in a multiemployer plan that provides pension benefits shall provide the following in its annual financial statements:

- **A narrative description** both of the general nature of the multiemployer plans that provide pension benefits and of the employer's participation in the plans that would indicate how the risks of participating in these plans are different from those of single-employer plans.
- **Tabular format disclosures:**
  (1) When feasible, the following information shall be provided in a *tabular format* while information that requires greater narrative description may be provided outside the table. For each *individually significant multiemployer plan* that provides pension benefits, an employer shall disclose the following:
    (a) Legal name of the plan
    (b) The plan's Employer Identification Number (EIN) and, if available, its plan number
    (c) For each statement of financial position presented, the most recently available certified zone status provided by the plan, as currently defined by the *Pension Protection Act of 2006* or a subsequent amendment of that Act

    The disclosure shall specify the date of the plan's year-end to which the zone status relates and whether the plan has utilized any extended amortization provisions that affect the calculation of the zone status. If the zone status is not available, an employer shall disclose, as of the most recent date available, on the basis of the financial statements provided by the plan, the total plan assets and accumulated benefit obligations, whether the plan was:

(1) Less than 65 percent funded
(2) Between 65 percent and 80 percent funded
(3) At least 80 percent funded.

(d) The expiration date(s) of the collective-bargaining agreement(s) requiring contributions to the plan, if any.

NOTE

If more than one collective-bargaining agreement applies to the plan, the employer shall provide a range of the expiration dates of those agreements, supplemented with a qualitative description that identifies the significant collective-bargaining agreements within that range as well as other information to help investors understand the significance of the collective-bargaining agreements and when they expire (e.g., the portion of employees covered by each agreement or the portion of contributions required by each agreement).

(e) For each period that a statement of income (or statement of activities for nonpublic entities) is presented:

(1) The employer's contributions made to the plan
(2) Whether the employer's contributions represent more than five percent of total contributions to the plan as indicated in the plan's most recently available annual report (Form 5500 for U.S. plans)

NOTE

The disclosure shall specify the year-end date of the plan to which the annual report relates.

(f) As of the end of the most recent annual period presented:

(1) Whether a funding improvement plan or rehabilitation plan (FIP or RP) (e.g., as those terms are defined by the Employment Retirement Security Act of 1974) had been implemented or was pending
(2) Whether the employer paid a surcharge to the plan
(3) A description of any minimum contribution(s) required for future periods by the collective-bargaining agreement(s), statutory obligations, or other contractual obligations, if applicable

NOTE

In determining whether a multiemployer plan is individually significant, factors other than the amount of the employer's contribution to a plan, such as the severity of the underfunded status of the plan, may need to be considered.

(2) The disclosures in (1)(a) through (f) above assume that this other information about the plan is available in the public domain such as plan information in Form 5500 being publicly available.

In circumstances in which plan level information is not available in the public domain, an employer shall disclose the following additional information about each significant plan, which shall be included in a separate section of the tabular disclosure required in (1)(a) through (f):

(a) A description of the nature of the plan benefits
(b) A qualitative description of the extent to which the employer could be responsible for the obligations of the plan, including benefits earned by employees during employment with another employer
(c) Other quantitative information, to the extent available, as of the most recent date available, to help users understand the financial information about the plan, such as total plan assets, actuarial present value of accumulated plan benefits, and total contributions received by the plan

(3) An employer shall disclose in a tabular format for each annual period for which a statement of income or statement of activities is presented, both of the following:

(a) Its total contributions made to all plans that are not individually significant
(b) Its total contributions made to all plans

NOTE

If the quantitative information in paragraphs (1)(c), (1)(e)(2), or (2)(c) cannot be obtained without undue cost and effort, that quantitative information may be omitted and the employer shall describe what information has been omitted and why. In that circumstance, the employer also shall provide any qualitative information as of the most recent date available that would help users understand the financial information that otherwise is required to be disclosed about the plan.

(c) Other disclosures:

(1) An employer shall provide a description of the nature and effect of any significant changes that affect comparability of total employer contributions from period to period, such as:
(a) A business combination or a divestiture
(b) A change in the contractual employer contribution rate
(c) A change in the number of employees covered by the plan during each year

STUDY QUESTION

4. If plan level information is ***not*** available in the public domain, which of the following is additional information that an employer must disclose?
   a. A qualitative description of the extent to which the employer could be responsible for the obligations of the plan
   b. A quantitative analysis of the extent to which the employer could be responsible for the obligations of the plan
   c. A probability-weighted analysis that provides the user with information as to the likelihood that the employer might be exposed to additional loss

Disclosures for employers of multiemployer plans that provide postretirement benefits other than pensions. Following are the new disclosures required by ASU 2011-09 for multiemployer plans that provide postretirement benefits other than pensions, such as health insurance.

An employer shall disclose the amount of contributions to multiemployer plans that provide postretirement benefits other than pensions for each annual period for which a statement of income or statement of activities is presented. The disclosures shall include a description of the nature and effect of any changes that affect comparability of total employer contributions from period to period, such as:

- A business combination or a divestiture
- A change in the contractual employer contribution rate
- A change in the number of employees covered by the plan during each year.

The disclosures also shall include a description of the nature of the benefits and the types of employees covered by these benefits, such as medical benefits provided to active employees and retirees.

Special rules for subsidiaries and not-for-profit entities. Under current U.S. GAAP, subsidiaries that participate in their parent entity's single-employer defined benefit pension plan and local chapters of not-for-profit entities that participate in their national organization's defined benefit pension plan have accounted for and disclosed their participation in such plans as multiemployer plans. Some of the disclosures required by the amendments in ASU 2011-09 are less relevant in these situations.

The FASB noted that stakeholders have not cited a lack of information about the subsidiaries' and not-for-profit chapters' involvement with these plans that would warrant significant changes to the historical disclosures. Consequently, the FASB, in ASU 2011-09, did amend the disclosure requirements for subsidiaries that participate in their parent entity's single-employer defined benefit pension plan and for local chapters of not-for-profit entities that participate in their national organization's defined benefit pension plan.

These subsidiaries and not-for-profit chapters are required to disclose only the name of the plan and the amount of contributions made to the plan in each annual period for which an income statement is presented. The parent entity should account for the pension plan as a single-employer pension plan in its consolidated statements.

STUDY QUESTION

5. Which of the following are requirements under ASU 2011-09 as they relate to subsidiaries and not-for-profit entities?

- **a.** Full disclosures under ASU 2011-09 apply to not-for-profit entities.
- **b.** Selected disclosures are required for subsidiaries and not-for-profit entities.
- **c.** The parent entity should account for the pension plan as a multiple-employer pension plan in its consolidated statements.

SAMPLE DISCLOSURE

Example 1: Disclosures for Multiemployer Plans That Provide Pension Benefits

The following sample disclosure was extracted from ASU 2011-09 and modified by the author.

Facts. Entity A contributes to numerous multiemployer defined benefit pension plans as required under collective-bargaining agreements. Following is a sample disclosure that is required under the amendments to ASU 2011-09.

Note X: Multiemployer Plans That Provide Pension Benefits

The Company contributes to a number of multiemployer defined benefit pension plans under the terms of collective-bargaining agreements that cover its union-represented employees. The risks of participating in these multiemployer plans are different from single-employer plans in the following aspects:

- Assets contributed to the multiemployer plan by one employer may be used to provide benefits to employees of other participating employers.

- If a participating employer stops contributing to the plan, the unfunded obligations of the plan may be borne by the remaining participating employers.
- If the Company chooses to stop participating in some of its multiemployer plans, the Company may be required to pay those plans an amount based on the underfunded status of the plan, referred to as a withdrawal liability. [Disclosure (a)(1)]

Entity A's participation in these plans for the annual period ended December 31, 20X0, is outlined in the table below reflective of the following data:

- **EIN/Pension Plan Number:** The "EIN/Pension Plan Number" column provides the Employer Identification Number (EIN) and the three-digit plan number, if applicable.
- **Certified zone information:** Unless otherwise noted, the most recent Pension Protection Act (PPA) zone status available in 20X0 and 20X9 is for the plan's year-end at December 31, 20X9, and December 31, 20X8, respectively. The zone status is based on information that Entity A received from the plan and is certified by the plan's actuary. Among other factors, plans in the red zone are generally less than 65 percent funded, plans in the yellow zone are less than 80 percent funded, and plans in the green zone are at least 80 percent funded. One of the plans, Plan Fund 46, utilized an extended amortization provision that affects the calculation of the zone status.
- **FIP/RP status:** The "FIP/RP Status Pending/Implemented" column indicates plans for which a financial improvement plan (FIP) or a rehabilitation plan (RP) is either pending or has been implemented. The last column lists the expiration date(s) of the collective-bargaining agreement(s) to which the plans are subject.

The number of employees covered by Entity A's multiemployer plans decreased by five percent from 20X9 to 20X0, affecting the period-to-period comparability of the contributions for years 20X9 and 20X0. The significant reduction in covered employees corresponded to a reduction in overall business. There have been no significant changes that affect the comparability of 20X8 and 20X9 contributions. [Disclosure (c)(1)]

Each multiemployer pension plan requires the Company to contribute to the plan a fixed contracted amount per hour worked by each employee covered by the collective-bargaining agreements. In future periods, the Company is not required to make any minimum contributions by the collective-bargaining agreements, or by statutory or other contractual obligations except that Fund 73 has a minimum annual contribution requirement of $1 million. [Disclosure (1)(f)(3)]

[(1)(a)] Legal Name of Pension Fund	[(1)(b)] EIN/ Pension Plan Number	[(1)(c)] Pension Protection Act Certified Zone Status		[(1)(e)] Contributions of Entity A			[(f)(1)] FIP/RP Status Pending/ Implemented	[(f)(2)] Surcharge paid to the plan	[(1)(d)] Expiration Date of Collective-Bargaining Agreement
		20X0	20X9	20X0	20X9	20X8			
Plans for which plan financial information is publicly available outside Entity A's financial statements:									
Fund 34	32-1899999	Red as of 9-30-X9	Yellow as of 9-30-X8	$1,883,000	$2,309,000	$2,226,000	Yes	Yes	12-31-20X13
Fund 37	52-5599999-002	Green	Yellow	3,342,000	3,609,000	3,586,000	No	No	12-31-20X12 to 12-31-20X13 **(a)**
Fund 40	92-3499999	Yellow	Yellow	5,798,000	6,435,000	6,374,000	No	No	12-31-20X15
Fund 43	82-4299999	Red	Red	3,539,000	3,234,000	3,218,000	Pending	Yes	12-31-20X14
Fund 46 **(b)**	82-6899999	Green	Green	778,000	816,000	833,000	No	No	12-31-20X13
Fund 49	52-6199999	Yellow	Yellow	534,000	547,000	491,000	No	No	12-31-20X12
Fund 52	72-8599999-001	Red	Green	1,349,000	1,134,000	1,050,000	Implemented	No	12-31-20X15
Fund 55	82-2999999	Green	Green	1,224,000	1,046,000	1,151,000	No	No	12-31-20X14
Other funds, individually not significant **[(3)(a)]**				147,000	160,000	169,000			
Plans for which plan financial information is not publicly available outside Entity A's financial statements:									
Fund 61 **(c)**	N/A	N/A	N/A	418,000	482,000	491,000	N/A	N/A	12-31-20X12
Fund 73 **(d)**	N/A	N/A	N/A	1,872,000	1,764,000	1,693,000	N/A	N/A	12-31-20X12
	Total contributions			**$20,884,000** **[(3)(b)]**	**$21,536,000** **[(3)(b)]**	**$21,282,000** **[(3)(b)]**			

(a) Entity A is party to two significant collective-bargaining agreements that require contributions to Fund 37. Agreements D and E expire on 12/31/20X12, and 12/31/20X13, respectively. Of the two, Agreement D is more significant because 70 percent of Entity A's employee participants in Fund 37 are covered by that agreement. Agreement E also is significant because its participants are involved in multiple projects that Entity A is scheduled to start in 20X14. [Disclosure (1)(d)—more than one collective-bargaining agreement]

(b) Fund 46 utilized the special 30-year amortization rules provided by Public Law 111-192, Section 211 to amortize its losses from 20X8. The plan recertified its zone status after using the amortization provisions of that law. [Disclosure (1)(c)—extended amortization provisions]

Plans for which plan level information is not available in the public domain: [Disclosures (2)(a)(b) and (c)]

Entity A has two plans, Funds 61 and 73, for which plan level information is not publicly available. Following is additional information about each of these two plans:

(c) **ABC Fund 61:** Plan information for Fund 61 is not publicly available. Fund 61 provides fixed, monthly retirement payments on the basis of the credits earned by the participating employees. To the extent that the plan is underfunded, the future contributions to the plan may increase and may be used to fund retirement benefits for employees related to other employers who have ceased operations. Entity A could be assessed a withdrawal liability in the event that it decides to cease participating in the plan. Fund 61's financial statements for the years ended June 30, 20X0 and 20X9 indicated total assets of $62 million and $51 million, respectively; total actuarial present value of accumulated plan benefits of $120 million and $110 million, respectively; and total contributions for all participating employers of $9 million and $8 million, respectively. The plan's financial statements for the plan years ended June 30, 20X0 and 20X9 indicate that the plan was less than 65 percent funded in both years.

(d) **ABC Fund 73:** Plan information for Fund 73 is not publicly available. Fund 73 provides fixed retirement payments on the basis of the credits earned by the participating employees. However, in the event that the plan is underfunded, the monthly benefit amount can be reduced by the trustees of the plan. Entity A is not responsible for the underfunded status of the plan because Fund 73 operates in a jurisdiction that does not require withdrawing participants to pay a withdrawal liability or other penalty. Entity A is unable to provide additional quantitative information on the plan because Entity A is unable to obtain that information without undue cost and effort. The collective-bargaining agreement of Fund 73 requires contributions on the basis of hours worked. The agreement also has a minimum contribution requirement of $1 million each year.

Entity A was listed in its plans' most recently available Forms 5500 as providing more than five percent of the total contributions for the following plans and plan years: [Disclosure (1)(e)(2)]

Pension Fund	Year Contributions to Plan Exceeded MoreThan Five Percent of Total Contributions (as of December 31 of the Plan's Year-End)
ABC Fund 34	20X9 and 20X8
ABC Fund 43	20X8
ABC Fund 52	20X8
ABC Fund 61	20X9

At the date the financial statements were issued, Forms 5500 were not available for the plan years ending in 20X0.

—End of disclosure—

EFFECTIVE DATE

For public entities, the amendments in ASU 2011-09 are effective for annual periods for fiscal years ending after December 15, 2011, with early adoption permitted.

For nonpublic entities, the amendments are effective for annual periods for fiscal years ending after December 15, 2012, with early adoption permitted. The amendments should be applied retrospectively for all prior periods presented.

STUDY QUESTION

6. Which of the following is true concerning the effective date of ASU 2011-09?

- **a.** For public entities, the amendments in ASU 2011-09 are effective for annual periods for fiscal years ending after December 15, 2012.
- **b.** For nonpublic entities, the amendments are effective for annual periods for fiscal years ending after December 15, 2013.
- **c.** Early adoption is permitted.
- **d.** The amendments should be applied prospectively only.

MODULE 3: CURRENT DEVELOPMENTS — CHAPTER 9

Balance Sheet Classification

LEARNING OBJECTIVES

Upon completion of this chapter, the reader will be able to:

- Recall basic concepts related to presenting a classified balance sheet
- Explain how to segregate debt that is current and noncurrent
- Apply criteria for offsetting assets and liabilities in a balance sheet
- Identify related disclosures

OVERVIEW AND BACKGROUND

Overview

Information about an entity's liquidity is critical to its stakeholders. To aid liquidity analysis, many entities present a balance sheet that segregates the entity's assets and liabilities between those that are current and those that are noncurrent (a *classified balance sheet*).

GAAP gives guidance on *how* (but not *when*) to classify a balance sheet. For example, entities in some industries (such as the financial services industry) typically present unclassified balance sheets. However, even an entity that presents an unclassified balance sheet must segregate certain assets or liabilities for disclosure purposes—for example, when disclosing the entity's debt maturities.

The FASB Accounting Standards Codification™ provides general guidance on classification of assets and liabilities between current and noncurrent in Topic 210, *Balance Sheet*, Section 210-10-45, which is addressed by this course. Guidance specific to particular assets, liabilities, and industries is given in various other Topics in the respective Other Presentation Matters Sections (Section 45). Of those, this course addresses the guidance specific to an entity's liabilities for its debt set forth in Topic 470, *Debt*, Section 470-10-45.

The overall presentation of a classified balance sheet is affected when an entity presents, as a net amount, a recognized asset and a recognized liability that are related. This course addresses the primary guidance on setting off (or netting) an asset and a liability that are related, which is provided in Topic 210, *Balance Sheet*, Section 210-20-45.

In addition to the general guidance addressed in this course, GAAP sets forth specialized industry requirements specific to balance sheet classification and offsetting. That guidance can be found in the following Balance Sheet Subtopics (Subtopic XXX-270) of the following specialized industry Topics of the FASB Accounting Standards Codification™:

- 912 Contractors—Federal Government
- 915 Development Stage Entities
- 942 Financial Services—Depository and Lending
- 946 Financial Services—Investment Companies
- 954 Health Care Entities
- 958 Not-for-Profit Entities

Background

In the ordinary course of business there is a continuing circulation of capital within an entity's current assets.

EXAMPLE

A manufacturer expends cash for materials, labor, and factory overhead that are converted into finished inventory. After being sold, inventory is usually converted into trade receivables. Upon collection those trade receivables are realized in cash.

The average time intervening between the acquisition of materials (or services) and the final realization of cash is referred to as an *operating cycle.* (ASC Master Glossary entry "Operating Cycle")

GAAP requires that an entity use one year as a basis for segregating current assets if more than one operating cycle occurs within a year. An entity that has no clearly defined operating cycle is also required to base its segregation of current assets on a one-year operating cycle. If an entity's operating cycle is longer than one year, the entity must base its segregation of current assets on the actual period of its operating cycle. (ASC Topic 210, *Balance Sheet,* paragraph 210-10-45-3)

PLANNING POINTER

Some entities have a *natural business year,* at the end of which the entity's activity, inventory, and trade receivables are at their lowest point. The end of the entity's natural business year is the point in time such an entity often selects as the end of its accounting period for financial reporting purposes.

STUDY QUESTION

1. Which of the following statements is ***false?***
   a. The average time elapsing between expending cash and receiving the cash back from the trade receivable is called an operating cycle.
   b. When the operating cycle is longer than a year, the operating cycle is used for segregating current assets.
   c. One year is used as a basis for segregating current assets when more than one operating cycle occurs within a year.
   d. An operating cycle of no more than 18 months is used for segregating current assets when there is no clearly defined operating cycle

BASIC CONCEPTS

Current Assets

GAAP defines *current assets* as resources or assets (including cash) that an entity reasonably expects it will consume, sell, or realize in cash during its normal operating cycle. (ASC Master Glossary, "Current Assets") Current assets are sometimes called *circulating assets* or *working assets.*

There are several basic types of current assets (ASC 210-10-45-1):

- **Cash available for current operations.** This includes money in any form, for example: cash on deposit, cash awaiting deposit, and cash funds available for use. This excludes cash and claims to cash that (a) cannot be withdrawn, (b) can only be spent for other-than-current operations, (c) are designated to be spent on noncurrent assets, or (d) are segregated for the liquidation of long-term debt. (ASC 210-10-45-4)
- **Cash equivalents.** These are short-term, highly liquid investments that are both (a) readily convertible to known amounts of cash and (b) so near their maturities that they present insignificant risk of changes in value because of changes in interest rates. (ASC Master Glossary "Cash Equivalents")
- **Certain marketable securities.** These are primarily marketable securities representing the investment of cash available for current operations, including debt securities and equity securities that an entity classifies as trading securities for GAAP purposes.
- **Receivables.** These include trade accounts receivable, notes receivable, acceptances receivable, certain installment or deferred accounts receivable, and certain receivables from officers and employees.
- **Inventories.** These include merchandise, raw materials, goods in process, finished goods, operating supplies, and ordinary maintenance material and parts.

OBSERVATION

An entity has to supplement the amounts at which inventories are reported as current assets with disclosures about:

- The various classifications of inventory items
- The basis upon which the amounts are stated
- If practicable, the method of determining the cost (for example, average cost, first-in first-out (FIFO), last-in first-out (LIFO), and so forth).

(ASC 210-10-50-1)

- **Prepaid expenses.** These include the prepayment of any of the following: insurance, interest, rents, taxes, advertising, unused royalties, and operating supplies. Prepaid expenses are segregated as current assets not because the entity expects to convert them to cash but because they would require the use of current assets during the operating cycle had they *not* been paid in advance. (ASC 210-10-45-2)

Current Liabilities

Current liabilities are obligations whose liquidation is reasonably expected to require either the use of current assets or the creation of other current liabilities. (ASC Master Glossary entry "Current Liabilities")

PLANNING POINTER

One way of identifying current liabilities is to consider the assets the entity expects to use to settle the liability. That is, liabilities the entity expects to settle during the normal operating cycle using current assets often are to be classified as current liabilities.

Be careful, however, to identify liabilities that are due in the near future but that must be classified as noncurrent because they will not require the use of current assets. For example:

A short-term obligation an entity expects to refinance over a longer term (ASC Topic 470, Debt, paragraph 470-10-45-12A)

A debt an entity plans to settle using resources it has accumulated in an account properly not classified as a current asset (ASC 210-10-45-12)

There are several basic types of current liabilities:

- **Payables from operations.** These include obligations for items that have entered the operating cycle, such as materials or supplies purchased to produce goods (or provide services) that the entity offers for sale and various accruals from operations (such as wages, rentals, royalties, or taxes). (ASC 210-10-45-8(a))

- **Debt maturities.** These include amounts the entity expects to settle during the current operating cycle, such as short-term notes and the currently maturing portion of long-term debt. (ASC 210-10-45-9)

OBSERVATION

An entity's classification of increasing-rate debt between current and noncurrent doesn't have to be consistent with the time frame used to determine periodic interest. Instead, the classification should reflect the entity's anticipated source of repayment—for example, from current assets, a new short-term obligation, a new long-term obligation, issuance of equity, a financing agreement, or so forth. (ASC 470-10-45-7)

- **Revenue received in advance.** This includes amounts the entity collects before delivering goods or performing services; for example, deferred revenue such as a subscription prepaid by a customer. An entity typically settles this type of current liability by delivering goods or services, not by paying cash. (ASC 210-10-45-8(b))
- **Other estimates or accruals.** These include estimates the entity accrues for payments within the coming year for known obligations that either (a) the entity can only determine approximately (for example, accrual of bonuses payable) or (b) for which the entity doesn't yet know specifically to whom payment will be made (for example, estimating costs related to warranty of a product). (ASC 210-10-45-6)
- **Obligations due on demand.** These are obligations that, by their terms, are either due on demand or will be due on demand within one year (or operating cycle, if longer) even if the entity doesn't expect to settle them within that period. (ASC 470-10-45-10)

PLANNING POINTER

An obligation that is due on demand permits the creditor to demand payment at any time, solely at the creditor's discretion. Following are two examples of wording that gives a creditor such permission:

"The term note shall mature in monthly installments as set forth therein or on demand, whichever is earlier."

"Principal and interest shall be due on demand, or if no demand is made, in quarterly installments beginning on...." (ASC 470-10-45-9)

Working Capital and Related Rules

Working capital is the excess of current assets over current liabilities. It helps measure an entity's liquidity. (ASC Master Glossary entry "Working Capital")

Changes in Each Element of Working Capital

The changes in each element of working capital are the increases or decreases in each current asset and current liability over the amounts in the preceding year.

Illustration of Determining Working Capital

	20X5	20X6	Working Capital Increase (Decrease)
Current assets:			
Cash	$10,000	$15,000	$5,000
Accounts receivable, net	25,000	35,000	10,000
Inventory	50,000	60,000	10,000
Prepaid expenses	1,000	500	(500)
Total current assets	$86,000	$110,500	$24,500
Current liabilities:			
Accounts payable	$10,000	$15,000	$(5,000)
Notes payable-current	20,000	15,000	5,000
Accrued expenses	1,000	1,500	(500)
Total current liabilities	$31,000	$31,500	$(500)
Net working capital	$55,000	$79,000	
Increase in working capital			$24,000

The *current ratio*, or *working capital ratio*, measures current position and is useful in analyzing short-term credit. The current ratio is computed by dividing the total current assets by the total current liabilities.

Illustration of Current Ratio

	20X5	20X6
Current assets	$86,000	$110,500
Current liabilities	(31,000)	(31,500)
Working capital	$55,000	$79,000
Current ratio	2.8 : 1	3.5 : 1

The *acid-test ratio* (also called the *quick ratio*) is determined by dividing those assets typically closest to cash by total current liabilities. The assets used to calculate this ratio consist of only the most liquid assets, typically cash, receivables, and marketable securities.

PLANNING POINTER

Only receivables and securities convertible into cash are included in the acid-test ratio; restricted cash and other securities are excluded.

Illustration of Acid-Test Ratio

	20X5	20X6
Cash	$10,000	$15,000
Accounts receivable, net	25,000	35,000
Total *quick* assets	$35,000	$50,000
Total current liabilities	$31,000	$31,500
Acid-test ratio	1.1 : 1	1.6 : 1

STUDY QUESTIONS

2. Which of the following is ***not*** a current asset?

a. Collections in advance of delivery of goods or performance of services
b. Secondary cash resources
c. Inventories
d. Prepaid expenses

3. Current liabilities ***exclude*** which of the following?

a. Payables from operations
b. Revenue received in advance of services
c. Debt maturities
d. Work-in-process

SEGREGATING DEBT AS CURRENT AND NONCURRENT

GAAP addresses several issues an entity must consider when segregating its debt between current liabilities and noncurrent liabilities:

- Short-term obligations expected to be refinanced long-term
- Callable obligations
- Subjective acceleration clauses
- Revolving credit arrangements.

Short-Term Obligations Expected to Be Refinanced Long-Term

Current liabilities *exclude* any short-term obligation for which the entity has both the intent and the ability to refinance that obligation over the long term. (ASC 470-10-45-14)

An entity might refinance a short-term obligation over the long term in several ways. The entity could replace the existing short-term obligation with either a long-term obligation or equity securities. Alternatively, the entity could renew, extend, or replace the existing short-term obligation with short-term obligations for an uninterrupted period extending beyond one year (or the operating cycle, if applicable) from the date of the entity's balance sheet. (ASC 470-10-45-12B)

An entity's ability to refinance a short-term obligation on a long-term basis must be evaluated and would be demonstrated in one of two ways:

- **Actual refinancing.** After the balance sheet date (but before the balance sheet was issued or available to be issued), the entity refinanced the short-term obligation with a long-term obligation or equity securities. (ASC 470-10-45-14(a)) This has to occur in one step; that is, the entity cannot apply this by settling the short-term obligation with current assets then replenishing those current assets with the long-term obligation or equity securities. (ASC 470-10-45-15)

OBSERVATION

Financial statements are considered...

Issued when they are widely distributed to shareholders and other financial statement users for general use and reliance in a form and format that complies with GAAP. (ASC Master Glossary entry "Financial Statements Are Issued")

Available to be issued when they are complete in a form and format that complies with GAAP and all approvals necessary for issuance have been obtained. (ASC Master Glossary entry "Financial Statements Are Available to Be Issued")

- **Financing agreement.** Before the balance sheet was issued (or available to be issued), the entity entered into an agreement under which it can refinance a short-term obligation on a long-term basis. The agreement must include some very specific elements:
  - The agreement cannot expire within one year (or operating cycle, if applicable) of the balance sheet date.
  - The other party to the agreement cannot cancel the agreement (and cannot call related obligations) unless the entity violates some provision of the agreement and the entity's noncompliance can be determined objectively.

PLANNING POINTER

An entity uses one year if either (a) more than one operating cycle occurs within a year or (b) the entity has no clearly defined operating cycle. An entity uses its operating cycle if its operating cycle is longer than one year. (ASC 210-10-45-3)

  - At the balance sheet date and thereafter but before the balance sheet is issued (or available to be issued), the entity was not in violation, nor was there any information that indicated a violation, of the agreement. If there was such a violation or such information, the entity has obtained a waiver for any such violation.

- The other party to the agreement is expected to be financially capable of honoring the agreement. (ASC 470-10-45-14(a))
- The entity intends to exercise its rights under the agreement (in the absence of other long-term financing alternatives). (ASC 470-10-45-20)
- The agreement doesn't contain (or let the other party to the contract establish) conditions that are unreasonable to the entity. (ASC 470-10-45-20)

The amount of the short-term obligation to be excluded from current liabilities cannot—for an actual refinancing—exceed the actual proceeds from the issuance of the long-term obligation or equity securities or—for a refinancing agreement—exceed the amount of available for refinancing under the agreement. (ASC 470-10-45-16 and ASC 470-10-45-17) The entity must further reduce the amount to be excluded for any limitations in a refinancing agreement that indicate the full amount obtainable will not be available to liquidate the short-term obligation. (ASC 470-10-45-18)

If the amounts available under a refinancing agreement will fluctuate, then the entity must estimate the minimum amount it expects to be available during the period. If the entity cannot make a reasonable estimate, then the entity cannot exclude any amount of the short-term obligation from its current liabilities. (ASC 470-10-45-19)

An entity may intend to seek alternative financing sources besides those in the established agreement when the short-term obligation becomes due. If alternative sources do not materialize, however, the entity must intend to borrow from the source in the agreement (ASC 470-10-45-20).

OBSERVATION

A financing agreement that allows the other party (that is, the prospective lender or investor) to set interest rates, collateral requirements, or other conditions that are unreasonable to the entity cannot be used to demonstrate the entity's ability to refinance. (ASC 470-10-45-20)

An entity can demonstrate its ability to refinance with a financing agreement that provides for renewal or extension of a short-term obligation for an uninterrupted period extending beyond one year (or operating cycle, if applicable) if that agreement otherwise meets the stated criteria. Any other replacement of a short-term obligation with another short-term obligation cannot demonstrate that ability. (ASC 470-10-45-21)

An entity that excludes a short-term obligation from current liabilities has to disclose the terms of the actual or expected refinancing (or the general terms of the financing agreement) that the entity uses to demonstrate its ability to refinance the short-term obligation on a long-term basis. (ASC 470-10-50-4)

Callable Obligations

GAAP addresses a variety of issues involving a debtor entity's current/noncurrent classification of debt that is callable by a creditor.

If an entity presents a classified balance sheet, the following guidance is used to determine whether the obligation should be classified as current or noncurrent. Whether or not an entity presents a classified balance sheet, the following guidance is used to determine the maturity dates of obligations disclosed in the notes to the financial statements.

EXAMPLE

An entity that prepares an unclassified balance sheet would include—as a long-term liability in its disclosure of debt maturities—a liability it determines is long-term based on the conditions in ASC 470-10-45-11(b). It also has to disclose the circumstances. (ASC 470-10-50-2)

A long-term obligation may contain various provisions with which the creditor must comply, including some that must be met on a quarterly or semiannual basis. A long-term obligation may provide for a grace period within which the debtor may cure a violation of a provision. The grace period usually begins after the occurrence of a violation of a provision.

EXAMPLE

By violation of a provision, GAAP refers to failure to meet a condition in a debt agreement (or a breach of a provision in the agreement) for which compliance is objectively determinable, whether or not a grace period is allowed or the creditor is required to give notice of its intention to demand repayment. (ASC Master Glossary entry "Violation of a Provision")

Except as discussed in the next paragraph, an entity (as debtor) has to include in its current liabilities any long-term obligation that meets either of the following conditions:

- It is callable by the creditor due to a debtor violation existing at the balance sheet date.
- It will be callable by the creditor if a debtor violation existing at the balance sheet date is not cured within the specified grace period.

The preceding guidance doesn't apply to a callable long-term obligation if either of the following conditions exists at the time the balance sheet is issued or available to be issued:

- The creditor has waived or lost its right (with respect to the entity's violation) to call the obligation for more than one year (or operating cycle, if longer) from the balance sheet date.
- It is *probable* that the entity will cure the violation within the specified grace period.

(ASC 470-10-45-11)

GAAP defines *probable* as *the future event or events are likely to occur*. (ASC Master Glossary entry "Probable") Consider a circumstance in which an entity (as debtor) violates a provision that would otherwise give the lender the right to call a long-term obligation. Assume the lender may waive its call right arising from the current violation for a period greater than one year while retaining future covenant requirements. Is the lender's waiver in this circumstance considered a grace period for purposes of determining the debt's maturity for classification and disclosure purposes? GAAP concludes that, unless facts and circumstances indicate otherwise, the entity shall classify the obligation as noncurrent, unless both of the following conditions exist:

- A covenant violation that gives the lender the right to call the debt has occurred at the balance sheet date or would have occurred absent a loan modification.
- It is probable that the borrower will not be able to cure the default (comply with the covenant) at measurement dates that are within the next 12 months.

(ASC 470-10-45-1; ASC 470-10-55-2 through 55-6)

Subjective Acceleration Clauses

A *subjective acceleration clause* allows a creditor to accelerate the scheduled maturities of an obligation *under conditions that are not objectively determinable*, for example, if the debtor fails to maintain "satisfactory operations" or if there is a "material adverse change" in circumstances. (ASC Master Glossary entry "Subjective Acceleration Clause")

EXAMPLE

The debt agreement might state that "if, in the opinion of the lender, the borrower experiences recurring losses or liquidity problems, the lender may at its sole discretion accelerate part or all of the loan balance...."

An entity has to consider the likelihood that the creditor would accelerate the dues dates of any long-term obligation that includes a subjective acceleration clause. Only if that likelihood is *remote*—for example, because the entity's financial position is strong and the creditor historically has not accelerated due dates of loans containing similar clauses—would there be no current financial reporting implication. (ASC 470-10-45-2)

On the other hand, if an entity has recurring losses or liquidity problems, the related long-term obligations must be classified as current liabilities. Other situations may require only disclosure of the subjective acceleration clause(s). (ASC 470-10-45-2)

Revolving Credit Agreements

An entity's classification of its obligation under a revolving credit agreement between current and noncurrent depends on whether that agreement involves a subjective acceleration clause or a lock-box arrangement or both.

PLANNING POINTER

A *lock-box arrangement* is, for GAAP purposes, any arrangement in which a debtor can't avoid using working capital to repay its outstanding obligation to a creditor because—in the ordinary course of business and without another event occurring—the agreement effectively requires that the debtor's cash receipts be used to repay the existing obligation.

An example of a lock-box arrangement is an arrangement requiring that a debtor's customers remit payment directly to the creditor with such payments reducing the outstanding obligation. (ASC Master Glossary entry "Lock-Box Arrangement")

If the lock box "springs," the debtor's cash receipts are remitted directly to the bank, but such payments don't reduce the outstanding obligation until and unless the creditor exercises the subjective acceleration clause. (ASC Master Glossary entry "Springing Lock-Box Arrangement") Because remittances do not automatically reduce the debt outstanding *without another event occurring*, a *springing lock-box arrangement* does not meet the GAAP definition of a *lock-box arrangement.* (ASC 470-10-45-6)

Absent a subjective acceleration clause or lock-box arrangement, an obligation under a revolving credit agreement is long-term if the borrowings are due at the end of a specified long-term period (for example, three years) rather than in a shorter term when the obligation rolls over (for example, 90 days). (ASC 470-10-45-4)

If a revolving credit agreement involves a subjective acceleration clause, but no lock-box arrangement, then it is like any other obligation for which the entity must assess the subjective acceleration clause.

If a revolving credit agreement involves a subjective acceleration clause *and* a lock-box arrangement (other than a lock-box arrangement at the discretion of the debtor or a *springing lock-box arrangement*), the entity must classify its obligation(s) under the revolving credit agreement as current unless it qualifies as being refinanced long-term. (ASC 470-10-45-5)

STUDY QUESTIONS

4. An entity can demonstrate its ability to refinance a short-term obligation on a long-term basis by taking any of the following actions before issuing its balance sheet ***except***:

   a. Actually refinancing the obligation with a long-term obligation
   b. Entering into qualifying agreement under which the entity can refinance on a long-term basis
   c. Actually repaying the obligation with current assets and replenishing those current assets by issuing equity securities
   d. Actually refinancing the obligation with equity securities

5. An entity has a long-term obligation that contains a clause under which the creditor may accelerate payment due dates if there are "material adverse changes in the borrower's operations." What is this clause called for GAAP purposes?

   a. Objectively determinable conditions
   b. Violation of a provision
   c. Right of offset
   d. Subjective acceleration clause

6. Which of the following describes how a typical *lock-box arrangement* works?

   a. A vendor's customers send their payments directly to the creditor, which then uses those payments to reduce the vendor's obligation to that creditor.
   b. A container is affixed (for example, to the door) of a property to provide secure access to the key(s) to that property.
   c. A vendor pledges to the creditor to remit the first 2 percent of its monthly cash receipts from its customers to repay its existing obligations to that creditor.
   d. A vendor's customers send their payments directly to the vendor, which then uses those payments to repay its obligation to its creditor.

BALANCE SHEET OFFSETTING

Offsetting allows an entity to present—as a net amount in its balance sheet—a recognized asset and a recognized liability that are related.

Offsetting is a presentation matter. It should not be confused with recognition matters (which involve whether or not a transaction is recorded in the balance sheet as an asset, liability, or equity) or derecognition matters (which involve whether or not a transaction should cause a recognized asset or a recognized liability to be removed from the balance sheet). This is true even though nonrecognition, derecognition (with no gain or loss), and offsetting (of an equal and offsetting asset and liability) each involve a net balance sheet amount of zero for the related asset and liability. (ASC 210-20-15-2)

It is a general principle of GAAP that an entity shouldn't offset a related recognized asset and recognized liability in the balance sheet except if a *right of setoff* exists. (ASC 210-20-05-1) That general principle applies in the context of unconditional receivables from and payables to another party. It also applies to contractual amounts that are conditioned on future interest rates, future exchange rates, future commodity prices, or other factors. (ASC 210-20-05-2)

A *right of setoff* is *a debtor's legal right (by contract or otherwise) to discharge all or a portion of the debt owed to another party by applying against the debt an amount that the other party owes to the debtor.* (ASC Master Glossary entry "Right of Setoff")

A *right of setoff* exists for GAAP purposes only if all of the following four conditions are met:

- Each of two parties owes the other determinable amounts.
- The reporting party has the right to set off the amount owed with the amount owed by the other party.
- The reporting party intends to set off.
- The right of setoff is enforceable at law. (ASC 210-20-45-1)

OBSERVATION

The phrase *enforceable at law* in the fourth criterion (ASC 210-20-45-1(d)) encompasses the idea that the *right of setoff* will be upheld in bankruptcy. Specifically, GAAP permits offsetting only if the available evidence, both positive and negative, indicates that there is reasonable assurance that the right of setoff would be upheld in bankruptcy. (ASC 210-20-45-9)

For example, a debtor having a valid *right of setoff* (based on the four criteria) may offset the related asset and liability and report the net amount in its balance sheet. (ASC 210-20-45-2)

PLANNING POINTER

GAAP identifies a unique circumstance in which a reporting entity may set off securities that a governmental entity will accept for the reporting entity's payment of taxes against the reporting entity's taxes payable to the governmental entity. Specifically, the reporting entity may set off when it is clear that the reporting entity's purchase of the securities is in substance an advance payment of taxes that will be payable to that governmental entity in the relatively near future. (ASC 210-20-45-6 and 45-7)

Beyond Subtopic 210-20, GAAP provides guidance for specific circumstances (which are beyond the scope of this course) that result in offsetting in the balance sheet or a balance sheet presentation that is similar to offsetting.

Guidance on those circumstances is addressed in the following parts of the FASB Accounting Standards Codification™:

- Leveraged leases (ASC 840-30-35-32 through 35-52)
- Accounting for pension plan assets and liabilities (ASC Subtopic 715-30)
- Accounting for plan assets and liabilities (ASC Subtopic 715-60)
- Net tax asset or liability amounts reported (ASC Subtopic 740-30)
- Trade date accounting for trading portfolio positions (ASC Subtopic 940-320)
- Advances received on construction contracts (ASC Subtopic 910-405)
- Reciprocal balances between banks (ASC 942-305-45-1).

Illustration of Balance Sheet Offsetting

The offsetting of a recognized asset and a recognized liability is an important issue to consider when determining financial statement presentation of current assets and current liabilities. Gross information and net information clearly differ.

Consider the following example:

Current Assets	
Receivable from M Co.	$100
Other assets	400
	$500

Current Liabilities	
Payable to M Co.	$75
Other liabilities	175
	$250
Current ratio (500/250)	2:1

Now, consider the same situation, except the $75 payable to M Co. is offset against the $100 receivable from M Co.:

Current Assets	
Net receivable from M Co. ($100 - $75)	$25
Other assets	400
	$425

Current Liabilities	
Other liabilities	$175
Current ratio (425/175)	2.4 : 1

When offsetting is applied, the individual amounts of the receivable and payable are offset and only the net amount of $25 is presented in the balance sheet.

Further, the current ratio is significantly altered by the offsetting activity. This is a simple example, but it illustrates the effect and importance of offsetting and the importance of an entity disclosing the effect or potential effect of its netting arrangements and rights to setoff.

Offsetting Derivative Instruments

GAAP allows an entity to offset certain amounts involving collateral for derivative instruments covered by a master netting arrangement without regard to whether the reporting party *intends* to set off the amounts. That is, it makes an exception such that the intent condition in ASC 210-20-45-1(c) doesn't have to be met for offsetting of certain derivative-related amounts. (Section 815-10-45)

A *master netting arrangement* is a contract between two parties that provides for the net settlement of all contracts between those parties through a single payment in a single currency in the event of either party's default on (or termination of) any one of the contracts. (ASC 815-10-45-5)

At any point in time, the single payment amount to net settle all contracts under a master netting arrangement represents a net loss to one party and a net gain to the other party. As a result, the master netting arrangement may require the party in a loss position to post cash as collateral for the party in the gain position. GAAP requires that cash collateral be recorded as an asset by the party receiving it (the secured party), together with a liability for the obligation to return it to the payer (obligor), whose asset is a receivable. (Topic 860, *Transfers and Servicing*, ASC 860-30-25-3)

Given all this, GAAP requires a reporting entity to adopt (and consistently apply) an accounting policy to either offset or not offset the following amounts related to derivative instrument transactions executed with the same counterparty under a master netting arrangement:

1. A fair value amount recognized for the derivative instrument
2. A fair value amount recognized for either of the following arising from that derivative instrument:
   a. The right to reclaim cash collateral (a receivable)
   b. The obligation to return cash collateral (a payable).

(ASC 815-10-45-5 and 45-6)

An entity cannot set off the fair value of a derivative instrument in a loss position against the fair value of a derivative instrument in a gain position unless all of the conditions in ASC 210-20-45-1 are met. Similarly, an entity cannot set off amounts recognized as accrued receivables against amounts recognized as accrued payables unless a *right of setoff* exists. (ASC 815-10-45-4)

None of the provisions in Subtopic 210-20-45 would support an entity's netting of a hedging derivative's asset (or liability) position against the hedged liability (or asset) position in the balance sheet. (ASC 815-10-45-2)

Offsetting Repurchase and Reverse Repurchase Agreements

Certain collateralized borrowing and lending agreements (such as *repurchase agreements* or *reverse repurchase agreements*) may also involve a master netting agreement between the parties. However, in this circumstance the intent criterion in ASC 210-20-45-1(c) must be met. Subtopic 210-20 establishes the following conditions to determine whether that criterion is met—that is, whether the reporting party intends to set off amounts under such agreements: (ASC 210-20-45-1(c), ASC 210-20-45-11 through 45-17)

- The agreements are executed with the same counterparty.
- The agreements have the same explicit settlement date specified at the inception of the agreement.
- The agreements are executed in accordance with a master netting arrangement.
- The securities under the agreements exist in *"book entry"* form and can be transferred only by means of entries in the records of the transfer system operator or securities custodian.
- The agreements will be settled on a securities transfer system that operates in a prescribed manner (ASC 210-20-45-14 through 45-17) and the entity has associated banking arrangements in place. Cash settlements for securities transferred are made under established banking arrangements that provide that the entity will need available cash on deposit only for any net amounts that are due at the end of the business day. It must be probable that the associated banking arrangements will provide sufficient daylight overdraft or other intraday credit at the settlement date for each of the parties.
- The entity intends to use the same account at the clearing bank (or other financial institution) to settle its receivable (i.e., cash inflow from the reverse purchasing agreement) and its payable (i.e., cash outflow to settle the offsetting repurchase agreement).

If these six conditions are met, the entity has the option to offset or not. That choice must be applied consistently.

The fourth criterion refers to *book-entry* form. This is a key element because it provides control over the securities. The operator of the transfer system maintains the controlling record for a *book-entry* security.

A securities custodian that has a security account with the transfer system operation may maintain *subsidiary* records of *book-entry* securities and may transfer the securities within its subsidiary records; however, a security cannot be traded from the account of that custodian to a new custodian without a *book-entry* transfer of the security over the securities transfer system. (ASC 210-20-45-14)

This form of accounting record facilitates repurchase and reverse repurchase agreement transactions on securities transfer systems.

For a transfer system for repurchase and reverse repurchase agreements to meet the fifth criterion, cash transfers must be initiated by the owner of record of the securities notifying its securities custodian to transfer those securities to the counterparty to the arrangement. (ASC 210-20-45-14)

Under associated banking arrangements, each party to a same-day settlement of both a repurchase agreement and a reverse repurchase agreement would be obligated to pay a gross amount of cash for the securities transferred from its counterparty, but the party would be able to reduce that gross obligation by notifying its securities custodian to transfer other securities to that counterparty the same day. (ASC 210-20-45-15)

GAAP defines *probable* (as used in the fifth criterion) as *the future event or events are likely to occur*. (ASC Master Glossary entry "Probable")

The phrase *"daylight overdraft or other intraday credit"* refers to the feature of the banking arrangement that permits transactions to be completed during the day when insufficient cash is on deposit, provided there is sufficient cash to cover the net cash requirement at the end of the day. (ASC Master Glossary entry "Daylight Overdraft")

Disclosures about Offsetting

Accounting Standards Update (ASU) 2011, *Disclosures about Offsetting Assets and Liabilities*, was issued in December 2011 to require disclosure information about offsetting and related arrangements to enable financial statements users to understand the effect of those arrangements on an entity's financial position. Under ASU 2011-11, an entity has to make certain disclosures about offsetting of derivative instruments, financial assets, and financial liabilities. (ASC 210-20-50-2 through 50-6) The disclosure objective is to help financial statement users evaluate the actual or potential effect(s) of netting arrangements on the reporting entity's financial position. (ASC 210-20-50-2) The disclosures apply to both of the following:

- Recognized financial instruments and derivative instruments that are offset
- Recognized financial instruments and derivative instruments that are subject to offset *whether or not* those derivative instruments have been offset for GAAP purposes. (ASC 210-20-50-1)

A financial instrument or derivative instrument may be subject to offset through a legal right of offset in the contract itself or in a master netting arrangement or similar agreement. (ASC 210-20-50-2)

PLANNING POINTER

The disclosure requirements apply to both financial instruments and derivative instruments. A contract that meets the GAAP definition of *derivative instrument* may or may not also meet the GAAP definition of *financial instrument*. Therefore, an entity needs to remember to consider any nonfinancial derivative instruments that are subject to offset.

An entity has to disclose a table of all of the following quantitative information for all assets (and separately for all liabilities) within the disclosure scope:

a. The gross amounts of the recognized assets (liabilities)
b. The amounts offset (in accordance with GAAP) to determine the net amounts presented in the balance sheet
c. The net amounts presented in the balance sheet
d. Both of the following amounts subject to offset but not otherwise included in item (b):
    1. The amounts related to recognized financial instruments and derivative instruments that either:
        i. The entity makes an accounting policy election not to offset
        ii. Do not meet any or all of the GAAP criteria for offsetting
    2. The amounts of any financial collateral (including cash collateral)
e. The net amount after deducting the amounts in item (d) from the amounts in item (c).

(ASC 210-20-50-3)

For any particular instrument, the amount in item (d) can't exceed the amount in item (c). (ASC 210-20-50-4)

For any recognized assets or recognized liabilities to which item (d) applies, the entity has to disclose its description (including the nature) of the associated rights of setoff. (ASC 210-20-50-5)

OBSERVATION

If the entity concludes that a format other than a table is more appropriate, it can use that other format. (ASC 210-20-50-4)

An entity has to apply the disclosure requirements for fiscal years beginning on or after January 1, 2013, and for interim periods within those annual periods. The entity has to provide the disclosures retrospectively for all periods presented for the balance sheet that begin before the date of the entity's initial application of the disclosure requirements. (ASC 210-20-65-1)

PLANNING POINTER

Given the effective date for the disclosures, an entity whose fiscal year is the calendar year has to first make the disclosures in interim financial statements for the quarter ending March 31, 2013, and annual financial statements for the year ending December 31, 2013. The entity also has to provide retrospective disclosures for the periods presented for the balance sheet.

GAAP requires that an entity disclose information about the fair value of its financial instruments. (ASC Topic 825, *Financial Instruments*, Section 825-10-50) The amounts the entity discloses are *after* giving effect to offsetting of the related balance sheet carrying amounts permitted under the general principle, for repurchase/reverse-repurchase agreements, and for derivative instruments. (ASC 825-10-50-15)

STUDY QUESTIONS

7. Which of the following describes a *right of setoff?*
   - **a.** A creditor's legal right to accelerate the due dates of some or all of a debt it is owed by the debtor
   - **b.** A creditor's legal right to apply a debtor's cash receipts to reduce existing obligations due the creditor
   - **c.** A debtor's legal right to discharge some or all of a debt it owes to another party by applying amounts the other party owes the debtor
   - **d.** A debtor's legal right to finance a short-term obligation on a long-term basis

8. Assuming all further conditions are met, an entity may offset which of the following amounts?
   - **a.** The fair value amounts of two derivative instruments (one in a loss position, the other in a gain position) that were not executed with the same counterparty
   - **b.** A fair value amount representing a hedging derivative asset and the recognized amount of the related hedged liability
   - **c.** A fair value amount recognized for a derivative instrument and a fair value amount arising from the right to reclaim related cash collateral for which there is a right of setoff
   - **d.** A fair value amount of a derivative instrument in a loss position and the fair value of another derivative instrument in a gain position for which there is no right of setoff

9. Which fact involving a repurchase agreement and reverse-repurchase agreement would *preclude* an entity from offsetting balance sheet amounts associated with those agreements?

   a. They are executed with different counterparties.
   b. They are executed in accordance with a master netting arrangement.
   c. They will be settled on a qualifying securities transfer system.
   d. They have the same explicit settlement date specified at their inception.

10. Which of the following is ***not*** subject to the scope of disclosures about offsetting?

    a. An asset recognized for a nonfinancial derivative instrument (a derivative instrument that does not meet the definition of a financial instrument)
    b. A liability recognized for a financial instrument
    c. An asset recognized for financial instrument
    d. An asset recognized for a nonfinancial instrument that does not meet the definition of a derivative instrument

MODULE 3: CURRENT DEVELOPMENTS — CHAPTER 10

FASB Selected 2010–2011 Accounting Standards Updates

LEARNING OBJECTIVES

Upon completion of this chapter, the reader will be able to:

- Determine what is considered a subsequent event and when it must be evaluated
- Discuss the scope of ASU 2010-20
- State how participant loans should be classified on the balance sheet for defined contribution pension plans
- Explain the pro forma disclosures required for business combinations

ASU 2010-09: SUBSEQUENT EVENTS AMENDMENTS TO CERTAIN RECOGNITION AND DISCLOSURE REQUIREMENTS

ASU 2010-09 was issued in May 2009 and amended in February 2010. The objective is to establish GAAP principles and requirements for subsequent events. ASC 855, *Subsequent Events* (formerly FAS 165), deals with:

- The period after the balance sheet date during which management of a reporting entity shall evaluate events or transactions that may occur for potential recognition or disclosure in the financial statements
- The circumstances under which an entity shall recognize events or transactions occurring after the balance sheet date in its financial statements
- The disclosures that an entity shall make about events or transactions that occurred after the balance sheet date

Scope

The Statement shall be applied to the accounting for and disclosure of subsequent events not addressed in *other applicable GAAP*.

NOTE

Other applicable GAAP may address the accounting treatment of events or transactions that occur after the balance sheet date but before the financial statements are issued or are available to be issued. If an event or transaction is within the scope of other applicable GAAP, then an entity shall follow the guidance in that applicable GAAP, rather than the guidance in this standard. Examples of other applicable GAAP that already addresses the accounting and disclosures for specific subsequent events include:

- ASC 740: *Accounting for Uncertainty in Income Taxes* (formerly FIN 48)
- ASC 260: *Earnings per Share* (formerly FAS 128)
- ASC 450: *Contingencies* (formerly FAS 5)

Definitions

Subsequent events are events or transactions that occur after the balance sheet date but before financial statements are *issued or are available to be issued.*

Financial statements are considered *issued* when they are widely distributed to shareholders and other financial statement users for general use and reliance in a form and format that complies with GAAP. Financial statements are considered *available to be issued* when:

- They are complete in a form and format that complies with GAAP
- All approvals necessary for issuance have been obtained, such as those from management, the board of directors, and/or significant shareholders

There are two types of subsequent events:

- *Type 1 subsequent events (recognized subsequent events)* consist of events or transactions that provide additional evidence about conditions that *existed at the date of the balance sheet*, including the estimates inherent in the process of preparing financial statements.
- *Type 2 subsequent events (nonrecognized subsequent events)* consist of events that provide evidence about conditions that *did not exist at the date of the balance sheet* but arose after that date.

SEC filer is an entity that is required to file or furnish its financial statements with either (a) the SEC or (b) with respect to an entity subject to Section 12(i) of the Securities Exchange Act of 1934, as amended, the appropriate agency under that Section. An SEC filer does not include an entity that is not otherwise an SEC filer whose financial statements are included in a submission by another SEC filer.

Revised financial statements consist of financial statements revised only for either of the following conditions:

- Correction of an error
- Retrospective application of U.S. GAAP

Rules

Subsequent event period. An entity that meets *either of* the following criteria shall evaluate subsequent events through the date that the financial statements are *issued*:

- It is a SEC filer.
- It is a conduit bond obligor for conduit debt securities that are traded in a public market (a domestic or foreign stock exchange or an over-the-counter market, including local or regional markets).

All entities other than those above shall evaluate subsequent events through the date that the financial statements are *available to be issued.*

Recognized subsequent events. An entity shall recognize in the financial statements the effects of all subsequent events that provide additional evidence about *conditions that existed at the date of the balance sheet*, including the estimates inherent in the process of preparing financial statements.

Nonrecognized subsequent events. An entity shall not recognize subsequent events that provide evidence about conditions that *did not exist* at the date of the balance sheet, but arose after the balance sheet date but before financial statements are issued or are available to be issued.

The Statement provides the following examples of non-recognized subsequent events:

- Sale of a bond or capital stock issued after the balance sheet date but before financial statements are issued or are available to be issued
- A business combination that occurs after the balance sheet date but before financial statements are issued or are available to be issued
- Settlement of litigation when the event giving rise to the claim took place after the balance sheet date but before financial statements are issued or are available to be issued
- Loss of plant or inventories as a result of fire or natural disaster that occurred after the balance sheet date but before financial statements are issued or are available to be issued
- Losses on receivables resulting from conditions (such as a customer's major casualty) arising after the balance sheet date but before financial statements are issued or are available to be issued
- Changes in the fair value of assets or liabilities (financial or nonfinancial) or foreign exchange rates after the balance sheet date but before financial statements are issued or are available to be issued
- Entering into significant commitments or contingent liabilities, for example, by issuing significant guarantees after the balance sheet date but before financial statements are issued or are available to be issued.

Disclosures

An entity that is not an SEC filer shall disclose the following:

- The date through which subsequent events have been evaluated by management
- Whether that date is the date the financial statements were issued or the date the financial statements were available to be issued

NOTE

An entity that is an SEC filer is not required to disclose the date through which subsequent events have been evaluated. This change alleviates potential conflicts between ASC Topic 855 and the SEC's requirements.

For those non-recognized subsequent events that are of such a nature that they must be disclosed to keep the financial statements from being misleading, an entity shall disclose the following:

- The nature of the event
- An estimate of its financial effect, or a statement that such an estimate cannot be made

Example of a disclosure. Following is a standard disclosure that is required for a non-public entity:

Note 4: Subsequent Events:

Company X has evaluated subsequent events through March 31, 20X3, which is the date through which the financial statements were available to be issued.

NOTE

The amendments found in ASU 2010-09 remove the requirement for an SEC filer to disclose a date in both issued and revised financial statements.

The SEC's requirements are clear on a registrant's responsibilities for evaluating subsequent events, and the entity is additionally subject to the SEC's continuous disclosure regime. There are certain entities whose financial statements are filed or furnished with the SEC by another entity in accordance with the SEC's requirements. As such, to clarify the requirements, the amendments remove any potential conflicts with existing SEC literature by no longer requiring disclosure of either the issuance date or the revised issuance date if an entity is an SEC filer. However, the FASB decided to clarify that ASU 2010-09 has no effect on disclosure of the issuance date for an entity that is not an SEC filer.

An entity also shall consider supplementing the historical financial statements with pro forma financial data. Occasionally, a non-recognized subsequent event may be so significant that disclosure can best be made by means of pro forma financial data. Such data shall give effect to the event as if it had occurred on the balance sheet date. In some situations, an entity also shall consider presenting pro forma statements, usually a balance sheet only, in columnar form on the face of the historical statements.

Effective Date and Transition

ASU 855 is effective for interim or annual financial periods *ending after June 15, 2009*, and shall be applied prospectively. All amendments in ASU 2010-09 are effective upon issuance of the final ASU (February 2010), except for the use of the issued date for conduit debt obligors which is effective for interim or annual periods ending after June 15, 2010. The provisions of the Statement do not apply to immaterial items.

STUDY QUESTION

1. Which of the following events would require that an entity recognize the effects of a subsequent event at the balance sheet date?
   - **a.** Inventory loss due to a fire that occurred after the balance sheet date and after the financial statements were issued
   - **b.** Loss on a receivable due to a condition arising after the balance sheet date but before financial statements are issued or available to be issued
   - **c.** A litigation loss based on events that took place before the balance sheet date
   - **d.** Settlement of litigation when the event giving rise to the claim took place after the balance sheet date but before financial statements are issued or are available to be issued

ASU 2010-20: DISCLOSURES ABOUT THE CREDIT QUALITY OF FINANCING RECEIVABLES AND THE ALLOWANCE FOR CREDIT LOSSES

ASU 2010-20 was issued in July 2010. The objective of the amendments is for an entity to provide disclosures that facilitate financial statement users' evaluation of the following:

- The nature of credit risk inherent in the entity's portfolio of financing receivables
- How that risk is analyzed and assessed in arriving at the allowance for credit losses
- The changes and reasons for those changes in the allowance for credit losses

Scope

ASU 2010-20 applies to all entities (public and nonpublic) and to various instruments and transactions that include the following:

- Trade accounts receivable
- Loans
- Loan syndications
- Factoring arrangements
- Standby letters of credit
- Financing receivables

NOTE

Although the ASU applies to all of the above instruments and transactions, several of the disclosures do not apply to trade accounts receivable, and receivables carried at fair value or lower of cost or market.

The ASU does not apply to the following transactions and activities:

- Mortgage banking activities
- A contract that is required to be accounted for as a derivative instrument

EXAMPLE

ASC 815, *Derivatives and Hedging,* states that commitments to purchase or sell mortgage loans or other types of loans at a future date shall be evaluated under the definition of a derivative instrument to determine whether ASC Subtopic 815-10 applies.

General Rules

Losses from uncollectible receivables. The inability to make a reasonable estimate of the amount of loss from uncollectible receivables prevents accrual and may, if there is significant uncertainty as to collection, suggest that the installment method, the cost recovery method, or some other method of revenue recognition be used.

Disclosures. The ASU provides the following disclosure guidance for receivables, off-balance-sheet credit exposures, and foreclosed and repossessed assets. Some of the disclosures have been retained from previous guidance while others are new. The list of disclosures follows:

- Accounting policies for loans and trade receivables
- Assets serving as collateral
- Nonaccrual and past due financing receivables
- Accounting policies for off-balance-sheet credit exposures
- Foreclosed and repossessed assets
- Allowance for credit losses
- Impaired loans
- Loss contingencies
- Risks and uncertainties
- Fair value disclosures
- Credit quality information
- Modifications

Effective Date and Transition

The following represents the transition and effective date information related to Accounting Standards ASU No. 2010-20, *Receivables (Topic*

310): Disclosures about the Credit Quality of Financing Receivables and the Allowance for Credit Losses:

For public entities:

- The amendments to disclosures as of the end of a reporting period shall be effective for the first interim or annual reporting period *ending on or after December 15, 2010.*
- The amendments to disclosures about activity that occurs during a reporting period is effective for the first interim or annual reporting period *beginning on or after December 15, 2010.*

For nonpublic entities, the amendments to disclosures shall be effective for the first annual reporting period *ending on or after December 15, 2011.*

An entity shall provide comparative disclosures for each reporting period ending after initial adoption.

ASU 2010-25: REPORTING LOANS TO PARTICIPANTS BY DEFINED CONTRIBUTION PENSION PLANS—A CONSENSUS OF THE FASB EMERGING ISSUES TASK FORCE

ASU 2010-25 was issued in September 2010 to clarify how loans to participants should be classified and measured by defined contribution pension benefit plans.

Background

Participants in a defined contribution plan can direct the investment of their plan account balance into an investment in a loan to themselves if the plan allows for participant loans. Although participant loans are by their nature receivables, for reporting purposes, participant loans are considered a plan investment.

Participant loans are currently classified as investments in accordance with the defined contribution pension plan guidance.

ASC Subtopic 962-325, *Planning Accounting-Defined Contribution Pension Plans- Investments-Other*, requires most investments held by a plan, including participant loans, to be presented at fair value. ASC 820, *Fair Value Measurements and Disclosures*, provides specific guidance on how fair value should be measured.

According to ASC 820, fair value of a plan investment is the price that would be received to sell an asset or paid to transfer a liability in an orderly transaction between market participants at the measurement date. Under ASC 820, plans can no longer assume that the outstanding principal balance of a loan approximates its fair value and, so, the valuation principles of ASC 820 should be applied.

In practice, most participant loans are carried at their unpaid principal balance plus any accrued but unpaid interest, which was considered a good faith approximation of fair value. However, some stakeholders questioned whether that measurement conforms to ASC 820, which requires the use of observable and unobservable inputs such as market interest rates, borrower's credit risk, and historical default rates to estimate the fair value of participant loans. Other parties have questioned whether the use of those assumptions would result in information that is decision useful.

The Emerging Issues Task Force (EITF) concluded in ASU 2010-25 that participant loans are unique plan assets that should be *classified as notes receivable* from participants, and not as investments. Further, the EITF concluded that classification of participant loans as receivables acknowledges that participant loans are essentially a participant borrowing against their own individual account. Further-more, EITF members noted that this classification best reflects the legal nature of the asset, which is a loan from the plan to the participant.

Because the participant loans are to be considered notes receivable, such loans should be reported at their unpaid principal balance plus any accrued but unpaid interest, instead of being recorded at fair value.

Scope

The ASU amendments apply to any defined contribution pension plan that allows participant loans.

Rules

The amendments in this ASU follow:

For reporting purposes, participant loans shall be classified as notes receivable from participants, and not as investments. The notes receivable should be segregated from plan investments.

The participant loans shall be measured at their unpaid principal balance plus any accrued and unpaid interest. The fair value disclosures required for investments under ASC 825-10-50-10 through 50-16, *Financial Instruments*, are not required for participant loans.

NOTE

The EITF discussed that the Department of Labor requires participant loans to be included as an investment on the supplemental schedule of assets held (measured as the unpaid principal balance plus any accrued but unpaid interest) to be included with the audited financial statements. The EITF noted that although for purposes of the supplemental schedule, participant loans will still be reported as investments, the current value included on the supplemental schedule for the participant loans will now be consistent with the measurement requirements in GAAP.

Participant loans are not as commonly observed outside the United States and International Accounting Standard (IAS) 26, *Accounting and Reporting by Retirement Benefit Plans,* does not specifically provide accounting guidance for participant loans. However, IAS 26 acknowledges that there may be some situations in which fair value may not be the most meaningful measurement attribute for plan investments, such as when securities that have a fixed redemption value are acquired to match the obligations of the plan or specific parts of the plan. It also states that estimates of fair value may not be possible in certain situations.

IAS 26 does not explicitly require a specific classification of the loans to participants as investments or receivables separately from investments. However, participant loans are generally carried at amortized cost by a plan applying international standards.

EXAMPLE

The following are illustrative financial statements and disclosures (Source: ASU 2010-25, as modified by the author):

	20X1	20X0
Assets:		
Investments (Note X)	$xx	$xx
Receivables:		
Employer contributions	xx	Xx
Participant contributions	xx	Xx
Notes receivable from participants	***xx***	***Xx***
Total receivables	xx	Xx
Total assets	xx	Xx
Liabilities:		
Accounts payable	xx	Xx
Accrued expenses	xx	Xx
Total liabilities	xx	Xx
Net assets available for benefits	$xx	$Xx

Effective Date and Transition

The amendments to ASU 2010-25 are effective for fiscal years ending after December 15, 2010, with early application permitted. An entity shall apply retrospectively the amendments in the ASU to prior years presented comparatively. Any disclosures required by ASC Topic 250-10-50-1 through 50-3, *Accounting Changes and Error Corrections*, shall be provided in the period an entity adopts the amendments.

STUDY QUESTION

2. How should participant loans be measured under ASU 2010-25?

   a. Fair value plus interest
   b. Unpaid principal balance plus interest
   c. Net realizable value
   d. Lower of cost or market value

ASU 2010-29: DISCLOSURE OF SUPPLEMENTARY PRO FORMA INFORMATION FOR BUSINESS COMBINATIONS

ASU 2010-29 was issued in December 2010 to address diversity in practice about the interpretation of the pro forma revenue and earnings disclosure requirements for business combinations.

ASU 2010-29 amends ASC Topic 805, *Business Combinations* (formerly FAS 141R), to do the following:

- Require that a public company present the pro forma revenue and earnings as if the business combination occurred at the beginning of the comparable prior annual reporting period
- Expand the supplemental pro forma disclosures to include a description of the nature and amount of material, nonrecurring pro forma adjustments directly attributable to the business combination(s)

Definitions

The following definitions, used in this ASU, are extracted from ASC Topic 805.

Acquiree. The business or businesses that the acquirer obtains control of in a business combination.

Acquirer. The entity that obtains control of the acquiree. However, in a business combination in which a variable interest entity is acquired, the primary beneficiary of that entity is always the acquirer.

Acquisition date. The date on which the acquirer obtains control of the acquiree.

Business combination. A transaction or other event in which an acquirer obtains control of one or more businesses. Transactions sometimes referred to as "true mergers" or "mergers of equals" also are business combinations as that term is used in this Statement.

Fair value. The price that would be received to sell an asset or paid to transfer a liability in an orderly transaction between market participants at the measurement date.

Rules

The amendments in this ASU affect any *public entity* as defined by ASC Topic 805 that enters into business combinations that are material on an individual or aggregate basis. The ASU amends ASC Topic 805 as follows with respect to *public* entities that have a business combination(s) within a period. Non-public entities are exempt from the ASU.

If a public entity presents comparative financial statements, the entity should disclose revenue and earnings of the combined entity as though the business combination(s) that occurred during the current year had occurred as of the beginning of the comparable prior annual reporting period only.

Supplemental pro forma disclosures are expanded to include a description of the nature and amount of material, nonrecurring pro forma adjustments directly attributable to the business combination included in the reported pro forma revenue and earnings.

The ASU provides a listing of revised disclosures required for the acquirer in a business combination.

Effective Date

The amendments in this ASU are effective prospectively for business combinations for which the acquisition date is on or after the beginning of the first annual reporting period *beginning on or after December 15, 2010.* Early adoption is permitted.

STUDY QUESTION

3. Which of the following must a public entity disclose in connection with a business combination?
   - **a.** Revenue of the combined entity in a business combination on a pro forma basis
   - **b.** Total assets and total liabilities on a pro forma basis
   - **c.** Consolidated balance sheets on a pro forma basis
   - **d.** A detailed pro forma income statement on a line-by-line basis

CPE NOTE: When you have completed your study and review of chapters 7–10, which comprise Module 3, you may wish to take the Quizzer for this Module.

Go to **CCHGroup.com/PrintCPE** to take this Quizzer online.

TOP ACCOUNTING ISSUES FOR 2013 CPE COURSE

Answers to Study Questions

MODULE 1 — CHAPTER 1

1. a. ***Correct.*** **ASC 330, *Inventory* (formerly FAS 151), amends the language in ARB No. 43 to be consistent with IAS 2, with respect to inventory costs.**
b. ***Incorrect.*** No changes have been made to the computation of EPS.
c. ***Incorrect.*** ASC 845, *Nonmonetary Transactions* (formerly FAS 153) eliminates the use of a book-value approach to account for the exchange of similar productive assets (e.g., real estate exchanged for real estate) in situations in which the transaction does not have commercial substance.
d. ***Incorrect.*** ASC 250, *Accounting Changes and Error Corrections* (formerly FAS 154) eliminates the use of the cumulative effect of an accounting change for implementation of a voluntary accounting change, replacing it with a required restatement of financial statements, applied retroactively.

2. a. ***Incorrect.*** The popularity of IFRS among U.S. investors is not one of the seven milestones.
b. ***Correct.*** **One of the milestones identified by the SEC is that there be education and training relating to IFRS. Another is the improvement in the ability to use interactive data for IFRS reporting.**
c. ***Incorrect.*** One of the milestones is the implementation of a mandatory (not optional) use of IFRS by U.S. issuers.

3. a. ***Incorrect.*** The proposal would not directly affect public and non-public companies.
b. ***Correct.*** **The proposal would not directly affect non-public companies but would directly affect public companies.**
c. ***Incorrect.*** The proposal directly affects one type of company.

MODULE 1 — CHAPTER 2

1. a. ***Incorrect.*** Investors stated that the FASB should move toward a fair value model.
b. ***Correct.*** **In *A Comprehensive Business Reporting Model,* investors stated, "Fair value information is the only information relevant for financial decision making." Decisions about whether to purchase, sell or hold investments are based on fair values. If financial statements are based on outdated historical costs, they are less useful for making such evaluations.**
c. ***Incorrect.*** Investors stated that the fair value model is more useful for making decisions, and not the historical cost model.

d. ***Incorrect.*** Investors stated that the historical cost model, and not the fair value model, is inconsistent with the way in which investors measure an entity.

2. a. ***Incorrect.*** Inputs used to measure fair value that result principally from or are substantiated with observable market data by correlation are an example of Level 2 inputs.
b. ***Incorrect.*** Observable inputs used to measure fair value that are other than quoted prices included in Level 1 are classified as Level 2 inputs.
c. ***Incorrect.*** Observable, unadjusted, quoted market prices in active markets for identical assets or liabilities that are accessible are classified as Level 1 inputs.
d. **Correct. Unobservable inputs used to measure fair value that should be used when observable inputs are unavailable are classified as Level 3 inputs.**

3. a. ***Incorrect.*** ASC 820 clarifies that the exchange price is the price that would be received for an asset or paid to transfer a liability in a transaction between market participants at the measurement date.
b. ***Incorrect.*** ASC 820 develops a three-level hierarchy for valuation.
c. **Correct. ASC 820 requires expanded disclosures about the use of fair value to remeasure assets and liabilities recognized in the statement of financial position, including information about the fair value amounts, how they were determined, and the effect of the remeasurements on earnings.**
d. ***Incorrect.*** ASC 820 requires that *in the absence of quoted prices for identical or similar assets or liabilities,* fair value be estimated using multiple valuation techniques consistent with the market approach, income approach, and cost approach whenever the information necessary to apply those techniques is available without undue cost and effort.

4. a. **Correct. *The Fair Value Option for Financial Asset and Financial Liabilities* creates the option of recording certain financial assets and liabilities at fair value for initial and subsequent measurement.**
b. ***Incorrect.*** *The Fair Value Option for Financial Asset and Financial Liabilities* defines the financial asset and financial liability, but not the exchange price.
c. ***Incorrect.*** *The Fair Value Option for Financial Asset and Financial Liabilities* requires the fair value election to be made on a contract-by-contract basis, and not on an annual basis.
d. ***Incorrect.*** *The Fair Value Option for Financial Asset and Financial Liabilities* would apply to all financial assets and liabilities except: investments that would otherwise be consolidated; assets and liabilities covered under

retirement and benefit plans; financial liabilities recognized under lease contracts under ASC 840; written loan commitments not accounted for as derivatives; and financial liabilities for demand deposit accounts.

5. a. ***Incorrect.*** A realized loss is recorded on the income statement if the investment is a non-security.
b. ***Incorrect.*** A realized loss is recorded on the income statement if the investment is a security.
c. ***Correct.*** **A realized loss is recorded on the income statement regardless of whether the investment is a security or non-security.**
d. ***Incorrect.*** ASC 320 indicates when a realized loss should be recorded on the income statement.

6. a. ***Incorrect.*** Debt securities held to maturity is one of the three categories and they are recorded at cost at the time of purchase.
b. ***Incorrect.*** Trading securities is one of the three categories and they are recorded at fair value at the time of purchase.
c. ***Incorrect.*** Available for sale securities is one of the three categories and they are recorded at fair value at the time of purchase.
d. ***Correct.*** **Undecided is a category under management intent for the purpose of determining accounting treatment for MBSs. It is not one of the three categories in which a security is placed when purchased.**

7. a. ***Incorrect.*** A security is impaired when the fair value is less than the carrying amount of the loan. A loan is not a security.
b. ***Incorrect.*** ASC 310 does not use a reasonably possible threshold to determine impairment.
c. ***Correct.*** **ASC 310 states that a loan is impaired if, based on current information and events, it is probable that a creditor will be unable to collect all amounts due according to the contractual terms of the loan agreement.**
d. ***Incorrect.*** There is no criterion that the interest rate dictates whether there is an impairment.

8. a. ***Incorrect.*** Present value of expected future cash flows is one of the three ways that ASC 310 states as a way to measure impairment of a loan.
b. ***Incorrect.*** Using the loan's market price is one of the three ways that ASC 310 states as a way to measure impairment of a loan.
c. ***Incorrect.*** Using the fair value of the collateral is one of the three ways that ASC 310 states as a way to measure impairment of a loan.
d. ***Correct.*** **Carrying value is not one of the three ways that ASC 310 states as a way to measure impairment of a loan.**

9. a. ***Correct.*** **Amortized Fair Value is *not* one of the three categories into which financial instruments should be separated. The three categories were included in a FASB revised document entitled, *Accounting for Financial Instruments, Summary of Decisions Reached to Date During Redeliberations.* This document will be the basis for final documents issued in the near future.**
b. ***Incorrect.*** Amortized Cost *is* one of the three categories. The business activity for financial assets in this category must meet three conditions, one of which is that they that are not held for sale at acquisition.
c. ***Incorrect.*** FY-OCI *is* one of the three categories. The business activity for financial assets in this category must meet two conditions, one of which is that they that are not held for sale at acquisition or issuance.
d. ***Incorrect.*** FY-NI *is* one of the three categories. The business activity for financial assets in this category must meet either of two conditions, one of which is that they are held for sale at acquisition.

MODULE 1 — CHAPTER 3

1. a. ***Incorrect.*** This is a disadvantage of using LIFO, but the IRS allows taxpayers using LIFO to report supplemental information to shareholders and creditors disclosing FIFO results, which makes the conformity requirement less burdensome.
b. ***Incorrect.*** This is a disadvantage of using LIFO. If a business's prices or volumes widely fluctuate, earnings may fluctuate without correctly reflecting operations.
c. ***Correct.*** **The most significant advantage of LIFO is the cash flow created from income tax savings. It generates substantial tax savings when inflation increases the value of inventory by charging the most recent costs to cost of goods sold.**

2. a. ***Incorrect.*** The primary income statement must be presented on a LIFO basis.
b. ***Correct.*** **This is true as long as long as the total of the interim statements does not aggregate to one annual statement.**
c. ***Incorrect.*** The balance sheet may be presented on a non-LIFO basis.

3. a. ***Incorrect.*** The proposed repeal would require the write up at a later date.
b. ***Correct.*** **The increase in gross income would be taken into account ratably over 10 years, starting with the first tax year beginning after December 31, 2013.**
c. ***Incorrect.*** The proposed repeal would require the write up before this date.

MODULE 2 — CHAPTER 4

1. a. ***Incorrect.*** Transactions involving trading securities are not part of other comprehensive income. However, certain foreign exchange transactions under ASC 830 are other comprehensive income items.
b. ***Correct.*** **Transactions involving available-for-sale securities go through stockholders' equity and are part of other comprehensive income.**
c. ***Incorrect.*** Transactions involving debt securities held to maturity are not part of other comprehensive income. One example of an other comprehensive income item is certain pension transactions under ASC 715.
d. ***Incorrect.*** Transactions involving non-security investments are not part of other comprehensive income. One example of an other comprehensive income item is certain derivative transactions under ASC 815.

2. a. ***Incorrect.*** Change in equity is not part of the comprehensive income.
b. ***Correct.*** **The formula for comprehensive income is: net income +- other comprehensive income. Comprehensive income consists of changes in equity that are from non-owner sources.**
c. ***Incorrect.*** Non-cash transactions have nothing to do with the comprehensive income formula.
d. ***Incorrect.*** The change in working capital has nothing to do with comprehensive income.

3. a. ***Incorrect.*** One example is unrealized gains and losses from transfers of securities from the held-to-maturity category to available-for-sale, not the other way around.
b. ***Incorrect.*** One example is a subsequent increase in the fair value of available-for sale securities previously written down as an impairment, but not as an other-than-temporary impairment.
c. ***Incorrect.*** One example is amounts recognized in other comprehensive income for debt securities classified as available-for-sale and held-to-maturity related to an other-than-temporary impairment recognized if a portion of the impairment was not recognized in earnings.
d. ***Correct.*** **Unrealized gains and losses on securities available for sale is an example of a transaction involving available-for-sale securities that would be part of other comprehensive income.**

4. a. ***Incorrect.*** GAAP requires a financial statement format and not just a disclosure of comprehensive income.
b. ***Correct.*** **One of the two format options is to present one single continuous statement of income and comprehensive income.**
c. ***Incorrect.*** Presenting comprehensive income as a section within the statement of stockholders' equity was one of the options previously available. However, ASU 2011-05 amended ASC 220 to eliminate this option.

5. a. *Correct.* **One presentation is to present each component net of its individual tax effect. Alternatively, this requirement can be satisfied by presenting the total tax expense as one line item assigned to other comprehensive income, with a separate note provided that discloses the breakout of income tax expense assigned to each other comprehensive income component.**
b. ***Incorrect.*** Although one presentation is to show the total other comprehensive income with one total allocation of income taxes, there is a requirement to present the tax effect of each component in the notes.
c. ***Incorrect.*** The tax effects are required to be allocated to other comprehensive income.
d. ***Incorrect.*** The tax effect must be presented in the financial statements.

6. a. ***Incorrect.*** The presentation must be made regardless of whether a single or two-statement format is used.
b. *Correct.* **The changes may be reflected in either the statement of stockholders' equity or the notes to the financial statements.**
c. ***Incorrect.*** Accumulated other comprehensive income must be presented as a separate component in the equity section of the balance sheet. The individual components need not be presented as long as they are presented elsewhere, such as in the statement of stockholders' equity or in the notes to the financial statements.

7. a. ***Incorrect.*** Such adjustments do not affect multiple financial statements.
b. *Correct.* **Reclassification adjustments avoid double counting of comprehensive income items that are presented as part of net income in one period, and as part of other comprehensive income in that period or prior periods.**
c. ***Incorrect.*** Reclassification adjustments have nothing to do with disclosures.
d. ***Incorrect.*** Reclassification adjustments do not deal with the particular line item in the statement of comprehensive income.

8. a. ***Incorrect.*** This requirement is not affected by ASU 2011-12.
b. ***Incorrect.*** Although ASU 2011-12 does defer certain ASU 2011-05 requirements, it does not affect all the requirements.
c. *Correct.* **ASU 2011-12 defers the application of the reclassification adjustments of ASU 2011-05 while the FASB has time to determine how to present reclassification adjustments. ASU 2011-12 does not affect any other requirements in ASU 2011-05.**

9. a. ***Incorrect.*** If a separate statement of comprehensive income or a combined statement of income and comprehensive income is used, the report wording must be changed to reflect the new statement.
b. ***Correct.*** **SSARS 19 requires that reference to the statement of comprehensive income should be made in the appropriate paragraphs.**
c. ***Incorrect.*** If a statement of comprehensive income is required, compilation and review reports, as well as audit reports, should be modified to include reference to the statement.

MODULE 2 — CHAPTER 5

1. a. ***Correct.*** **The FASB cites that accounting policy disclosures are too general to be informative. The revenue project will help alleviate some of the generality related to revenue disclosures.**
b. ***Incorrect.*** The FASB cites that despite the large number of revenue recognition pronouncements, there is little guidance for service activities, which is the fastest growing part of the U.S. economy.
c. ***Incorrect.*** The FASB cites that U.S. GAAP contains *no* comprehensive standard for revenue recognition that is generally applicable.
d. ***Incorrect.*** The FASB cites that U.S. GAAP for revenue recognition consists of more than 200 pronouncements by various standard-setting bodies that is hard to retrieve and sometimes inconsistent.

2. a. ***Incorrect.*** A contract signed is not identified as a triggering event under the proposed revenue recognition standard.
b. ***Incorrect.*** The proposal does not address whether a critical stage has to be surpassed in order for there to be revenue recognition.
c. ***Correct.*** **The core principle of the proposed standard is that an entity shall recognize revenue when the entity satisfies a performance obligation by transferring a promised good or service to a customer.**
d. ***Incorrect.*** The proposal does not deal with a percentage-of-completion approach to revenue recognition.

3. a. ***Incorrect.*** The contract must have commercial substance. Therefore, the entity's future cash flows should be expected to change as a result of the contract
b. ***Incorrect.*** *All* the parties to the contract must have approved the contract (in writing, orally, or in accordance with other customary business practices) and be committed to perform their respective obligations.
c. ***Incorrect.*** A contract exists only if the entity can identify each party's enforceable rights regarding the goods or services to be transferred.
d. ***Correct.*** **One of the criteria is that the entity can identify the payment terms for those goods or services. Another criterion is that the contract must have commercial substance.**

4. a. ***Incorrect.*** Variable consideration is identified as one of the four elements. If the promised amount of consideration in a contract is variable, an entity would estimate the transaction price by using one of two methods.
b. ***Incorrect.*** Time value of money is listed as one of the four elements. An entity would adjust the promised amount of consideration to reflect the time value of money if the contract has a significant financing component.
c. ***Correct.*** **The specific level of demand for a product or service would not be an element that would be used to determine the transaction price in a contract. However, demand might be considered by the purchaser prior to agreeing on the transaction price.**
d. ***Incorrect.*** This is one of the four elements. If an entity expects to pay consideration to or on behalf of a customer that the customer can apply against amounts owed to the entity, the entity would account for the consideration payable to the customer as a reduction of the transaction price unless the payment is in exchange for a distinct good or service.

5. a. ***Incorrect.*** The customer having a conditional obligation to pay is not an indicator. The entity having a present right to payment for the asset is a proposed rule for recognizing revenue over time.
b. ***Incorrect.*** The customer having an option to obtain legal title is not an indicator. The customer *having* legal title is a proposed rule for recognizing revenue over time.
c. ***Correct.*** **One of the indicators is that the customer has the ability to direct the use of the asset and obtain substantially all of the remaining benefits from the asset.**

6. a. ***Correct.*** **Under the exposure draft, costs that are incurred only because the entity entered into the contract (e.g., payments to subcontractors) should be recorded as an asset.**
b. ***Incorrect.*** Under the exposure draft, costs that relate to satisfied or partially satisfied performance obligations in the contract (i.e., costs that relate to past performance) should be recorded as expense.
c. ***Incorrect.*** Under the exposure draft, costs that relate to remaining performance obligations that the entity cannot distinguish from costs that relate to satisfied performance obligations should be recorded as expense items.
d. ***Incorrect.*** Under the exposure draft, costs of wasted materials, labor, or other resources to fulfill the contract that were not reflected in the price of the contract should be recorded as expense.

MODULE 2 — CHAPTER 6

1. a. ***Incorrect.*** The market is not indifferent and actually looks at a restatement negatively.

b. ***Correct.*** **The market reacts quite negatively to a restatement by penalizing the stock price for the three-day period after the restatement announcement.**

c. ***Incorrect.*** The study does not make any correlation between a restatement and the impact of a company going bankrupt, which would have a devastating result.

2. a. ***Incorrect.*** In 2008 and 2007, the United States did not require that companies adhere to all international accounting standards.

b. ***Incorrect.*** Auditors were actually more, not less, demanding and assertive in requiring companies to make adjustments.

c. ***Incorrect.*** Materiality thresholds were reduced, not increased, in fear of heightened scrutiny.

d. ***Correct.*** **A possible reason for the decrease in restatements in 2008 and 2007 was that companies implemented Section 404 of Sarbanes-Oxley and rectified internal control issues in years prior to 2007. Years 2007 and 2008 represented a two-year period after Section 404 corrections had been made.**

3. a. ***Incorrect.*** The SEC did not prosecute a Section 304 case until 2007. Since then, the number of cases has increased.

b. ***Incorrect.*** Sixty-four percent, not 18 percent of those companies have clawback provisions, and of those companies 18 percent apply to all employees, not just executives.

c. ***Correct.*** **This is due to several reasons including the high cost of litigation and bad publicity.**

d. ***Incorrect.*** The requirement is that this be allowed at least once every *three* years.

MODULE 3 — CHAPTER 7

1. a. ***Incorrect.*** Goodwill is an intangible asset. Therefore, it is not expensed in the year a company acquires it in a business acquisition.

b. ***Incorrect.*** Unlike other intangible assets with a finite life, goodwill is not amortized over its useful life.

c. ***Incorrect.*** Before FAS 142 (now Topic 350), goodwill was amortized over its useful life, which could not exceed 40 years. Goodwill is no longer accounted for in such a manner.

d. *Correct.* **Goodwill must be capitalized and analyzed for impairment at least annually. If the goodwill has become impaired, the company must record a loss and write down the carrying value of the goodwill.**

2. a. *Correct.* **The impairment loss for goodwill is equal to its carrying value over its implied fair value. A company uses implied fair value rather than fair value because the company cannot directly determine the fair value of goodwill.**
b. ***Incorrect.*** If the implied fair value of goodwill exceeds its carrying value, no impairment of the goodwill has occurred.
c. ***Incorrect.*** Net realizable value is the estimated sales price minus the costs of disposal. A company cannot sell goodwill directly. Therefore, a company does not use net realizable value in computing an impairment loss for goodwill.
d. ***Incorrect.*** A company cannot directly determine the fair value of goodwill because a company cannot sell goodwill by itself.

3. a. ***Incorrect.*** Notice that in this example, there is no impairment.
b. ***Incorrect.*** In the first step, the company compares the carrying amount of the reporting unit to its fair market value, including goodwill. If the carrying value is less than its fair value, no impairment exists.
c. *Correct.* **Because it is more likely than not that the fair value is not less than its carrying amount, there is no impairment and the entity may bypass the two-step test for impairment.**
d. ***Incorrect.*** If impairment exists, the company performs the second step to determine the amount of the impairment loss.

MODULE 3 — CHAPTER 8

1. a. ***Incorrect.*** This is true of single-employer plans but not multiemployer plans. Assets contributed by one employer for its own employees in a multiemployer plan may be used to provide benefits to employees of other employer plans.
b. ***Incorrect.*** In a multiemployer plan, if a participating employer fails to make its required contributions, the unfunded obligations of the plan may be borne by the remaining employers. This is not an issue with single-employer plans.
c. *Correct.* **A company that withdraws from a plan may be required to make a final payment to the plan called a withdrawal liability.**
d. ***Incorrect.*** A multiemployer plan consists of more than one employer, not a single employer, as in a single-employer plan.

2. a. ***Incorrect.*** These disclosures must be kept separate to increase transparency for the user.
b. ***Incorrect.*** The disclosures apply to nongovernmental plans and not governmental plans.

c. ***Incorrect.*** The changes apply to multiemployer plans but not single-employer plans.
d. ***Correct.*** **The ASU expands disclosures for multiemployer other post-retirement benefit plans.**

3. a. ***Correct.*** **Multiemployer plans are usually administered by a board of trustees composed of management and labor representatives.**
b. ***Incorrect.*** Some, but not all, such plans involve a union.
c. ***Incorrect.*** Most multiemployer plans involve employers with a common industry bond.
d. ***Incorrect.*** A characteristic of multiemployer plans is that assets contributed by one employer may be used to provide benefits to employees of other participating employers since assets contributed by an employer are *not* segregated in a separate account or restricted to provide benefits only to employees of that employer.

4. a. ***Correct.*** **One of the additional disclosures is a qualitative description of the extent to which the employer could be responsible for the obligations of the plan, including benefits earned by employees during employment with another employer.**
b. ***Incorrect.*** The additional disclosures do not include a quantitative analysis of the extent to which the employer could be responsible for the obligations of the plan. However, other available quantitative information should be disclosed to help users understand the financial information about the plan.
c. ***Incorrect.*** This is not one of the additional disclosures. One of the disclosures that *is* required is a description of the nature of the plan benefits.

5. a. ***Incorrect.*** The ASU states that both subsidiaries and not-for-profit organizations are not required to make the full set of disclosures.
b. ***Correct.*** **The ASU requires only two disclosures for subsidiaries and not-for-profit entities. They are the name of the plan and the amount of contributions made to the plan in each annual period for which an income statement is presented.**
c. ***Incorrect.*** The parent entity should account for the pension plan as a *single*-employer pension plan in its consolidated statements.

6. a. ***Incorrect.*** For public entities, the amendments in ASU 2011-09 are effective for annual periods for fiscal years ending after December 15, *2011*.
b. ***Incorrect.*** For nonpublic entities, the amendments are effective for annual periods for fiscal years ending after December 15, *2012*.
c. ***Correct.*** **Early adoption is permitted for both public and nonpublic entities.**
d. ***Incorrect.*** The amendments should be applied *retrospectively* for all prior periods presented.

MODULE 3 — CHAPTER 9

1. a. ***Incorrect.*** This statement is true. The average time between purchasing or acquiring inventory or services and receiving cash proceeds from its eventual sale is considered an operating cycle.
b. ***Incorrect.*** This is statement is true. The operating cycle is used for segregating current assets when the operating cycle is longer than one year. You must consider cash flow when defining an operating cycle.
c. ***Incorrect.*** This statement is true. One year is used as a basis for segregating current assets when more than one operating cycle occurs within a year. For example, an entity that was considered to have four operating cycles in a given year would still segregate current assets based on a one-year cycle.
d. ***Correct.*** **This statement is false. An entity that has no clearly defined operating cycle is required to base its segregation of current assets on a one-year operating cycle.**

2. a. ***Correct.*** **Such collections are classified as current liabilities because they are obligations that normally will be liquidated in the ordinary course of business by the delivery of goods or performance of services. They are not current assets.**
b. ***Incorrect.*** Secondary cash resources (for example, marketable securities) are indeed current assets.
c. ***Incorrect.*** Inventories (including raw materials, semi-finished goods, and finished goods) are indeed current assets.
d. ***Incorrect.*** Prepaid expenses (including prepaid insurance, interest, rents, taxes, advertising, and operating supplies) are indeed current assets.

3. a. ***Incorrect.*** Payables from operations are classified as a liability for which payment is expected to require the use of current assets during the operating cycle.
b. ***Incorrect.*** This revenue is classified as a liability for which repayment is expected to require the use of current assets during the operating cycle. It is therefore a current liability.
c. ***Incorrect.*** Debt maturities include amounts expected to be liquidated during the current operating cycle, such as short-term notes and the currently maturing portion of long-term debt, and therefore are current liabilities.
d. ***Correct.*** **Work-in-process is a component of inventory and is therefore recognized as a current asset.**

4. a. ***Incorrect.*** Actually refinancing the short-term obligation with a long-term obligation before its balance sheet is issued clearly demonstrates the entity's ability to refinance on a long-term basis.
b. ***Incorrect.*** A financing agreement entered into before the balance sheet is issued demonstrates the entity's ability to refinance on a long-term basis (assuming the agreement otherwise meets the qualifying criteria).

c. *Correct.* An actual refinancing has to occur in only one step, not two. That is, an entity cannot view the combination of its use of current assets to settle its short-term obligation (step one) and its replenishment of those current assets with equity securities (step two) as refinancing on a long-term basis.

d. *Incorrect.* Issuing equity securities to actually refinance the obligation before the balance sheet is issued clearly demonstrates the entity's ability to refinance on a long-term basis.

5. a. *Incorrect.* Whether there has been a "material adverse change in the borrower's operations" is not objectively determinable because different evaluators may disagree about what constitutes a change, whether a particular change is material, and which changes are adverse.

b. *Incorrect.* A *violation of a provision* is a failure to meet a condition in a debt agreement.

c. *Incorrect.* A *right of offset* relates to an entity's ability to set off an amount owed to another party with an amount that other party owes the entity.

d. *Correct.* A *subjective acceleration clause* allows acceleration of debt under conditions that are not objectively determinable. Whether there has been a "material adverse change in the borrower's operations" is not objectively determinable because different evaluators may disagree about what constitutes a change, whether a particular change is material, and which changes are adverse.

6. a. *Correct.* Under a lock-box arrangement, an entity can't avoid using working capital to repay its outstanding obligations because the agreement requires that cash receipts be used to repay the entity's existing obligations.

b. *Incorrect.* This is a lock box, not a lock-box arrangement.

c. *Incorrect.* Such an arrangement would not effectively require the debtor's cash receipts be used to repay the existing obligation.

d. *Incorrect.* In this circumstance, the vendor has decided at its discretion to send receipts to the creditor.

7. a. *Incorrect.* This right is part of an acceleration clause that a creditor may be allowed to exercise under certain objectively determinable or subjective conditions.

b. *Incorrect.* A creditor's right to apply a debtor's cash receipts to reduce existing obligations is a feature of a lock-box arrangement.

c. *Correct.* A right of setoff is a legal right (by contract or otherwise) that allows the debtor to net such amounts.

d. *Incorrect.* When included in a financing agreement that meets certain other criteria, such a right is relevant to whether the debtor can exclude certain short-term obligations from its current liabilities.

8. a. ***Incorrect.*** An entity can't set off such amounts unless all applicable conditions are met, including that there are only two parties involved.
b. ***Incorrect.*** An entity cannot net in the balance sheet a hedging derivative's asset (or liability) position against the hedged liability (or asset) position.
c. ***Correct.*** **An entity may offset such amounts in the balance sheet even if it does not intend to offset them.**
d. ***Incorrect.*** The general principle is that amounts shouldn't be offset in the balance sheet unless a right of setoff exists.

9. a. ***Correct.*** **An entity cannot offset such agreements if they are not executed with the same counterparty.**
b. ***Incorrect.*** Agreements that are not executed in accordance with a master netting arrangement cannot meet the intent criterion needed for offsetting.
c. ***Incorrect.*** GAAP is very specific about the required attributes of the securities transfer system through which the agreements will be settled.
d. ***Incorrect.*** This attribute is a prerequisite for offsetting of assets and liabilities associated with such agreements.

10. a. ***Incorrect.*** All derivative instruments (whether or not they meet the definition of a financial instrument) are subject to the scope of the disclosures.
b. ***Incorrect.*** A financial instrument in a liability position is subject to the disclosures.
c. ***Incorrect.*** A financial instrument in an asset position is subject to the disclosures.
d. ***Correct.*** **The disclosure does not apply to a contract that doesn't meet the definition of either a financial instrument or a derivative instrument.**

MODULE 3 — CHAPTER 10

1. a. ***Incorrect.*** Because the loss occurred after the balance sheet date, the effect would not be recognized at the balance sheet date. Moreover, its effect was not discovered until the financial statements were issued.
b. ***Incorrect.*** The condition that resulted in the loss occurred after the balance sheet date so that its effect would not be recognized at the balance sheet date.
c. ***Correct.*** **Because the loss was based on events that took place before the balance sheet date, its effect would be recorded at the balance sheet date.**
d. ***Incorrect.*** The settlement was based on an event that took place after the balance sheet date. The result is that its effect should not be recorded at the balance sheet date.

2. a. ***Incorrect.*** The fair value model does not apply to participant loans under ASU 2010-25.
b. ***Correct.*** **The ASU requires that participant loans be measured at the unpaid principal balance plus accrued and unpaid interest.**

c. ***Incorrect.*** Net realizable value is not used for the measurement of participant loans under ASU 2010-25. It is sometimes used for inventory valuation.
d. ***Incorrect.*** The ASU does not provide for use of lower of cost or market value for the measurement of participant loans as it is sometimes used for other items balance sheet items.

3. a. ***Correct.*** **ASU 2010-29 requires that a public entity disclose revenue and earnings of the combined entity in a business combination on a pro forma basis.**
b. ***Incorrect.*** GAAP does not require that pro forma information be disclosed about an entity's total assets, total liabilities or combined equity.
c. ***Incorrect.*** Although the combined entities might issue consolidated balance sheets, there is no requirement that they be disclosed and certainly no requirement to present them on a pro forma basis.
d. ***Incorrect.*** There is no requirement to disclose a detailed pro forma balance sheet or income statement on a line-by-line basis.

TOP ACCOUNTING ISSUES FOR 2013 CPE COURSE

Index

B

C

G

H

I

S

TOP ACCOUNTING ISSUES FOR 2013 CPE COURSE

CPE Quizzer Instructions

This CPE Quizzer is divided into three Modules. To obtain CPE Credit, go to **CCHGroup.com/PrintCPE** to complete your Quizzers online for immediate results and no Express Grading fee. There is a grading fee for each Quizzer submission.

Processing Fee:	**Recommended CPE:**
$60.00 for Module 1	5 hours for Module 1
$72.00 for Module 2	6 hours for Module 2
$72.00 for Module 3	6 hours for Module 3
$204.00 for all Modules	17 hours for all Modules

Instructions for purchasing your CPE Tests and accessing them after purchase are provided on the **CCHGroup.com/PrintCPE** website.

To mail or fax your Quizzer, send your completed Answer Sheet for each Quizzer Module to **CCH Continuing Education Department, 4025 W. Peterson Ave., Chicago, IL 60646,** or fax it to (773) 866-3084. Each Quizzer Answer Sheet will be graded and a CPE Certificate of Completion awarded for achieving a grade of 70 percent or greater. The Quizzer Answer Sheets are located at the back of this book.

Express Grading: Processing time for your mailed or faxed Answer Sheet is generally 8-12 business days. To use our Express Grading Service, at an additional $19 per Module, please check the "Express Grading" box on your Answer Sheet and provide your CCH account or credit card number **and your fax number.** CCH will fax your results and a Certificate of Completion (upon achieving a passing grade) to you by 5:00 p.m. the business day following our receipt of your Answer Sheet. **If you mail your Answer Sheet for Express Grading, please write "ATTN: CPE OVERNIGHT" on the envelope.** NOTE: CCH will not Federal Express Quizzer results under any circumstances.

Recommended CPE credit is based on a 50-minute hour. Participants earning credits for states that require self-study to be based on a 100-minute hour will receive ½ the CPE credits for successful completion of this course. Because CPE requirements vary from state to state and among different licensing agencies, please contact your CPE governing body for information on your CPE requirements and the applicability of a particular course for your requirements.

Date of Completion: If you mail or fax your Quizzer to CCH, the date of completion on your Certificate will be the date that you put on your Answer Sheet. However, you must submit your Answer Sheet to CCH for grading within two weeks of completing it.

Expiration Date: December 31, 2013

Evaluation: To help us provide you with the best possible products, please take a moment to fill out the course Evaluation located after your Quizzer. A copy is also provided at the back of this course if you choose to mail or fax your Quizzer Answer Sheets.

CCH is registered with the National Association of State Boards of Accountancy (NASBA) as a sponsor of continuing professional education on the National Registry of CPE Sponsors. State boards of accountancy have final authority on the acceptance of individual courses for CPE credit. Complaints regarding registered sponsors may be addressed to the National Registry of CPE Sponsors, 150 Fourth Avenue North, Suite 700, Nashville, TN 37219-2417. Web site: www.nasba.org.

CCH is registered with the National Association of State Boards of Accountancy (NASBA) as a Quality Assurance Service (QAS) sponsor of continuing professional education. State boards of accountancy have final authority on the acceptance of individual courses for CPE credit. Complaints regarding registered sponsors may be addressed to NASBA, 150 Fourth Avenue North, Suite 700, Nashville, TN 37219-2417. Web site: www.nasba.org.

One **complimentary copy** of this course is provided with certain copies of CCH publications. Additional copies of this course may be downloaded from **CCHGroup.com/PrintCPE** or ordered by calling 1-800-248-3248 (ask for product 0-4285-500).

TOP ACCOUNTING ISSUES FOR 2013 CPE COURSE

Quizzer Questions: Module 1

1. More than ____companies are now using IFRS worldwide.

a. 12,000
b. 25,000
c. 50,000
d. 100,000

2. By the year ____, it is likely that all countries, including the United States, will adopt the IFRS format.

a. 2013
b. 2014
c. 2015
d. 2016

3. In a recent AICPA survey of executives, ____of those surveyed noted that they were preparing in some manner for IFRS adoption.

a. 25 percent
b. 55 percent
c. 75 percent
d. 95 percent

4. In accordance with the convergence to international accounting standards, the second phase is referred to as the long-term convergence project that addresses all of the following ***except:***

a. Consolidations
b. Investments
c. Revenue recognition
d. Financial performance reporting

5. Which of the following is true as it relates to how certain elements are accounted for under U.S. GAAP as compared with IFRS?

a. Under its rules-based approach, U.S. GAAP has more extensive disclosures than IFRS.
b. IFRS uses a one-step approach versus U.S. GAAP's two-step approach for impairment of long-lived assets.
c. Both IFRS and U.S. GAAP deal with uncertain tax positions.

   d. U.S. GAAP guidance on revenue recognition is limited while IFRS has significant guidance.

6. Which of the following is a current challenge to a fair value model noted by its critics?

   a. The historical cost model is more relevant.
   b. Fair value accounting introduces a degree of volatility to the model.
   c. Fair value accounting is too objectives-based.
   d. Fair value accounting will reveal an entity's true value from period to period.

7. Which of the following items is ***not*** measured at fair value under existing GAAP?

   a. Asset retirement obligations
   b. Fixed assets
   c. Hedging derivatives
   d. Intangibles other than goodwill with finite lives

8. Under the fair value hierarchy, which of the following is a description of a Level 1 input?

   a. Quoted prices for identical assets or liabilities in active markets
   b. Other than quoted prices for identical assets or liabilities
   c. Quoted prices for similar assets and liabilities in active markets
   d. Quoted prices for identical or similar assets and liabilities in markets that are not active

9. ASC 825 is:

   a. Always required
   b. Optional
   c. Required only in certain circumstances

10. Under ASC 320, what would be the accounting treatment of an unrealized loss on trading securities?

    a. Disclosed in the footnotes to the financial statements only
    b. Presented on the balance sheet only with a direct hit to retained earnings
    c. Presented on the income statement

11. Facts: A bank has investments in an MBS that it buys and sells on a regular basis. How should this investment be categorized under ASC 320?

a. Held to maturity
b. Trading securities
c. Available for sale
d. Other than temporary

12. Facts: Bank Y made a loan in the amount of $600,000 secured by a first mortgage on a borrower's home.

- The borrower has continued to make timely $4,000 per month payments and there are no other defaults related to the loan. All indication is that the borrower will continue to make payments on the loan.
- At December 31, 20X1, the fair value of the borrower's home has declined to $400,000.
- The Bank's strategy is to hold the loan and collect the monthly mortgage payments until maturity.

How should this loan be accounted for under GAAP?

a. There is no impairment so there is no writedown.
b. There is an impairment so the loan should be written down to $400,000 which is the fair value of the collateral.
c. There is an impairment, but there is no writedown.
d. It is unclear whether there is an impairment.

13. The SEC's 2009 study on mark-to-market accounting concluded that:

a. The accounting for investments in financial assets is too simple and should be expanded.
b. ASC 820 and mark-to-market requirements are satisfactory.
c. ASC 820 and mark-to-market requirements should be suspended.
d. Fair value accounting did not appear to play a meaningful role in bank failures.

14. A fair value measurement assumes that an asset or liability is exchanged in a/an ______.

a. Orderly transaction
b. Open-ended transaction
c. Inactive transaction
d. Confidential transaction

15. Which of the following factors may contribute to the determination that there has been a significant decrease in the volume of activity for an asset?

    a. Price quotations are stable.
    b. Indices that previously were uncorrelated with the fair value of the asset are demonstrably correlated with recent indications of fair value for that asset.
    c. There is a wide bid-ask spread in the bid-ask spread.
    d. A great amount of information is publicly available.

16. Circumstances that may indicate that a transaction is ***not*** orderly include all of the following ***except:***

    a. The transaction price is an outlier when compared with other recent transactions for the same asset.
    b. There was a customary marketing period in which the seller marketed the asset to a wide market.
    c. The seller was required to sell to meet regulatory requirements.
    d. The seller is near bankruptcy.

17. What criteria has the FASB determined should be used in determining the classification and measurement of financial assets?

    a. Characteristics of the financial asset only
    b. An entity's business strategy only
    c. Both the characteristics of the financial asset and an entity's business strategy
    d. Neither the characteristics of the financial asset nor an entity's business strategy

18. A financial asset that is held for sale at acquisition would fall into which of the following categories on the financial statements?

    a. Amortized Fair Value
    b. Amortized Cost
    c. FV-OCI
    d. FV-NI

19. The FASB has stated that debt securities should be categorized in which of the following categories?

    a. Amortized Fair Value
    b. Amortized Cost
    c. FV-OCI
    d. FV-NI

20. The FASB has stated that an entity should separately present the following items in net income for both financial assets measured at fair value with changes in value recognized in other comprehensive income and financial assets measured at amortized cost ***except:***

a. Current-period interest income
b. Current-period credit losses
c. Realized gains and losses
d. Unrealized gains and losses

21. During periods of rapidly increasing costs, LIFO tends to minimize profits from the turnover of low cost inventories and thereby:

a. Reduces income tax liabilities
b. Increases income tax liabilities
c. Discourages companies from electing to use the LIFO method
d. Causes the stock market to fall due to lower net income reports

22. Which of the following is true?

a. IFRS permits use of LIFO inventory in most cases.
b. IFRS does not permit use of LIFO inventory.
c. IFRS permits use of LIFO inventory in all cases.
d. IFRS follows U.S. GAAP in determining whether LIFO is permitted and when.

23. According to a 2008 study, how many U.S. companies use LIFO?

a. 24%
b. 36%
c. 50%
d. 78%

24. The political landscape points toward repeal of LIFO with a(n) ____ phase-in of the LIFO recapture.

a. Two to five-year
b. Three to five-year
c. Eight to 10-year
d. 15 to 20-year

25. The 2013 budget proposal repeals which of the following inventory valuation methods?

a. LIFO only
b. FIFO only
c. Lower of cost or market only
d. Both LIFO and lower of cost or market

TOP ACCOUNTING ISSUES FOR 2013 CPE COURSE

Quizzer Questions: Module 2

26. Which of the following is an example of an other comprehensive income item that under present accounting literature bypasses the income statement and is recorded directly to stockholders' equity?

- **a.** Certain foreign exchange transactions
- **b.** Certain purchases of long-lived assets
- **c.** Certain transactions involving intangible assets
- **d.** Certain transactions involving long-term debt

27. The definition of comprehensive income is a change in equity from ________________.

- **a.** Non-owner sources
- **b.** Investor sources
- **c.** Lender sources
- **d.** Equity holder sources

28. Which of the following accurately describes differences between how U.S. GAAP and IFRS present comprehensive income?

- **a.** IFRS allows three alternatives for presenting comprehensive income, whereas GAAP only allows two.
- **b.** U.S. GAAP requires a consecutive presentation of the statement of income and comprehensive income but IFRS does not.
- **c.** IFRS allows three alternatives for presenting comprehensive income, whereas GAAP only allows one.
- **d.** IFRS requires that reclassification adjustments from other comprehensive income to net income be presented on the face of the financial statements. U.S. GAAP allows the option to present those adjustments in the notes to financial statements.

29. There are essentially ____categories of other comprehensive income items.

- **a.** Two
- **b.** Three
- **c.** Four
- **d.** Five

30. Which of the following would ***not*** be included in other comprehensive income?

- **a.** Gains associated with postretirement benefits that are not recognized immediately as a component of net periodic benefit cost
- **b.** Realized losses on available-for-sale securities
- **c.** Gains on derivative instruments that are designated as cash flow hedges
- **d.** Foreign exchange translation adjustments

31. If a company's financial statements are being compiled and management has elected to omit substantially all disclosures and the statement of cash flows, then:

- **a.** The company is exempt from complying with ASC 220 because it is not presenting a full set of financial statements.
- **b.** The company must present comprehensive income in a financial statement only if it has other comprehensive income items.
- **c.** Even if the company has other comprehensive income items, it is not required to present comprehensive income in a financial statement or modify the compilation report.

32. If statements are prepared on an OCBOA (income tax basis), a statement of comprehensive income __________.

- **a.** Is required
- **b.** Is not required
- **c.** May be required because other comprehensive income items may be present
- **d.** May be added if a special election is made in the report

33. Which of the following is an example of the caption that should be presented for the total of other comprehensive income on the balance sheet?

- **a.** Accumulated other comprehensive income
- **b.** Total other comprehensive income
- **c.** Aggregate other comprehensive income
- **d.** Cumulative other comprehensive income

34. ASU 2011-05 allows how many options for presenting comprehensive income?

a. Four
b. Three
c. Two
d. One

35. Which of the following are exempt from ASC 220, as amended by ASU 2011-05?

a. Investment companies, because they are exempt from providing a statement of cash flows
b. Defined benefit pension plans, because they are exempt from providing a statement of cash flows
c. Entities that only have items of other comprehensive income in one of two periods presented.
d. Not-for-profit organizations that must follow the provisions of ASC Subtopic 958-205

36. Which of the following is ***not*** true regarding the tax effects of other comprehensive income items?

a. An entity may present components of other comprehensive income in the statement in which other comprehensive income is reported net of tax effects.
b. An entity may present components of other comprehensive income in the statement in which other comprehensive income is reported before the tax effects with one amount shown for the total income tax expense allocated to total other comprehensive income.
c. An entity must present the amount of income tax expense allocated to each component of other comprehensive income in the notes to financial statements.
d. The income tax expense allocated to each component of other comprehensive income may be presented parenthetically for each component of other comprehensive income in the statement in which other comprehensive income is presented.

37. Which of the following is true under ASU 2011-05 regarding reclassification adjustments?

a. An entity may determine reclassification adjustments for all components of other comprehensive income together.
b. The reclassification adjustment for foreign currency translation adjustments is limited to translation gains and losses realized upon sale or upon complete or substantially complete liquidation of an investment in a foreign entity.
c. An entity may present reclassification adjustments in the notes to financial statements.
d. Reclassification adjustments are only allowed for prior period adjustments

38. Public entities are required to apply the ASU 2011-12 deferral for fiscal years, and interim periods within those years, beginning after:

a. December 15, 2011
b. December 15, 2012
c. December 31, 2012
d. December 31, 2013

39. Nonpublic entities should begin applying the ASU 2011-12 deferral for fiscal years and interim and annual periods ending after:

a. December 15, 2011
b. December 15, 2012
c. December 31, 2012
d. December 31, 2013

40. If an entity has a non-controlling interest in another entity, how should comprehensive income be presented?

a. Before the non-controlling interest, but not after it
b. After the non-controlling interest, but not before it
c. Before and after the non-controlling interest
d. Comprehensive income is ignored in this situation

41. Examples of recognition of revenue prematurely include all of the following ***except:***

   a. Channel stuffing
   b. Improper use of the percentage-of-completion method
   c. Reporting revenue when significant services have not been performed
   d. Reporting revenue when the goods are shipped and title passes

42. SAB No. 101 concluded that revenue should ***not*** be recognized until it is realized. Realization occurs when four criteria have been met that include all of the following ***except:***

   a. Delivery has occurred
   b. Persuasive evidence of an arrangement exists
   c. The sale has been collected in cash
   d. The seller's price to the buyer is fixed and determinable

43. Which of the following is a step in applying the proposed revenue standard?

   a. Deliver the goods or services
   b. Collect the consideration
   c. Determine the transaction price
   d. Recognize revenue once the contract is signed

44. An entity would ***not*** combine two or more contracts entered into near the same time with the same customer and account for the contracts as a single contract if:

   a. The amount of consideration to be paid in one contract depends on the price of the other contract.
   b. The services promised in the contracts are separate performance obligations but all must be met.
   c. The contracts are negotiated as a package with a single commercial objective.

45. Under the revenue recognition proposal:

   a. Some companies may record revenue earlier in their sales cycle as compared with current GAAP.
   b. All companies will record revenue later than with existing GAAP.
   c. When revenue is recorded will not change from existing GAAP.
   d. Revenue can only be recorded when the price is fixed and determinable.

46. If an entity transfers control of a good or service over time, it recognizes revenue over time if:

- **a.** The entity's performance creates work in process that the customer controls as the asset is created.
- **b.** The entity's performance creates an asset with an alternative use to the entity.
- **c.** The entity's performance does not create an asset with an alternative use to the entity and the customer receives and consumes the benefits of the entity's performance when the performance is completed.
- **d.** The entity's performance does not create an asset with an alternative use to the entity and the entity has no right to payment for performance completed to date and it expects to fulfill the contract as promised.

47. A performance obligation is onerous if the _____cost of settling the performance obligation _____the amount of the transaction price allocated to that performance obligation.

- **a.** highest, is less than
- **b.** highest, exceeds
- **c.** lowest, is less than
- **d.** lowest, exceeds

48. Which of the following statements is true under the revenue recognition proposal?

- **a.** An entity shall recognize as expense the incremental costs of obtaining a contract with a customer if the entity expects to recover those costs.
- **b.** An asset recognized for a contract cost would be amortized on a regular basis that is consistent with the transfer of the goods or services to which the asset relates.
- **c.** Costs to obtain a contract that would have been incurred, regardless of whether the contract was obtained, should be recognized as an asset.
- **d.** An entity's promise to be ready to accept a returned product during the return period would be accounted for as a separate performance obligation in addition to the obligation to provide a refund.

49. Detailed disclosures that would be required for public companies under the revenue recognition proposal do ***not*** include:

a. The amount of any liability recognized for onerous performance obligations
b. A reconciliation of the opening and closing balances of assets recognized from the costs incurred to fulfill a contract with a customer in total
c. Information about its performance obligations in contracts with customers
d. A reconciliation from the opening to the closing aggregate balance of contract assets and contract liabilities presented in the statement of financial position

50. The FASB has decided that the proposed revenue recognition standard would ***not*** be effective for public companies sooner than the annual reporting periods beginning on or after:

a. January 1, 2013
b. January 1, 2014
c. January 1, 2015
d. January 1, 2016

51. Based on one study noted in the text, the leading accounting issues resulting in restatements include which one of the following?

a. Receivables adjustments
b. Inventory adjustments
c. Consolidation adjustments
d. Debt and equity securities issues

52. What did Glass Lewis report with regard to financial restatements?

a. Restatements by companies audited by the Big Four were about half those by other firms.
b. Lease accounting errors are declining as a cause of restatements.
c. The number of restatements by overseas companies that do business in the U.S. decreased significantly.
d. The number of restatements in 2010 was more than double the amount in 2008.

53. A consistent hypothesis is that the decline in restatements from 2007 to 2009 was a result of:

a. Increased litigation
b. Internal control improvements
c. Clawback provisions
d. Fewer executive bonuses

54. The courts and SEC have been inconsistent as to when Section 304 of Sarbanes-Oxley can be used because:

a. It is unclear as to whether the SEC can use Section 304 to recover bonuses.
b. It is uncertain whether third parties can sue under Section 304.
c. The definition of the term "misconduct" in Sarbanes-Oxley is not consistent with the definition of the term within other securities statutes.
d. Section 304 can clearly be used against a CEO even when the CEO has no knowledge of an employee's misconduct.

55. Which of the following is true in comparing the key differences between the Sarbanes Section 304 and Dodd-Frank Section 954 clawback provisions?

a. Section 304 of Sarbanes only applies to a CEO and CFO, while Section 954 of Dodd-Frank applies to "any current or former executive."
b. Section 954 requires that the misstatement be due to misconduct, while Section 304 does not require misconduct.
c. Section 304 goes back two years, while Dodd-Frank extends back only six months from the year of restatement.
d. The two provisions are identical as Section 954 was written to mirror Section 304.

TOP ACCOUNTING ISSUES FOR 2013 CPE COURSE

Quizzer Questions: Module 3

56. Internally generated goodwill is:

- **a.** Capitalized and amortized over its useful life
- **b.** Capitalized and amortized over 40 years
- **c.** Capitalized and analyzed for impairment
- **d.** Not recorded in the accounts

57. Goodwill purchased in the acquisition of another company is:

- **a.** Capitalized and amortized over its useful life
- **b.** Capitalized and amortized over 40 years
- **c.** Capitalized and analyzed periodically for impairment
- **d.** Not recorded in the accounts

58. Changes in the carrying amount of goodwill during the period must be disclosed showing all of the following separately ***except:***

- **a.** Net exchange differences arising during the period
- **b.** Adjustments resulting from the subsequent recognition of deferred tax liabilities during the period
- **c.** Gross amount and accumulated impairment losses at the beginning of the period
- **d.** The gross amount and accumulated impairment losses at the end of the period

59. ASU 2011-08 does which of the following?

- **a.** Provides a special goodwill impairment test carryforward rule
- **b.** Provides the option to first make a qualitative assessment to determine whether it is necessary to perform the two-step goodwill impairment test
- **c.** States that the quantitative disclosures about significant unobservable inputs used in fair value measurements categorized within Level 3 of the fair value hierarchy are required for fair value measurements related to the financial accounting and reporting for goodwill after its initial recognition in a business combination

60. In making the qualitative assessment while testing goodwill for impairment, a qualitative factor to consider includes which of the following?

a. Stable foreign exchange rates
b. Abundance of capital
c. A change in key personnel
d. A decrease in the competitive environment

61. ASU 2011-09 requires an employer to provide ___________.

a. Additional qualitative disclosures only
b. Additional quantitative disclosures only
c. Additional quantitative and qualitative disclosures
d. No additional qualitative or quantitative disclosures

62. The amendments in ASU 2011-09 apply to:

a. Both multiemployer pension plans and multiemployer plans that provide postretirement benefits other than pensions
b. Neither multiemployer pension plans, nor multiemployer plans that provide postretirement benefits other than pensions
c. Multiemployer pension plans, but not multiemployer plans that provide postretirement benefits other than pensions
d. Multiemployer plans that provide postretirement benefits other than pensions, but not multiemployer pension plans

63. How does U.S. GAAP compare to IFRS in recognition and measurement of an employer's participation in multiemployer plans for plans that provide pension benefits and those that provide other postretirement benefits?

a. They are identical.
b. They differ for both pension and other postretirement benefit plans.
c. They are the same for pension plans but differ for other postretirement plans.
d. They are different for pension plans but the same for other postretirement plans.

64. After the issuance of ASU 2011-09, U.S. GAAP disclosures for multiemployer plans are _______ the IFRS disclosures.

a. Identical to
b. Completely different from
c. Similar to

65. A ______________ consists of aggregations of single-employer plans, combined to allow participating employers to pool plan assets.

- **a.** Multiple-employer plan
- **b.** Aggregated-employer plan
- **c.** Multiemployer plan
- **d.** Combined employer plan

66. Which of the following information does ***not*** have to be disclosed in a tabular format under ASU 2011-09?

- **a.** Legal name of the plan
- **b.** The plan's Employer Identification Number (EIN)
- **c.** The expiration date(s) of the collective-bargaining agreement(s) requiring contributions to the plan
- **d.** The number of employees covered by the plan segregated by age, gender, and years of employment

67. One disclosure required by ASU 2011-09 is ______________ provided by the plan.

- **a.** Certified Zone Status
- **b.** Certified Environmental Status
- **c.** Recommended Funding Status
- **d.** Minimum Funding Zone Initiative Status

68. For multiemployer plans that provide postretirement benefits other than pensions, an employer must disclose all of the following under ASU 2011-09 ***except:***

- **a.** A description of the nature of the benefits
- **b.** Categories of distributions from the plan
- **c.** The amount of contributions to the plan
- **d.** The types of employees covered by the benefits

69. What are the disclosure requirements under ASU 2011-09 as they relate to subsidiaries and not-for-profit entities?

- **a.** They are the same as for public entities.
- **b.** Subsidiaries and not-for-profit entities are exempt from the disclosure requirements.
- **c.** Only not-for-profit entities are exempt from the disclosure requirements.
- **d.** Subsidiaries and not-for-profit entities must make limited disclosures.

70. ASU 2011-09 is effective for public companies for annual periods for fiscal years ending after:

- **a.** December 15, 2011
- **b.** December 31, 2011
- **c.** December 15, 2012
- **d.** December 31, 2012

71. Which of the following is false?

- **a.** Current assets are resources expected to be realized in cash, sold or consumed during the next year or longer operating cycle.
- **b.** Current assets are sometimes called circulating assets.
- **c.** Cash that is restricted as to its withdrawal or use for other than current operations is classified as a current asset.
- **d.** Current assets are sometimes called working assets.

72. When the operating cycle of an entity is shorter than one year, which of the following is used to segregate current assets?

- **a.** A calendar year
- **b.** A fiscal year
- **c.** The operating cycle
- **d.** One year

73. Which of the following statements about an entity's refinancing a short-term obligation on a long-term basis is false?

- **a.** The entity must classify the short-term obligation as noncurrent if it has both the intent and the ability to refinance it on a long-term basis.
- **b.** The entity must support its ability to refinance on a long-term basis with either an actual refinancing or a financing agreement.
- **c.** The entity must amend any associated master netting arrangement to eliminate any right of offset for the existing short-term obligation.
- **d.** The entity must disclose the terms of an actual refinancing (or financing agreement) that demonstrate its ability to refinance on a long-term basis.

74. Under which conditions is it likely that a long-term obligation must be included in an entity's current liabilities?

a. The entity has not violated any provision of the agreement.
b. The entity has violated a provision, but the creditor lost its right to call the obligation for more than 18 months.
c. The entity has violated a provision but cured the violation before the grace period ended.
d. The entity has violated a provision that cannot be cured absent a loan modification.

75. Which of the following triggers would be consistent with a subjective acceleration clause?

a. The debtor fails to achieve a specified occupancy rate for a specified rental property at a specified date.
b. The debtor fails to maintain satisfactory operations.
c. The debtor fails to submit a copy of its audited financial statements by a specified date.
d. The debtor fails to make a contractual interest payment as of the contractual due date.

76. Which of the following describes a lock-box arrangement?

a. Any arrangement in which a depositor can store valuables in a depository institution vault
b. Any arrangement in which a debtor can't avoid using working capital to repay its outstanding obligation to a creditor
c. Any arrangement in which a customer prepays a purchase before receiving the related goods from the retailer
d. Any arrangement in which a regulated entity must maintain an objectively determinable minimum amount of capital

77. The criteria for offsetting determine whether or not an entity should:

a. Present, as a net amount in its balance sheet, a recognized asset and recognized liability that are related
b. Recognize a transaction in its balance sheet as an asset (or liability)
c. Remove a recognized asset or recognized liability from its balance sheet
d. Recognize periodic income (expense) on a recognized asset (liability)

78. Balance sheet offsetting does ***not*** affect which of the following items of financial information?

a. Line item amounts presented and ratios based on those amounts
b. Subtotal amounts presented and ratios based on those amounts
c. Footnote disclosures
d. The amount at which the recognized asset and related recognized liability are measured

79. Even if the reporting party does ***not*** intend to exercise its right of setoff, GAAP allows that reporting party to offset a recognized asset and a related recognized liability associated with which of the following?

a. A repurchase agreement and related repurchase agreement under a master netting arrangement
b. A derivative instrument and related cash collateral under a master netting arrangement
c. An unconditional receivable from and unconditional payable to a counterparty
d. A receivable from and payable to another party for contracts for which the settlement amount depends on future interest rates

80. An entity has to make certain disclosures about offsetting of all derivative instruments, financial assets, and financial liabilities ***except:***

a. Those that have been offset in the balance sheet
b. Those that are subject to a master netting arrangement but that have not been offset in the balance sheet
c. Those that are not subject to a master netting arrangement and have not been offset in the balance sheet
d. Those that are subject to offset and have been offset in the balance sheet

81. Subsequent events involve financial statements that are issued or are ___________.

a. Ready to be issued
b. Available to be issued
c. Considered for issue
d. Expected to be issued

82. Which of the following entities must evaluate subsequent events through the date that the financial statements are issued? An entity that ________________.

a. Is a closely held entity
b. Is a conduit bond obligor for conduit debt securities traded in a public market
c. Issues private placement investments
d. Is a non-SEC filer

83. ASU 2010-20 does ***not*** apply to which of the following?

a. Mortgage banking activities
b. Factoring arrangements
c. Standby letters of credit
d. Loan syndications

84. Under the amendments in ASU 2010-25, how should participant loans be classified on the balance sheet for defined contribution pension plans?

a. As a note receivable
b. As an investment
c. As a trade receivable
d. As a deferred asset

85. Which of the following entities must include disclosures of pro forma revenue and earnings under ASU 2010-29?

a. A not-for-profit organization that is non-public and has a business combination in the current year
b. A not-for-profit organization that is public but does not have a business combination in the current year
c. A public organization that has a business combination in the current year
d. A not-for-profit organization that is non-public and does not have a business combination in the current year

TOP ACCOUNTING ISSUES FOR 2013 CPE COURSE (4589-8)

Module 1: Answer Sheet

NAME ______________________________

COMPANY NAME ______________________________

STREET ______________________________

CITY, STATE, & ZIP CODE ______________________________

BUSINESS PHONE NUMBER ______________________________

E-MAIL ADDRESS ______________________________

DATE OF COMPLETION ______________________________

Please go to **CCHGroup.com/PrintCPE** to complete your Quizzer online for instant results and no Express Grading Fee. A $60.00 processing fee will be charged for each user submitting Module 1 for grading.

If you prefer to mail or fax your Quizzer, remove both pages of the Answer Sheet from this book and return them with your completed Evaluation Form to: CCH Continuing Education Department, 4025 W. Peterson Ave., Chicago, IL 60646-6085 or fax your Answer Sheet to CCH at 773-866-3084. You must also select a method of payment below.

METHOD OF PAYMENT:

☐ Check Enclosed ☐ Visa ☐ Master Card ☐ AmEx

☐ Discover ☐ CCH Account* ______________________________

Card No. ______________________________ Exp. Date ______________

Signature ______________________________

EXPRESS GRADING: Please fax my Course results to me by 5:00 p.m. the business day following your receipt of this Answer Sheet. By checking this box I authorize CCH to charge $19.00 for this service.

☐ Express Grading $19.00 Fax No. ______________________________

* Must provide CCH account number for this payment option

CCH
a Wolters Kluwer business

TOP ACCOUNTING ISSUES FOR 2013 CPE COURSE (4589-8)

Module 1: Answer Sheet

Please answer the questions by indicating the appropriate letter next to the corresponding number.

1. ___	8. ___	14. ___	20. ___
2. ___	9. ___	15. ___	21. ___
3. ___	10. ___	16. ___	22. ___
4. ___	11. ___	17. ___	23. ___
5. ___	12. ___	18. ___	24. ___
6. ___	13. ___	19. ___	25. ___
7. ___			

Please complete the Evaluation Form (located after the Module 3 Answer Sheet) and return it with this Quizzer Answer Sheet to CCH at the address on the previous page. Thank you.

TOP ACCOUNTING ISSUES FOR 2013 CPE COURSE (4589-9)

Module 2: Answer Sheet

NAME ______________________________

COMPANY NAME ______________________________

STREET ______________________________

CITY, STATE, & ZIP CODE ______________________________

BUSINESS PHONE NUMBER ______________________________

E-MAIL ADDRESS ______________________________

DATE OF COMPLETION ______________________________

Please go to **CCHGroup.com/PrintCPE** to complete your Quizzer online for instant results and no Express Grading Fee. A $72.00 processing fee will be charged for each user submitting Module 2 for grading.

If you prefer to mail or fax your Quizzer, remove both pages of the Answer Sheet from this book and return them with your completed Evaluation Form to: CCH Continuing Education Department, 4025 W. Peterson Ave., Chicago, IL 60646-6085 or fax your Answer Sheet to CCH at 773-866-3084. You must also select a method of payment below.

METHOD OF PAYMENT:

☐ Check Enclosed ☐ Visa ☐ Master Card ☐ AmEx

☐ Discover ☐ CCH Account* ______________________________

Card No. ______________________________ Exp. Date ______________

Signature ______________________________

EXPRESS GRADING: Please fax my Course results to me by 5:00 p.m. the business day following your receipt of this Answer Sheet. By checking this box I authorize CCH to charge $19.00 for this service.

☐ Express Grading $19.00 Fax No. ______________________________

* Must provide CCH account number for this payment option

CCH
a Wolters Kluwer business

TOP ACCOUNTING ISSUES FOR 2013 CPE COURSE (4589-9)

Module 2: Answer Sheet

Please answer the questions by indicating the appropriate letter next to the corresponding number.

26. ____	34. ____	42. ____	49. ____
27. ____	35. ____	43. ____	50. ____
28. ____	36. ____	44. ____	51. ____
29. ____	37. ____	45. ____	52. ____
30. ____	38. ____	46. ____	53. ____
31. ____	39. ____	47. ____	54. ____
32. ____	40. ____	48. ____	55. ____
33. ____	41. ____		

Please complete the Evaluation Form (located after the Module 3 Answer Sheet) and return it with this Quizzer Answer Sheet to CCH at the address on the previous page. Thank you.

TOP ACCOUNTING ISSUES FOR 2013 CPE COURSE (4590-0)

Module 3: Answer Sheet

NAME ____________________

COMPANY NAME ____________________

STREET ____________________

CITY, STATE, & ZIP CODE ____________________

BUSINESS PHONE NUMBER ____________________

E-MAIL ADDRESS ____________________

DATE OF COMPLETION ____________________

Please go to **CCHGroup.com/PrintCPE** to complete your Quizzer online for instant results and no Express Grading Fee. A $72.00 processing fee will be charged for each user submitting Module 3 for grading.

If you prefer to mail or fax your Quizzer, remove both pages of the Answer Sheet from this book and return them with your completed Evaluation Form to: CCH Continuing Education Department, 4025 W. Peterson Ave., Chicago, IL 60646-6085 or fax your Answer Sheet to CCH at 773-866-3084. You must also select a method of payment below.

METHOD OF PAYMENT:

☐ Check Enclosed ☐ Visa ☐ Master Card ☐ AmEx

☐ Discover ☐ CCH Account* ____________________

Card No. ____________________ Exp. Date ____________

Signature ____________________

EXPRESS GRADING: Please fax my Course results to me by 5:00 p.m. the business day following your receipt of this Answer Sheet. By checking this box I authorize CCH to charge $19.00 for this service.

☐ Express Grading $19.00 Fax No. ____________________

* Must provide CCH account number for this payment option

CCH
a Wolters Kluwer business

TOP ACCOUNTING ISSUES FOR 2013 CPE COURSE (4590-0)

Module 3: Answer Sheet

Please answer the questions by indicating the appropriate letter next to the corresponding number.

56. ___	64. ___	72. ___	79. ___
57. ___	65. ___	73. ___	80. ___
58. ___	66. ___	74. ___	81. ___
59. ___	67. ___	75. ___	82. ___
60. ___	68. ___	76. ___	83. ___
61. ___	69. ___	77. ___	84. ___
62. ___	70. ___	78. ___	85. ___
63. ___	71. ___		

Please complete the Evaluation Form (located after the Module 3 Answer Sheet) and return it with this Quizzer Answer Sheet to CCH at the address on the previous page. Thank you.

TOP ACCOUNTING ISSUES FOR 2013 CPE COURSE (4285-5)

Evaluation Form

Please take a few moments to fill out and mail or fax this evaluation to CCH so that we can better provide you with the type of self-study programs you want and need. Thank you.

About This Program

1. Please circle the number that best reflects the extent of your agreement with the following statements:

	Strongly Agree				Strongly Disagree
a. The Course objectives were met.	5	4	3	2	1
b. This Course was comprehensive and organized.	5	4	3	2	1
c. The content was current and technically accurate.	5	4	3	2	1
d. This Course was timely and relevant.	5	4	3	2	1
e. The prerequisite requirements were appropriate.	5	4	3	2	1
f. This Course was a valuable learning experience.	5	4	3	2	1
g. The Course completion time was appropriate.	5	4	3	2	1

2. This Course was most valuable to me because of:

____ Continuing Education credit
____ Relevance to my practice/ employment
____ Price
____ Other (please specify) ____________________
____ Convenience of format
____ Timeliness of subject matter
____ Reputation of author

3. How long did it take to complete this Course? (Please include the total time spent reading or studying reference materials and completing CPE Quizzer).

Module 1 ____ Module 2 ____ Module 3 ____

4. What do you consider to be the strong points of this Course?

5. What improvements can we make to this Course?

TOP ACCOUNTING ISSUES FOR 2013 CPE COURSE (4285-5)

Evaluation Form *cont'd*

General Interests

1. Preferred method of self-study instruction:
   ____ Text ____ Audio ____ Computer-based/Multimedia ____Video

2. What specific topics would you like CCH to develop as self-study CPE programs? ____

3. Please list other topics of interest to you ____

About You

11. Your profession:

____ Accountant
____ Controller
____ Enrolled Agent
____ Other (please specify) ____
____ Auditor
____ CPA
____ Risk Manager

2. Your employment:

____ Self-employed
____ Service Industry
____ Banking/Finance
____ Education
____ Public Accounting Firm
____ Non-Service Industry
____ Government
____ Other ____

3. Size of firm/corporation:
   ____ 1 ____ 2-5 ____ 6-10 ____ 11-20 ____ 21-50 ____ 51+

4. Your Name ____
   Firm/Company Name ____
   Address ____
   City, State, Zip Code ____
   E-mail Address ____

THANK YOU FOR TAKING THE TIME TO COMPLETE THIS SURVEY!

NOTES